VANISHED FLEETS

First published in 1931

First published in this edition in 1974
Reprinted in 1975

Library of Congress Catalog Card Number 74–11929

ISBN 0 684 14112 4

Printed and bound in Great Britain
at the University Printing House, Cambridge,
for the publishers, Charles Scribner's Sons,
New York

VANISHED FLEETS

SEA STORIES FROM
OLD VAN DIEMAN'S LAND

BY

ALAN VILLIERS

ILLUSTRATED WITH PHOTOGRAPHS AND MAPS

CHARLES SCRIBNER'S SONS
NEW YORK

HOBART, CAPITAL CITY OF TASMANIA, "BRITAIN'S FURTHEST ISLAND"

To

EDWIN H. WEBSTER

GENTLEMAN

CONTENTS

BOOK I: EARLIER DAYS

BOOK II: THE CONVICT SHIPS

BOOK III: THE WHALERS

BOOK IV: CLIPPERS, AND LATER DAYS

ILLUSTRATIONS

INTRODUCTION TO NEW EDITION

I FIRST VISITED Tasmania in the barque *James Craig*, which was the proper way to come to that island. Later I was in the ketch *Hawk*, trading there from Melbourne. In 1923, I was in port ashore when the Norwegian pelagic whale-ship *Sir James Clark Ross* put in at Hobart, bound on the pioneer whaling voyage into the big whales' last retreat, beyond the pack-ice into the Ross Sea. Roald Amundsen – that most competent professional among the Polar men – had told the Norwegian whaleman Carl Anton Larsen about the whales down there, and recommended Hobart as the best base for Ross Sea voyages. The astute Norwegian had chosen it himself rather than New Zealand as it was to windward, and so offered the Roaring Forties on his starboard beam to get the little *Fram* down south, unlike Scott's choice of New Zealand, which brought them on his starboard bow. The difference was of importance in Polar planning, for the explorers used very small square-rigged ships, and Larsen had five whale-ships of a couple of hundred tons each to harpoon the big blue whales. He had to get them to the Ross Sea, too.

Amundsen saw the whales down there and knew what he was looking at. He told Larsen also of the whaling traditions of old Tasmania. So Larsen called at Hobart to recruit survivors from the old days: there were none, but he picked up a dozen men. I joined with these as A.B.-Whaleman: I spoke a kind of Norwegian with a Finnish accent. It was a wild voyage. Real Tasmanians there (excellent chaps) told me something of their island's maritime history and traditions, its minute clippers that once sailed in the London trade like the *Harriett McGregor* of some 300 tons, the old whale-ships which wandered adventurously in the South Pacific, the sealers of the sub-Antarctic, the grim old convict days (transportation had ceased only 70 years before), escapes by sea, and remarkable local voyages.

Tasmania in the 1920s was still somewhat off the world's beaten tracks. Life could be difficult not only there, for there was a world-wide depression. After the Ross Sea voyage I settled in Hobart for a while, working for the morning *Mercury* as a sort of reporter, taking on Pitman's shorthand at night school as this was required of reporters in those days. But the stirring maritime past of the island was the real attraction. Why report the dull daily round when all that stirring stuff was going to waste? It dawned on me that a book was often nothing but a long and, preferably, well thought-out 'report' that no desk-bound sub or re-write man could trim, mutilate, or otherwise 'improve'. Well, really good books were more than that – often infinitely more (like Conrad's: his only command lay a lowly coal-hulk serving steamers there in Hobart, for he'd been a real sailor too).

I was young, then – very young, in the early '20s. I should not be thinking of producing books at all, but some optimistic American publisher *had* written asking me to write a book for him on that whaling voyage with C. A. Larsen into the Ross Sea, and I had perpetrated that. So I set about gathering new material, and there was plenty. I wrote much of this book later in the Finnish ship *Grace Harwar*, an under-manned old killer in the grain trade from South Australia to North

Europe. She killed my shipmate, drove an officer out of his mind, leaked, was 57 days to the Horn and another 80 on to Ireland. That long Horn run was in winter, and she was short of food. But I wrote the book. I wish I had written it better and had been able to study the subject for years rather than months. Indeed, I could still be in Tasmania doing just that. But the Finnish ship's voyage was a moving story, too.

Many friendly Tasmanians helped me, though they already had enough to do. Chief among them were Mr Edwin Webster, a descendant of the pioneers; Mr J. D. A. Collier, then the Librarian at the Public Library in Hobart; Sir William Crowther, who was an expert in Tasmanian whaling history; and Mr Thomas Dunbabin, a Tasmanian Rhodes Scholar who wrote several fine books in the field of Tasmanian maritime (and general) history. It was Dunbabin who had the first outside news of the success of Amundsen's dog-sled dash for the South Pole when poor Scott was still bravely but wearily floundering on to find that odd place, for Amundsen brought his *Fram* to Hobart, and Dunbabin was sent aboard to help draft his famous dispatches in English 'cable-ese' for transmission to *The Times*. He and all the others of the *Mercury* had to wait for the news to come back again from London, which took several days. They waited patiently and faithfully, as became good Tasmanians.

I am glad that I lived among those same good Tasmanians for a year or two while I got my shore-side bearings, and the material for this book.

The illustrations used are mainly those from the original edition, with some new material kindly supplied from his own collection by Sir William Crowther, and a few from my own Hobart-based whaling voyage into the Ross Sea in the whale-ship Sir James Clark Ross, of Sandelfjord, in 1923–24.

ALAN VILLIERS

Oxford, May 1, 1974

BOOK I

EARLIER DAYS

CHAPTER I

THE ROMANCE OF THE RIVER

Where do Derwent waters flow
When the light is leaving;
Eager for the to and fro,
Of the ocean's heaving?

OUT of the world's beaten tracks, in the far south of the southernmost state of the Commonwealth of Australia, the Derwent River flows quietly and steadily on for the sea, through a valley of surpassing beauty, even in a land of wonderful beauty everywhere. Steep, gaunt-peaked hills, wooded almost to the water's edge, line the countless bays and little havens into which the backwaters slowly sweep as the main stream goes on its voyage; here and there narrow strips of golden beach kneel for the kiss of the blue water, here weathered cliffs rise grimly from the breast of the great river; there orchard and farm, and township and hamlet, dip down to the sea.

In the background are the blue encircling hills that fling out wide arms over southern Tasmania; where the river bends to wash the feet of sweet old Hobart Town a mountain rises high into the clear air, and often from its tree-embroidered sides the blue smoke of the bush fire arises. It is not unlike Table Mountain, of better known Cape Town, this tall Mount Wellington whose name is scarcely known beyond the limits of the city over which its black and watchful crags mount ceaseless guard, but for the beauties of the river sweeping down close by there is no analogy. It is unique, this river! By the world little known, with the world little concerned, its waters now drift softly on for the freedom of the sea so close outside. Now and then the wake of a firewood barge, heeling to the fresh offshore breeze, leaves a white line for a while that soon is gone; the deep waters suffer unperturbed the throbbing and the thrashing of the propellers of the steamers.

But it was not always so, this river! It has not always flown on peacefully, through peace and quietude. It has played a part as stirring as any of these New World streams in the molding of man's destiny, the more interesting since old world and new world alike know so little of it; for Derwent River and its port have been great in their day, and will be great again. How many know that once this Derwent, 12,000 miles and more from England, at the very end of the world—for none may venture further from Home there, unless they would voyage to the South Pole—this quiet, sleepy, peaceful, beautiful old Derwent, was once a greater shipbuilding center than the famous Clyde? That once it was the greatest whaling port south of the Line? That its wooded banks and shelving shores have heard the cries of man adventurous, man courageous, man suffering more than human frame can stand? That here half a hundred whalers lay, fitting out for sea; that here, in these waters, under these mountains, men hunted giant whales in tiny boats, and won at times and sometimes lost; that here a score-odd graceful clippers first felt the bosom of the sea, and set out upon great voyages? That into this port countless crippled ships have limped, seeking haven from the shrieking of the westerly gales outside; that from here Polar expeditions have set proudly forth, many never to return? Now the blue waters wash quietly on, and the steamers belch their scorning smoke; but here once was Life, and Romance, and Adventure—colorful, amazingly interesting, glorious indeed!

The Derwent River was first discovered in 1793 by Rear Admiral Bruni d'Entrecasteaux and Captain Huon de Kermandée. D'Entrecasteaux called the river Rivière du Nord; but the following year a Captain Hayes came in, from India

—looking probably for some place for wood and water—and, unaware of its previous discovery, gave it the name of Derwent. The French did not colonize these shores, and Derwent is the name the river has kept. In 1803 the river was first entered by colonists, though the most of these were convicts from Port Jackson. (It is said the colony was first founded in this way to forestall the French.) The early years of the settlement were hard; food was short, supplies did not arrive, and starvation stared the pioneers in the face. This first settlement was further up the river from the present site of the city of Hobart, at a point opposite where now a great industry is established. The land there was bleak and the situation and the outlook both not promising. Some wanderers who had been sent to form a colony in what is now the state of Victoria, not liking that place, happened to come on to the Derwent, and it was their leader who first selected the site of Hobart. This was in 1804, and almost from that year the new country and its river thrived.

First convicts came, for much of the colonization was in this way, and as the older state of New South Wales began to assert its independence and its free settlers to object to the importation of convicts, more and more of them were sent from England to Tasmania. Even when all the other states of Australia had ceased to take convicts, Tasmania had to take them. The island itself made an excellent natural prison from which the only possible escape was by sea, and in those stormy, ice-infested latitudes, that was hard. For, if they were successful in the seizing of a ship, or even in the construction of one, where might the adventurers go? They could not make for the mainland of Australia, for there was too great a risk of apprehension: they could not pit their craft against the viciousness of the wild west winds, and make for Africa. If they stood to the east they would fetch New Zealand, but here again the red coats were in possession. What then? They could make up into the Pacific, and seek sanctuary among the islands; but the horror of the convict system had spread even here and the shadow of Norfolk Island was a blot in the sunshine of the South Seas. They might endeavor to reach South America if they were brave enough, but they must also be very fortunate if ever they were to escape thence. And when they got there—if they did—there were mines to fear, and the chain gang, and all the terrors of the bad old days on the hot and terrible West Coast. All the world was a prison then, to the wretch who once bore the brand of the irons.

Yet some did escape. They built their own craft, or seized ships. Many were drowned without getting out of sight of the prison island; many were shot down in the attempt; many were lost utterly in the bitter seas, and neither ship nor men heard of again. Yet some managed to get clear away, and reached the England from which they had been banished, and wreaked torment, one hopes, upon those who had so fiendishly tormented them. Sometimes they mutinied in the ships that brought them out, and sometimes won: and more than one stout, red coat-guarded, convict-filled sailer set out from the Thames mouth or Dungeness mysteriously to disappear from the face of the waters.

Sometimes the ships were wrecked, and then were tragedies harrowing beyond description. In places now not far from where Derwent waters so quietly flow, once men were shot down in their chains while their ship pounded itself to pieces on the rocks. At low tide now the rock ledges show above the surface, while all around the waters break, and fret, and worry, and swirl in ceaseless misery as if they were condemned forever to torment for the part that they had played in these tragedies—tragedies which they only began, and man ended. *George III* and *Actæon!* Even to-day, after one hundred years have gone, men recall these names with a shudder. In *George III*, grim convict-freighted ship from England, one hundred and thirty-four lives were lost: the story of the *Actæon* is filled, too, with horror.

There were other wrecks. Once a proud full-rigged ship, filled with women convicts out from England, piled herself on Derwent mouth because the wind came ahead, and the crew was too spent to summon up the energy to put her about . . .

And then the whalers! Not so tragic a chapter, this, but richly colorful and full of life. First the whales were so thick in the river, when they came to breed that they could be hunted profitably there and for twenty years and more a good thing was made out of this "bay whaling."

"The river so filled with beastly whales it was dangerous to make a crossing," wrote a peevish cleric in his diary during the year 1820. These were black whales, easy prey to the skilled hunters in those sheltered waters, and the slaughter was so great that the whales retired to an ocean retreat at Recherché, farther down the coast. Here the hunters still pursued them, though now the hunting was more difficult and much more dangerous, and a good many lives were lost.

The season for bay whaling was from July until September, and so just nicely gave a winter occupation for those who were engaged in sperm whaling or in sealing over the summer months. Eventually, however, the whales either decided that Tasmania was no place for them or were all killed out, and after about 1841 bay whaling seems to have died.

In these old days there were some famous contests in the river, and the colonists were often treated to the thrilling sight of a boat's crew fighting with a bad-tempered bull whale. There were tragedies, too, for the whales did not always lose, and the waters of the Derwent are perilously cold in winter.

When bay whaling died, that was not the end. For years

after that whaling was the most important industry in Tasmania, and the very lifeblood of the Derwent and its port. Those who had their money in whaling ventures fitted out their ships for sperm whaling throughout the year, and built bigger and better ships for the purpose. By 1849 there were 38 deep sea ships owned in Hobart, and these were only a portion—and a small portion too— of the fleet that used Hobart as the base for its whaling operations.

The New Bedford whalers, and the old English whalers that still kept the seas—these more rarely—were visitors and ship chandling and various other businesses not so prosaic flourished. The American flag was as common in the port as the Red Ensign that flew from the Colonial and English vessels: on Good Friday, 1847, there were no less than 47 deep water whalers lying in the Derwent, either just in from sea or refitting to go out again, and the bulk of these were American. The sperm whales flourished around the Tasmanian coast, and not even the shriek of the almost continuous westerly gales that swept unchecked from the bitterness of Cape Horn to the wild west coast of Tasmania could keep the whalers from their harvest. But it was no game for weaklings. Those whalemen were men— hard drinking, hard swearing, hard fighting, for the most part, but men.

The port was cosmopolitan then, with nothing of the sleepy air about it, or the quiet spirit of the grim pioneer. The dregs of the earth came to the old streets of quaint Hobart Town: around the taverns of the water front— and the whole town then was little more than water front— Mexicans with rings in their ears and knives in their shirts drank hilariously, quarreled madly, fought bitterly, lurched drunkenly, with pale faced Nordics, slow to fight but quick in the thirst: Spaniards jostled African negroes—great handsome, muscular fellows who were grand on shipboard— and derelict Englishmen (and splendid Englishmen too) paid for the drinks of Peruvians, and Finns, and Germans, and Hollanders, and Turks, and Irishmen, and loud-voiced Americans, and suffered sometimes with a bored air, to have drinks paid for them. When the whalers were in port there was life! The ale flowed in the gutters, blood, too, afterwards: and the village policemen, if they were wise, retired to a game of bowls.

For many years whaling prospered and a greater and greater proportion of the fleet operating out of the Derwent was Hobart owned. Many a stately clipper, ousted from some crack run by a faster vessel, found her last employment here, and many a sinking old derelict, too, that was as leaky as a crayfish pot and a hundred times as smelly. There was money in it: fortunes were made, and some were lost again. Gradually the sperm whales learned to fight shy of the Tasmanian waters, and the whalers had to push out further and further for them. To New Zealand, to the far southern waters of the ice-rim of the Antarctic, to Campbell and Macquarie Islands, to Kerguelen and the warm waters off the Madagascar coast, to Cape Town and Saldanha Bay, to the Islands of the South Pacific—further and further afield the whale ships had to go, and longer and longer were their voyagings.

Through the years, then, the fleets declined, and those who were wise sold their ships and kept their money: there came a time when sperm oil was no longer the chief means of illumination, and whalebone was needed no more by corsetmakers, and even ambergris was looked upon askance. The stout old whalers still kept the seas, however, and fished now mostly in Behring Straits—a long cry from Hobart. Off the coast of Japan they fished, too, and put in sometimes to try to sell the blubber-stripped carcasses to the natives, who were partial to that sort of diet: expeditions were sent to endeavor to penetrate the ice-wastes of the Antarctic, and see if there were profitable whaling grounds there. Some of these expeditions were epic in their way.

Ships were lost and wrecked, and seized in mutiny. As profits declined the trade became more difficult, and sometimes a whaler preferred to turn her attentions to blackbirding in the South Sea Islands, and such other nefarious pursuits as might be depended upon to bring in something of a profit. Other old whaling captains grew tired of the ceaseless efforts to earn dividends, and took their ships and all their crews to some remote island in the Pacific where they took themselves native wives, renounced civilization and all its obligations, and proceeded to live happily ever after—or until some marauding tribe came and converted them into soup. Some of the stolidly recorded adventures of these days are now almost unbelievable.

So the whalers came, and after nearly a hundred years, went again. The last cruise out of the port was made by the old barque *Helen*, in 1899, and since her return from that voyage Hobart has had none of its ships engaged in whaling. As a base for Norwegian operations in the Antarctic, in recent years it has again come into some prominence in the time-honored industry, but now its interest is impersonal and passing. There is yet a third phase of the port's greatness—the clipper ships it built and sent out to sea. When sail declined in the latter part of the last century, and sailing ships were driven off the main trade routes which they had held so long, there still remained more or less profitable voyagings that they might make, in routes where the steamer did not care to compete or did not think it worth while.

The trade between Hobart and England came in this category, and even before that the Tasmanian barques and little full-rigged ships were well known in the Thames. Some of them were built first as whalers; others were built to convey oil home to the markets, and the wool that the new country produced, and the tin and the gold. Ships were chartered for this work at first, but it was not long before the astute colonists asked themselves why if they could freight ships they could not buy their own. They bought ships, and then—they had the timber and the sail lofts—decided that they could build for themselves, as well as find cargoes for them. And this they did, in a small way at first, with tops'l schooners, brigantines and brigs, that were sent out whaling or in the trade with New Zealand, Australia, and Mauritius; these prospered, and they built for deep water.

Hobart is peculiarly favorably situated for sailing ships, lying in a good harbor right in the belt of the Roaring Forties, so that ships may run there from the Cape, or run from there to the Horn, with no fear of long delays in the changeable winds beyond the westerlies belt. Trading with London, the sailers made the outward voyage round the Cape of Good Hope and the homeward round the Horn, so that even if the passages of the North and South Atlantic were slow at times, they could always depend upon a quick running of their easting down, with no northing to make at the end of it.

The colonists made excellent shipbuilders and turned out, with their native woods, sweet little craft that sat beautifully upon the water, and flew cleanly through it with anything of a breeze. Some of these little ships—their average size was between 300 and 400 tons, which is not big for Cape Horn—made very fast voyages. A little Hobart barque called *Harriet McGregor* was for years known as the yacht of the London docks. She was only about 330 tons, but for 15 years she was in the Cape Horn trade—Hobart to London, London to Hobart—and in all that time her average for the voyage was 88 days. That is not clipper time but it is good. Quite recently there was a good deal of romantic fuss about a Finnish four-masted barque which made the voyage from Australia to the Channel in 96 days, and that big Finn was more than ten times the size of the little *Harriet McGregor*—although, incidentally, she carried only about the same crew.

But 3,000-ton four-masted barques, steel to the trucks, with brace winches, halliard winches, and all the other devices to lighten their work, find the Cape Horn road a hard one and many of them have been overwhelmed in the great seas that race down there. How, then, must the tiny 300-tonners have fared! It is remarkable that they remained in this worst trade in the world so long, and were not lost—though a few of them were—and infinitely more remarkable that they made such splendid voyages.

The *Harriet McGregor* is not alone. There are many others—*Ethel, Lufra, Wagoola, Loongana*, and the rest of them, all sweet little ships and regular London traders. It was a little Hobart-owned ship, too, that made a famous passage of 64 days from Australia to the Ushant, beating the time of the famous *Cutty Sark* by three days for the same voyage. That was the full-rigged ship *Heather Bell*, of only 479 tons, and for many years she was owned and traded regularly out of the port of Hobart.

The old colonists had a deep pride in these little ships of theirs, and the whole town was interested in their arrivals and their departures, and all the little tidings that were to be learned about them. The hoisting of a signal flag denoting that the little *Harriet*, or the old *Ethel*, was once more off the Derwent mouth was the signal for a general gathering round the waterfront to watch the sailer come up to her berth; as the little vessels always did that under sail, the sight must have been a beautiful one.

But the port fell upon bad days. The builders of the Old Country looked coldly upon these graceful craft from overseas, as if they considered it their unquestioned right to a monopoly in ship construction for the new lands of the far south. They overlooked no means, in harassing restrictions, unfair classings, and the like, of making their disapproval very plain. When *Harriet McGregor* first came to London she was made to strip the whole of her copper, and, though as stout and strongly built a vessel as came to London river in those days, she was classed for only 10 years against the 15 years granted to countless less sturdily constructed English ships.

That policy was rigidly pursued, and might have led to trouble had not the economic conditions also taken a hand, in the shape of steam which steadily and overwhelmingly drove the sailing ships from the seas. The great English companies, taking to steam, were easily able to capture the Tasmanian trade from the little sailers; the *Harriet* and the rest of them were hulked, or sold, or sent for a year or two into the trade with New Zealand, Mauritius, China, the Islands and the East, and the number of Hobart barques steadily declined. None came to take their place, and it is some years now since the last of them disappeared.

But their story will go on.

There are many stirring stories out of this port, and of the ships that sailed upon this river—stories of wreckers of King Island, and the pirates of Bass Strait; stories of shipwreck, and mutiny, and suffering, and privation, and human courage almost unbelievable. When the westerly gale shrieks by overhead and the storm clouds gather round the high crest of Mount Wellington, the listener who knows may hear, through the moaning of the wind, the ghastly shrieks of tortured and dying convicts, the throaty shouts of sturdy whalers, and the sweet chanteys of the wind ships' men taking their craft to sea. Now to Derwent River nothing comes save steamers, and yet perchance still, in the darkness of the night, one may hear the thrashing of the sailer's sails and the music of strong wind in stronger rigging, and catch some ghostly glimpse of the tall ships that have long since made their departure. . . . The dark waters swirl softly on, and by the quay-side a blackened coal hulk, still sweet of line and graceful-bowed, drags fretfully at her moorings.

CHAPTER II

ROUND TASMANIA IN A WHALEBOAT

ONE of the most hazardous of the early voyages round Tasmania was that made by James Kelly, who in 1815 sailed right round the island with a crew of four men, two of whom were natives, in a whale boat, discovering Port Davey and Macquarie Harbour on the way. Port Davey was later to become famous as a whaling station for the off-shore whalers; Macquarie Harbour became infamous as one of the worst convict settlements the world has known.

It was summer when Kelly made his voyage, but even in summer the wild west coast of Tasmania is dangerous and stormy, and the little boat—a "small sized open five-oared whale boat," we are told—was at sea 49 days. The dangers from weather were the least of the hazards. There were natives to be met, many of whom were hostile—largely because of the treatment they had received at the hands of the whites, who were to exterminate them within 50 years—and bushrangers to fear, for the little craft had to put in frequently into wild places where bushrangers might lurk; and to such gentry she might fall an easy prey. They were stirring days in old Tasmania then, and escaped convicts from the prison settlements, who had taken to the bush with what arms they could find and murder in their hearts, were a menace to the safety of the outlying communities.

Kelly's diary, which is still preserved in the library of the Royal Society at Hobart, contains staidly written accounts of adventure with blacks, with storms, with treacherous currents, and bushrangers which must have been dangerous in the extreme. The lives of the little party were

14

in constant danger throughout their voyage; they several times escaped from savage blacks by the barest luck or the coolest daring; at one time the whole of them were arrested by militia who were scouring the countryside for a gang of notorious marauders, and all but shot on sight before they could establish their innocence.

Even to-day, when there are large settlements on the west coast of Tasmania and the north-west and east coasts are thickly populated, no one cares to wander round the island in a whaleboat. Now and then some particularly adventurous party, eager for a thrill from the sea beyond the limits of ordinary yachting, sets off in a well-found yawl or schooner for Port Davey, and is apt to consider itself lucky if it ever reaches the place. Fishermen go round there at times, in stoutly rigged craft, and parties of prospectors are landed to explore the still largely unknown and untouched south-west; and sometimes the fishermen and prospectors do not come back. It is no coast to take risks with. Not even for steamships, which often prefer, if they are bound from Hobart to Adelaide or to Fremantle, to go out of their way up the east coast and to the westward through Bass Strait rather than stand into the teeth of the winds that come roaring off the great seas that sweep unchecked from the Horn to the west coast of Tasmania.

James Kelly knew that this was no coast to fool with, for he had gone to sea as a cabin boy at the age of nine and remained there until he rose to be a commander.

It was on December 12, 1815, that he and his little band set out, and his diary records the fact that his crew was as follows:

> John Griffiths, a native of the Colony.
> George Briggs,   do.
> William Jones, Englishman.
> Thomas Toombs,   do.

Where John Griffiths and George Briggs found their English names is not explained, but at any rate they appear to have made excellent sailors, although their presence on board did not save the party from being driven back on their first attempt to land, the day after they left Hobart, by a party of natives who hurled stones and spears at them. This was at Recherché Bay, and received in that manner— not wholly unexpectedly—James Kelly stood on and, eluding these stone-throwing and spear-hurling natives, landed somewhere else for the night. His references to these encounters with natives appear frequently in the diary, and are of especial interest in view of the fact that within a comparatively few years the Tasmanian aborigine had been wiped out. His lot with the conquering white man does not appear ever to have been easy, and although the natives easily evaded the punitive expeditions sent against them— there is the famous case of the "cordon" of whites which was formed to comb the island in a kind of human dragnet, and actually did comb it and manage to catch two sick and very aged gins *—they fell a hopeless victim to changed conditions. They did not long survive the coming of the whites, and as early as 1869 the last full-blooded male Tasmanian native died, to be followed seven years later by Trucaninni, last of the Tasmanians.

After the stone-throwing incident Kelly appears to have fallen in with friendly natives, though throughout his story he does not hide the fact that he was always pretty suspicious of the friendliness of these blacks. In his queer style, which, illiterate, ungrammatical, and quaint as it is, still gives a vivid impression of the facts, he writes:

On the morning of the 14th launched and proceeded round the south coast of Van D. Land, with a fresh breeze at south east. At sunset the same evening hauled up in a small sandy bay to the northward of the largest of the De Witts Isles. Here we had a friendly reception from a large number of natives. We made them a few presents of some sugar and biscuit, but the disgusting sight of them pulling virmin by handfulls from their heads and beards and eating them, which they

* Gins—Native women.

seemed to enjoy more than the sugar and biscuit, did not please us. In fact it seemed like a rejoicing at them seeing their new visitors, but they did not seem the least hostile as they brought down their women and children to see us, which denotes friendship in these savages. At dusk they took their leave of us and pointed to a small rising hill about a mile distant, signifying that they intended to sleep there. We thought it was only a decoy to put us off our guard but we kept a good watch during the night in case of an attack, but we saw no more of them.

On the next day there were further encounters, with "two native aborigines which seemed very much alarmed at seeing us; they were over six feet in height their stomachs verry large, legs and arms verry thin and seemed as if they were nearly starved."

Kelly gave them some black swans to eat, having a good supply of them in the boat, and they went away pleased. He did not stay at the spot where he met the natives, but stood out to sea again and went on further before coming ashore for the night.

After that came gales, which lasted over Christmas Day, and the weather was wet and miserable beyond words. However, the crew refused to be downhearted and honored their Christmas in the old established way. "This day we had a glorious feed for dinner, two black swans, one roasted (stuck up), the other a sea pie—a three decker—in the large iron pot; a first rate Christmas dinner on the west coast of Van Diemen's Land." That three-decker sea pie of black swans stewed in the "large iron pot" was an historical meal, being the first Christmas dinner ever eaten by white men in that part of the world, and it was fitting that it should have been so appropriate to the occasion.

On Boxing Day the gales still blew, but feeling energetic after that three-decker sea pie the adventurers put to sea again, standing on as close to the coastline as they dared.

The gale abated, and so they advanced along the west coast until the 28th December, when it was impossible to make a landing because of the bush fires which raged along the shore. "The whole face of the coast was on fire, and lucky for us it was," the diary states (though utterly without punctuation or any regard to syntax, spelling or grammar), "for the smoke was so thick we could not see a hundred yards ahead of the boat. On pulling into a narrow entrance to an inlet we heard a large number of natives shouting and making a great noise as if they were hunting kangaroos, and had the natives seen the boat passing through the narrow entrance it is possible they would have killed every person on board by volleys of stones and spears in their usual way."

Then came Macquarie Harbour, then in virgin quietude save for the moaning of the gale through the wet gaunt treetops and the splashing of the almost incessant rain on the dull shore. Here within a few years men in the last stages of despair were to cry aloud for death, to seek it in the horror of the cold sea or the greater horror of the pitiless bush as their only deliverance from that accursed place of torment. Here the sigh of the lash singing through the air, the screams of the tortured wretches who felt its maddening thrash, the sounds of misery and torture, human suffering and woe beyond description, were to rise into the sad, rain-dulled skies; now only the gale softly moaned and the heavens rained their tears. And to-day the gale still moans in from the sea through the Hell's Gates of Macquarie Harbour, and the heavens still rain their tears, in memory of those frightful days of fiendishness and pain, though for fourscore years and more no broad-arrowed convict has been here. . . .

More storms beset the little craft when she stood out of this haven. Here is the entry in the log:

On the morning of 1st January, 1816, we left Macquarie Harbour with a fresh breeze at south east. This day we ran a long distance to the north west having a strong fair wind. At 8 P.M. attempted to get into a river which was named Retreat River, being nearly lost on the bar in a heavy surf. During the night of the 1st January it blew a strong gale from the southward. We were obliged to heave the boat to by a raft made of the oars with about forty five fathoms of rope, where she lay verry snug during the night, the men taking it in turns to attend to the steer oar to keep the boat end on to the sea, and having a good tarpaulin that covered the boat all over she lay very dry. At daylight of the morning of the 2nd January hauled the raft in, set the reefed lug and steered in for the west point of Van D. Land with a heavy sea running. As we neared the shore we had to pass through heavy tide rips; the tide running to the southard against the wind made it more dangerous.

We got within 500 yards of the shore when the boat was pooped by a heavy sea that filled her to the thwarts *—and had it not been for the precaution taken before we left Hobarton (that was of having three good buckets slung with lanyards and fastened to the thwarts for the purpose of bailing the boat on such an emergency), we must all have been lost. However, by the quick use of the buckets the boats was soon bailed out, and we got under the lee of the point and landed on a small sandy beach.

Such is the prosaic and illiterate account of the log. What a night that must have been! With a little five-oared whaleboat, lying to a sea anchor no more stable than her oars lashed together and payed out on the end of a line, pitching in the huge seas that run off the west coast of Tasmania, almost overwhelmed at times but always rising buoyantly, flung high into the murky, storm-filled sky at times and again deep into the troughs of treacherous seas, fighting bravely in a wild sea with an infinitely wilder and more dangerous coast in perilously close proximity—and, as like as not, prowling round that coast tribes of natives whose welcome would be the waddy and the spear.

And then when the little craft was pooped—a desperate moment! Kelly's seamanship must have been perfect, else there should have been no return to Hobart Town, and no entries in that picturesque log. It was very much more

* The diary spells them "thoughts."

than luck that saved the little whaleboat when she filled up
to the "thoughts."

Landing on that small sandy beach did not bring an end
to these adventures, as the log recounts:

We now thought we were safe so far and had just got a
large fire made to dry ourselves, when to our great astonishment we were accosted by six huge men, black natives, each of
them about six feet high and verry stout, thair faces greased
and blacked. They had a spear in each of thair right hands
and two in their left. They were quite naked and appeared
quite ready for war or mischief. Our men got greatly alarmed
and called out what was to be done. It was thought best to
make gestures to them to come closer to us; they were standing
behind a low thick scrub and did not seem inclined to come any
nearer. Our arms all wet and no means of defending ourselves,
we were in a verry dangerous situation.

It happened that luck was still at our side. We had 9 or 10
black swans and a large wombat in the boat that we brought
from Macquarie Harbour for fresh provisions. On showing
them one of the swans they seemed delighted and came nearer
to the boat. After they came out of the scrub we saw more
of thair war impliments as each of them had a spear between
the great toe of each of their feet, dragging them along the
ground. We supposed they had never seen a white man before.
It was thought best to try to barter with them for their spears,
for if we got possession of them they could not hurt us. We
luckily succeeded, and gave them four swans and the wombat
for all their spears. They seemed much pleased with thair
bargain; they went away holding up one hand as a sign of
friendship. We were equally pleased when they were gone and
we saw no more of them. During the evening a great number
of smoaks were made along the coast which we thought to be
signals between the natives.

We remained on the beach that night and got our arms dried
and put in firing order, keeping a good watch in case the natives should pay us another visit.

There was little rest for the adventurers, though now the
worst of the journey was over. They rounded the north-
western corner of the triangular island that is Tasmania
and stood along the northern coast. Here there were more

encounters with natives, that were both interesting and dangerous. Thus the entry in the log for January 4:

About noon rounded Cape Grim. We passed between two pinnical rocks that lie near the Cape. We were nearly filled in a tide rip going through, but luckily escaped. We pulled along shore to the eastward until we came to the south end of the largest Hunters Island. We landed on a point opposite on the main land on a large flat of pebble stones to boil our kittle and take a rest. There *was* a great many fires along the shore and we kept the boat afloat and the arms ready in case of an attack by the natives. Tooms and Jones were left to take care of the boat and have the arms in readiness. We had just got a fire lighted when we saw a large body of natives, at least fifty in number, standing at the edge of the bush about fifty yards from us. They were all armed with spears and waddies. We immediately brought the arms from the boat and put ourselves in a state of defence near the fire. They began to advance slowly towards us. We held up our pieces and made signs to them not to come any closer. They held up their spears in return with loud laughing and jeering at us, as if they thought we were afraid of them.

At seeing them so formidable we thought it best to retreat to the boat, when all of a sudden they laid down thair spears and waddies in the edge of the bush and holding up both their hands as if they did not mean any mischief, at the same time making signs to us to lay down our arms which we did to satisfy them, for if we had retreated to the boat quickly they must have killed every one before we could have got out of the reach of their spears.

They then began to come to us one by one, holding up both their hands to show they had no weapon, but we kept a good lookout that they had no spears between thair toes as they had on a former occasion, but they had none. There were twenty two came to the fire (we made signs to them that no more should come). Upon that being understood two more came from the bush together. One of them seemed to be a chief, a stout good-looking man about six feet high, 30 years of age; the other an old man about six feet seven inches high with scarcely a bit of flesh on his bones.

When the chief came he ordered them all to sit down on the ground which they did and formed a sort of circle round the

fire. The chief ordered the old man to dance and sing, as if
to amuse us, which he did, making ugly faces and putting himself into most singular attitudes. While the old man was engaged in his dancing and singing we found out it was only to
take our attention off what the chief and his men were doing.
He ordered them to gather pebble stones about the size of hen's
eggs and put them between their legs where they sat for the
purpose, as we supposed, to make an attack on us with the
stones. At this our men began to get alarmed and expecting
some mischief would be done we planned it to give them a few
swans and get off as well as we could, and Briggs brought two
swans from the boat, one under each arm.

When the chief saw them he rushed at Briggs to take the
swans from him but did not succeed. He then ordered his men
to give us a volley of stones which they did by him giving them
the time in most beautiful order by him calling with the swing
of the arm three times Yah, yah, yah; and a severe volley it
was. I had a pair of large dueling pistols in my coat pocket
loaded with two balls each, and seeing there was no alternative
I fired one amongst them, which dispersed them. The other I
fired after them as they ran away. Two of them dragged
Briggs along the ground a little distance to get the swans from
him but did not succeed. The chief and his men run into the
bush and were quickly out of sight.

On looking round after they had all ran away we found the
6 feet 7 inch dancing gentleman laying on his back on the
ground. We thought of course he was dead but on turning
him over to examine his wounds found he had not a blemish on
him, his pulse was going at 130. It must have been the report
of the pistols that frightened him. We then set him on his
feet to see if he could walk; he opened his eyes and trembled
very much. We led him a few steps towards the bush. He
stood up straight, looked around him and took one jump towards the bush; the next leap he was out of sight. As soon
as he was out of sight the hills around echoed with shouts of
joy from the voices of men women and children that the dancing gentleman had escaped. We measured the first jump the
old man took; it was exactly eleven yards,* but the second one
must have been more. This was more like the jump of a
kangaroo than a man.

---

* One must admit an entire lack of personal knowledge of natives
who can leap eleven yards.

This must surely have been the chief Medicine Man of the district.

The next adventure was arrest on suspicion of being escaping bushrangers, a nasty hole out of which the party was lucky to scramble. This was at the early settlement of George Town, quite close to the entrance of the Tamar River, and the welcome which the adventurers received was to be greeted by a man in the uniform of a military officer who hailed them "What boat is that?", and before they could reply eight men rushed out from behind a building with muskets and fixed bayonets. These grim individuals told Mr. Kelly and his crew that if they moved they would get a musket ball through them, not to mention an exploratory poke in the abdomen with the business end of a bayonet. The officer was in uniform but the rest were in kangaroo skins, "and a ruffianlike mob they were" says the insulted diarist. Kelly and his crew were taken out of the boat, handcuffed, and led ashore, too taken aback for the moment to make it all out.

"Now, my lads," said the officer, "I have been looking for you for a long time. You are the colleagues of Michael Howe, the bushranger, and if you do not give me all the information where we can find Howe and his party I will send you all to Hobart Town in double irons."

Kelly said they were on a voyage of discovery round Tasmania, and was laughed at for his pains. The situation looked nasty for a time, and the military gentleman would listen to no explanations, pleased, no doubt, that at last they had arrested somebody and not much concerned whether the arrest was justified. To be just, they had it on their side that small boats were not in the habit of wandering round Tasmania, either then or at any other time in that island's history, and the last thing they might have expected in that faraway corner of the earth was that a whaleboat full of legitimate and peaceful explorers should come into the river-mouth and visit them.

At last, after numerous protests that nearly got him shot on sight, Kelly was able to unlock the box of the little ship's papers and to produce his clearance from the authorities at Hobart Town.

This curious document was as follows:

> Commandant's Office,
> Military Barracks,
> Hobart Town.
>
> These are to certify to all whome it may concern that the boat *"Elizabeth,"* commanded by Mr. James Kelly, was cleared out for the West Coast of Van Diemen's Land on a Voyage of Discovery after having paid the accustomed dues.
>
> Given under my hand this 11th Day of December, 1815 in the absence of the Lieutenant Governor.
>
> WM. NAIRN,
> Captain 46th Regiment,
> Commandant.

Even then the officer was not much impressed, and it was not until the obvious sincerity of his prisoners forced the conclusion into his mind that they were really telling the truth that he consented grudgingly to allow them to be released, though his soldiers still kept a watchful eye on them. Kelly, however, actually knew this officer, and was able in the evening to convince him that they had had some grog together on various occasions in the hostelries of Hobart Town. Thereupon the officer opened up his heart and his stores as well—seeing that they were provided by the government—and gave the wanderers food and blankets, of both of which they were in sore need. They stayed with the soldiers for a while and learnt all they could of the movements of Mr. Howe, who was known to be in the neighborhood and they did not wish to meet with any one with so unsavory a reputation. The officer seized the opportunity to forward a despatch to the Governor by Kelly's boat, since opportunities for establishing communication with his headquarters were rare. Howe held a strong position in the

bush, from which he was in the habit of sending curt epistles
to military officers, whenever he felt like it, informing them
that he would open all despatches and the messengers who
conveyed them "he would hang up by the heels to a tree let
thair intrils out and leave them hanging just as he would
a kangaroo," adding that he would serve any one else who
crossed his path in the same way. Now and again, just to
show he was in earnest, he did things like that.

Hoping that they would see nothing of the ferocious Mr.
Howe, having naturally a strong desire to take their "intrils" back with them to Hobart Town, and a distaste for
being strung up by the heels in the bush, Kelly and his crew
pushed on. They rounded the north-eastern point of the
island without further adventure, except for an encounter
with a gale or two which was nothing compared with Mr.
Howe or any of his sympathetic natives.

Apparently the natives, by means of smoke signals, had
sent the news right round the island that the circumnavigators were to be expected, and Kelly makes frequent refer-
ence to these signal fires. He had some cause to distrust
the natives before hearing of Howe, and now he set out to
avoid them altogether if it were at all possible. But his
little boat had to come into the land often, and he could not
avoid the natives who were pretty sure to be watching her
every movement from the hilltops, and signaling her whereabouts all along the coast.

On January 13 they fell in with a chief, named Lamanbunganah, who wanted them to fight on his side against
another chief named Tolobunganah, who happened to be
his brother.

Tolobunganah, according to Lamanbunganah, was in
league with Howe and everything else that was bad, and
nothing would satisfy him but that Kelly and his men
should muster all their arms and proceed immediately to the
slaughter of Tolo and his tribe, and the confiscation of his
goods and all his wives. To this Kelly gave a curt refusal,

not wishing to be mixed in any tribal brawls, but Laman would brook no refusal and immediately summoned some 50 of his braves who, suddenly springing from nowhere, surrounded the travelers and placed them in a thoroughly nasty corner.

Here, however, inspiration came from a most unexpected source. Briggs, one of the natives in the boat, discovered that he was married to the daughter of no less a personage than Chief Laman himself; he had also other wives and numerous progeny, of course, but that was beside the point. Inquiries were made upon the spot, and it was established that what Briggs said was quite true. Not only the chief's daughter, but several others of his wives were not 50 yards away; Laman fell upon his son-in-law's neck and wept copiously, and in the general hullaballoo Kelly and the gang got away. They lay off the coast that night and Briggs, fresh from a reunion with his wives, managed to get out to them with the news that they had better go on. They had been aware of that, however, and went.

Then, as ill luck would have it, head winds delayed them further down the coast and they fell in with the tribe of Laman's brother Tolo. To prevent any possible encounter with Howe, or complications that would follow the desire of Tolo to conscript him into his army in the war with Laman, Kelly acted warily here and preferred to beat on and off the shore in the dangers that he knew rather than to stand in and face the dangers that he did not know. The wind remained ahead and they had to go somewhere or be driven out to sea and maybe fetch up at New Zealand, so they put in to a small island around which seals were playing, and hauled the boat up on the beach.

Here they were held by the wind for several days, during which Tolo and his tribe remained on the beach of the mainland not far away and Kelly kept a careful watch, filling in the days by clubbing seals and flaying them. Their skins were valued at £1 apiece in Hobart Town, and were consequently worth having. Kelly wished to discover all he could as to Howe and his whereabouts and wished to communicate with the natives and for that purpose took the boat in close enough one day for Briggs to talk. Tolo swore complete and everlasting ignorance of Howe and all his works, expressing the suspicion that he was actually with Laman, but Kelly was suspicious and refused all overtures to come ashore.

He must have been a pretty good business man, however, in addition to his other qualities, for he bartered, from the safety of the boat, the carcasses of the seals for the kangaroo skins of the natives. He insisted that only a few natives should swim out to the boat with the skins while he threw the carcasses overboard for them to rescue, and trade was good —so good, indeed, that on the suggestion of Tolo Kelly and the crew took over six women to the island to help with the sealing operations, and stayed there longer. It was on the 16th January that Kelly first put in at this seal island, and it was not until the 23rd that he left. The log records the fact that on this information being given to Tolo—that Kelly intended to leave,—"the whole mob seemed filled with sorrow and the women all began to cry." Tolo would not allow his friends to go, however, without a dance in their honor, and it was held round a fire on the beach on the night before they went. The dance must have been a famous one, and the diarist's description of it is most interesting.

The whole mob, about three hundred in number, formed a line in three divisions, the men in one, the women in one, and the children in one. Tolobunganah then gave the signal to commence the dance, and a most singular dance it was; the women began in the centre with a song, joining thair hands, forming a circle, and dancing round the heap of dead seals, then throwing themselves down on the sand and putting themselves into most singular attitudes, beating the lower part of thair bodies with thair hands and kicking the sand over each other with thair feet, the men and children laughing verry much seeming to enjoy the sport. The women then all sat down. The children had a similar dance to the women and sat down. The men then commenced a sort of sham fight with spears and waddies, then dancing round the heap of dead seals.

After that there were no further adventures, and Kelly gave all the natives that he saw the widest berth possible. The boat was well laden with seal and kangaroo skins, so that the voyage would be profitable from the point of view of commerce as well as from that of discovery, and Kelly meant to reach Hobart Town. This he did, on January 30, 1816, coming up the blue Derwent as if he had just returned from a fishing trip down the river, and it was some time before the news went round that the circumnavigators were back. Most people had been skeptical of their fate and never expected to see them again; and indeed the wanderers themselves were considerably surprised at their good fortune.

Such is the story of what must rank as one of the most interesting and hazardous open boat voyages of those hazardous and adventurous days.

CHAPTER III

THE COLORFUL CAREER OF CAPTAIN KELLY

THIS same James Kelly who circumnavigated the island in a whale boat and afterwards was harbor master of Hobart for many years was one of the outstanding maritime figures of the early days of the port of Hobart. Many stories of his adventures have been told, and he certainly appears to have been a courageous and enterprising character. He had vessels principally in the inter-colonial trade, going up to Sydney and across to New Zealand. New Zealand in those days was a wild place, wilder than Tasmania, and ships putting in there often had to take their chance as to what kind of reception was given them.

Of course, as in nearly all cases of the kind, if the whites of some vessel came in to find a seething inclination to murder them on sight on the part of the natives, the possession of that inclination was nearly always solely attributable to the visit of some previous whites who had done enough to cause it. Not all mariners treated the people decently in the places where they landed, and if they went ashore for wood and water at some quiet, hitherto untouched spot, they were likely to carry off some of the native maidens—if they could get them—for their own uses, and to murder such of the unfortunate natives who might bravely come to the rescue of their folk. There were shipmasters who frowned upon this practice and all its attendant evils—Kelly himself was foremost among these—but there were others whose principal interest in them was to set the worst example possible, which they proceeded to do with great gusto upon every possible occasion.

Could it be wondered at that the simple-minded natives grew to look upon the white man—all white men—with horror and aversion, and felt only when they saw him an inclination to murder him on sight? This inclination they at first were wont to indulge in, until the unfortunate wretches found that the white fiend's guns gave them no chance and it was always they who were murdered, and not the white man. Then they resorted to strategies, and it was at this stage of New Zealand and Polynesian development generally that there are so many stories of massacres, missing ships, and murdered crews. Often the good whites suffered for the bad, for the natives could make no distinction; nor were they aware that there was much cause for making any.

In the end, of course, they were beaten, just as they were beaten everywhere else, and they had to bow before an advancing conquest of the whites that could never prove of benefit to them. In Tasmania the whole of the natives were wiped out; in Australia the years will show that they fared little better, and even to-day their state in that fair continent is a deplorable one. In New Zealand the superior intelligence and loftiness of the Maoris—quite a different kind of people from the blacks of Australia—have given them some chance, and their lot has not been so bad.

Kelly did a fair bit of trading round the coasts of New Zealand in the days when the Maoris had just become aware of the danger of the whites. He was mixed up in a few adventures in that colorful but unfortunate period.

On November 12th, 1817, he set out from Hobart Town in his brig *Sophia*, bound on a sealing voyage, that he intended would include a visit to New Zealand. A month out he anchored in Otago Harbor, on the south-eastern coast of New Zealand, where Port Chalmers and Dunedin stand to-day. Then the place was known as Port Daniel and had been first visited by whites only seven years before. Kelly went ashore the same day and was met in an apparently friendly way by the natives, although afterwards he attributed the fact largely to the inclusion in his boat's crew of a sailor named W. Tucker, whom the Maoris knew from previous visits and whom they called *Wioree*. That day the natives were most friendly and gave no hint that they ever intended to be any other way; Kelly asked them where he would find seals, and they told him of a place called Small Bay, outside the harbor's mouth, where they said he would have plenty.

Tucker was very pleased with the reception the boat's crew received and spoke at length on the merits of trusting the natives. He urged that on all occasions the boats' crews should go about unarmed, in order that the natives would see that they were totally trusted and no underhand strategy was thought of. Kelly listened to Tucker's advice, and when the brig came to Small Bay next day he, with a boat's crew of six, went ashore without any firearms or other weapons. He bitterly regretted it before long, as also did the unfortunate Tucker, who lost his life through his confidence.

The natives of Small Bay received the whites with broad welcoming smiles and everything appeared to be going well. They called to Tucker by his name of *Wioree*, at which he was delighted. Kelly gave the old chief a piece of iron for a present, and marched off with him and five of his men to barter for potatoes, leaving one man in charge of the boat by the beach. The natives were very thick round the bay, but the significance of that fact did not strike anybody. The first occurrence to cause any suspicion was when Kelly reached the chief's hut, where he saw a man who was obviously not a native. This man was a Lascar, and when he saw a chance he whispered to Kelly that he was the only survivor of the brig *Matilda*, the whole of whose crew had been murdered and eaten by these same Maoris, not very long before. They had not killed him because he was not white, and he was regarded as something of a curiosity among them.

Kelly pricked up his ears at the Lascar's yarn, obviously

only too true, and wished that he had not been so ready to
leave his arms behind. However, there was nothing for it
now but to put a bold face on it and keep smiling. *Wioree*
and the others had still no suspicion. Kelly knew that it
was of no use to run for the boat, for there were hundreds
of Maoris between the chief's tent and the beach and they
were well cut off. Unarmed amongst that mob! He smiled
serenely and chatted with the chief, and sought to buy potatoes; inwardly he was in the tightest corner of his life,
and knew it.

There was not long to wait before the true position was
made known. Some sixty or more natives had crowded into
the chief's yard and all the women were absent, which was
a significant thing. The natives were pressing round,
watching the bartering for potatoes, noting with delight
that the whites really were unarmed. Suddenly, without the
slightest warning, while Kelly was casting about for some
scheme by which they could make a retreat, there was a fearful yell and the whole place became a chaos of shrieking
natives and flying spears. Kelly and two of his men were
thrown instantly, not being killed because, probably, of the
greater delights to be obtained from torturing them. The
other two never rose again but Kelly was quickly on his feet
in the struggling, roaring, fuming mob.

Tucker and the other two were also seized but, being on
the edge of the compound, got out of the captor's arms and
made a mad bolt for the beach. On the way one was brought
down with a flying spear, and all of them would surely have
been murdered had not the natives had a greater interest in
securing Kelly. As it was, the unfortunate *Wioree* was
taken on the beach by some fleet-footed natives who pursued
him, and struck him down. He called to them loudly to
remember who he was and to have mercy, but they cut him
limb from limb and carried the trunk that remained away
on a spear. The man who had been guarding the boat they
had taken from behind and clubbed, but he was not sense-

less, and with the other survivor managed to launch the boat and get off.

In the meantime the fight was raging in the chief's compound, and all hope of Kelly's escape appeared quite gone. The two who had got off in the boat lay-to a while, since the natives rushed back to the compound and left them, and wondered why the shrieking and the yells did not cease. Then they saw Kelly tearing madly along the beach towards them! Two hundred natives were at his heels, but every now and then Kelly turned and flailed around him with a billhook which he fortunately had been carrying; and brought them down by the sheer force of his arm, and cowed them for the instant by the strength of his determined personality. Spears and clubs flew thick around him and he was struck more than once, but not badly; there seemed to be a pact between all the natives that he should be taken alive, probably because of an idea that he would taste better that way.

When Kelly saw that the boat had gone, his spirits must have sunk within him, but he did not give in. He formed the center of a large circle that swayed about the beach, in the midst of which his towering figure stood with the flail of the billhook wreaking death, and such was the force of his blows that he was able actually to make a breach in all that mob and reach the water. Here the boat had been backed in to give him a chance and he sped into the surf. Eager hands grasped him and pulled him aboard, and the boat was off swifter than it had ever been propelled in its career before.

But that was not the end of the day's adventures, by any means. It was only the desperate beginning. Kelly wondered that the natives did not pursue the boat as hotly as they might have done, but his mind was cleared on that point when, rounding a point, he saw his brig lying at anchor with a hundred bloodthirsty natives swarming all over her. For the instant he thought the *Sophia* had been already taken, and the whole of the horrible plot forced itself home to him. These natives aboard the ship were from another part of the harbor, and it was obvious there had been a concerted plan to take those who landed in the chief's compound while the other natives came, still under the guise of friendliness, out to the ship and made a bloody butchering there. It was all so confoundedly easy! The ship's people would not know of the fate of their friends in the boat for they could not hear the yells and in any case would not know what full significance to attach to them: they would not repulse the natives who came out to their ship, and they would be able to get aboard in their full strength without the slightest hindrance. Kelly inwardly felt a spark of admiration for the native strategy, while he cursed . . .

Then he saw that the *Sophia* was not yet taken. There was his crew, walking unarmed about the decks grinning with the natives. Apparently the time for the attack had not yet come, but the situation was desperate enough. When they saw Kelly and the other survivors returning, the natives might make a wild swoop and that would be the end.

Kelly determined once again to put a bold face on it, and came on, whistling. He mounted the rope ladder and came aboard as if nothing had happened, and offered no explanation either for the fact that so few had returned or for his own wounds. At this the natives, who had expected to see nothing further of him but his well-broiled corpse, were nonplused; they could not make it out. They asked Kelly what had become of the others? He said they were coming out with potatoes, and smiled with the chief; in the meantime he was desperately warning his crew of the real position, and getting them gradually aft where they could have arms. They did not appear to have any chance at all against the grinning hordes of savages who sat about in their rigging and looked smilingly on.

But the next thing those savages saw was a solid square

of the crew formed on the poop beneath the main boom, armed to the teeth and not looking friendly at all.

At this their chief, a huge brute called Corockar, swung out of the rigging with a shriek and summoned his men to the battle: the friendliness on their faces turned to a furious blood-lust and they swept aft. The little brig was so crowded with shrieking, swaying natives that they could not move properly and the battle became a hand-to-hand one. In this affray the tactics of the trained whites, in the narrow space of their own decks, were superior; they could not use their fire-arms after the first volley—that was devastating enough—so they took the huge sealing knives that were slung by their sides and set to with these wholeheartedly.

Each man had two large sealing knives in his belt, for flaying the seals, and these were most excellent weapons. Kelly himself had a capstan bar with which he committed most efficient slaughter; the natives began to fall so fast that the decks were slippery with their blood, and the others could not stand up. These long knives were beyond them: their spears and clubs were of little use at such close quarters, and despite the fact that they were so outnumbered the whites gained a decisive victory. If such an encounter had been fought in the open bush ashore, of course, they would have had no chance, but on their own decks they were at an advantage they well knew how to use.

Now many of the natives began to jump overboard in fear, and most of these were drowned. A strong ebb was running and the brig was a fair distance from the shore. Corockar saw that he was beaten and ordered a general retreat; but he was seized as a hostage and flung into the cabin, which was bolted and battened over him. The other natives who still lived leapt over the side, and a few reached the shore. Forty or fifty had been slain with the knives: twice that number must have been drowned. The square of whites stood together solidly throughout the encounter and the only casualties they suffered were two wounded.

When the natives had gone they washed the blood off the decks and Kelly sat down to think things out. It was a flat calm, then, and they could not get out; in any case they had come for seals and seals they meant to have. They warped the brig out a little further and let her be; Corockar remained under hatches.

That night Kelly kept a good watch but nothing happened.

In the morning, however, it appeared that quite half the natives of the province of Otago had gathered on the beach, and there was such a shrieking going on that it was dreadful to hear. Apparently the natives thought that Corockar had been eaten, and when he was led, well bound, out on deck for their inspection—they could see the ship's decks from the beach, which was still not far away—they uttered wild howls of joy. They had two score canoes on the beach, and it looked as if they would take to these and surround the ship, which they could still easily have taken.

But they feared that if they made too great a show of hostilities Corockar would be killed.

That was exactly the fear Kelly meant them to have, and he found ways of imparting that knowledge to Corockar himself. He was still without both his potatoes and his seals, and he allowed Corockar to know that a good life-sized canoe full of potatoes, and no funny business, would secure his freedom. Corockar yelled to the shore to send out all the potatoes in the country. A very large canoe was chosen and the watchers aboard the brig saw great loads of potatoes being put into it, with mats underneath; what they did not see being embarked were some two-score huge warriors, armed to the teeth, who were hidden under the mats. A queer movement among the mats as the canoe was almost alongside, however, gave the keen-witted Kelly warning, and without waiting for any official inquiries or anything else he provided material for an inquest by letting those mats have a broadside, good and proper.

The effect was electrical. Immediately the forty warriors arose and pitched the potatoes overboard; another broadside and they leapt overboard themselves—but not in retreat. Swimming along beside the canoe, which they quickly maneuvered so that it gave them shelter, they headed towards the brig and swam strongly for her. Arms were of little use now since the target was so poor, and once again Kelly and his men were up against it. The brig now mustered only 14 hands, and the chances of repelling the natives were really slight. They saw other canoes being launched from the beach; the situation was desperate. The calm was flat and stagnant, and if they slipped their cable all that they could do would be to drift ashore.

The natives came steadily on; a few were picked off by gunfire. The crew were stationed with boarding pikes around the brig's sides and gave the first arrivals such a reception that the lot of them soon hauled off, without one having been able to reach the decks. In the meantime Corockar left to his own devices, leapt overboard to join his fellows but was shot in the neck before he had gone far. Obviously badly wounded, two of his fellows swam to him and supported him to the shore, with such a show of bravery about it—for it was a brave thing to do; they had to swim right under the guns' fire to reach their chief—that Kelly ordered that no one should shoot in their direction. The wounding of the chief put an end to the encounter, and all the natives retired to the beach with their canoes and their wounds. Ashore, they carried Corockar into the bush, where he shortly afterwards died. As soon as they had gone Kelly landed nine men and sawed up the whole of their canoes—42 of them—into firewood, which he took on board. Then he set fire to the native village and, a breeze having sprung up off the land, weighed anchor and stood away for Chatham Island.

That New Zealand episode, of course, was not by any means the first or the last of Captain Kelly's adventures.

He was born at Parramatta, New South Wales, on December 24, 1791, so that he must have been one of the first whites born in Australia, or at least among the earliest of them. What he did in his early days it is impossible now to say, but the period was a colorful one and the times stirring. Quite early he turned his attention to whaling and between 1812 and 1815 appears to have been whaling out of the port of Sydney, probably as master. After that he came to Hobart Town, and, taking a liking to the place, remained there and sailed out of the far southern port for the rest of his life, dying in the street outside his home on April 20, 1859.

In 1818 a ship of his which was lying in Port Jackson was seized by escaping convicts, and if it had been anybody else's ship but Kelly's they probably would have got away with it. However, with Kelly it was a different matter and, after a desperate fight, he was able to retake his ship from the desperadoes before they were clear of the harbor. In those days Sydney was a lawless hole, and queerer things happened there even than in old Hobart.

After that Kelly sailed ships in the colonial trade for some years, and for a while brought up the Huon pine from Macquarie Harbour—which he had discovered—to Hobart. In 1819 he was appointed Harbormaster and pilot at Hobart Town, and was one of the foremost followers of bay whaling. In 1830 his job as Harbormaster was taken from him, but he retained his pilot's berth, and for many years was pilot in the River Derwent and Storm Bay. At the same time he was still interested in whaling ventures and in ordinary trading vessels, and for years was most successful in practically everything he undertook.

In 1821 or thereabout there is a record of him having sent a brig—the *Venus*—after whales from Hobart Town down to the ice pack at the edge of the Antarctic. The *Venus* penetrated to 72° South, right in the heavy ice at the entrance to the Ross Sea, and conducted whaling operations in that sea which was destined, over a hundred years later, to become the world's best and perhaps last whaling ground.   To-day Norwegian fleets of 12,000 and 14,000 ton steamers, with their broods of little 70-ton whale catchers, hunt the whales in these icy seas that Kelly first exploited, but the difficulties appear to have been too much for the *Venus* and she did not go again that way.   Kelly found sealing islands of his own in the stormy sub-Antarctic waters, too, and sent out ships for unknown destinations, with the masters bound upon a £5,000 bond never to disclose whence they obtained their seals.

Kelly turned to farming, too, and held large areas at Bruni Island, off the south-east coast of Tasmania; in Hobart itself he acquired considerable property.   To-day a street in Battery Point, a suburb of Hobart most of which he once owned, bears his name, and the oldest stone steps in the old colonial seaport, leading from Kelly street down to the neighborhood of the wharves, have been Kelly's Steps from time immemorial, though most of the local inhabitants seem convinced that the name was taken from some murder that occurred there or from a woman who cut her throat, and have long since forgotten poor, adventurous Kelly.

Kelly was always enterprising but not always successful, and in the thirties adversity came to him heavily.   He lost badly on whaling; his ships were unfortunate and his cruises unprofitable; he was let down by bad masters and worse crews: his property slipped from him.   He lost one of his ships on the Tasmanian coast.   But he was never once beaten, throughout his long life; whatever happened, he was always prepared to begin again.   The wealth that he had earned so hardly from the seas slipped through his hands, and his favorite son was drowned at whaling.   His job as pilot went and he turned to wharfinger.   He still was interested in shipping and able to lay his plans; right at the time of his death he was planning a further venture in his ship *Dogo*, which had been lying out of commission for some time.

Although he looked always to the future right up to the end, for some years he had been ready for his death and kept a sum of money in the bank sufficient to meet his funeral expenses. He used to say that he hoped he would die at sea in order that that money might be saved, but he dropped dead in the street on his way to the wharves one morning. For some years he had had his name and "all particulars except the date" carved ready on the gravestone above the vault which sheltered his wife in the quiet cemetery at St. David's. Cathedral, in old Hobart Town, and when he died he was buried there and the date of his death added incorrectly.

CHAPTER IV

THE DOLLARS OF DEATH

BLIGH'S adventures in Australia and his call at Tasmania are fully dealt with in the history books. But one little sidelight seems to have escaped the historians—the fact that it was one of Bligh's men who was the first to grow potatoes in Tasmanian soil. William Portlock was his name, and when the *Bounty* was in Adventure Bay he filled some tubs that were lying about the deck with good Tasmanian earth, and in these tubs he grew potatoes on the way to Tahiti. The first actual tiller of the soil—Tasmanian soil in Tasmania—was also a mariner: one Charles Bishop, I believe, who was with Bass and Flinders in 1798 and remained behind to do some sealing in the Bass Strait Islands. He found that peas and potatoes and so on flourished.

Perhaps these were poor pursuits on the part of hardy mariners, but they show that at least they also knew how to make use of the soil, as well as to discover it.

But they were usually interested in much more romantic affairs than the growing of potatoes. There is the case of Captain William Smith, for instance. Captain Smith owned a little schooner, the *Caledonia*, in which he was wont to engage in such trades as paid him, asking no questions, taking what commissions came his way. He sailed mostly out of Launceston and consorted with the evil gentry who sealed in Bass Strait; but if he consorted with them he was prepared to accept more profitable employment, if any came his way. One day a gentleman called to see him, one Roberton, who told strange stories of Peru and the Chilean coast where he said he had served quite a time.

Roberton came to Smith aboard the *Caledonia* and proposed to him certain schemes, about which he was pretty furtive, and Smith was unable to find out much despite the frequency with which he treated his guest to good rum. But at least he did know that Roberton wanted to charter the *Caledonia:* he spoke airily of thousands of pounds. Apparently Roberton knew of some place where trade was good and money was to be picked up easily. Whatever was afoot, Smith accepted the proffered employment and, with Roberton safe and sound in the best cabin in the ship, the little schooner dropped down the River Tamar one night early in 1826.

Smith did not know where they were going, but from time to time Roberton, who rather liked drink, gave him some further spot in the wide Pacific to steer for. As he reached each successive point, another was set. Roberton disclosed that he was willing to pay Smith 14,000 Mexican dollars for the work he wanted him to do for him, if all went well. Smith was pleased at first, but later he noticed that when in his cups Roberton raved about much greater sums than a mere 14,000 dollars. Captain Smith began to think there was a pretty big treasure attached to the expedition.

He spoke to Roberton about it, politely suggesting that 14,000 dollars would be a poor reward if they succeeded in retrieving so great a treasure as Roberton was seeking. Roberton told him to go to hell.

There were words at that. There were frequently "words," after that, between Mr. Smith and Mr. Roberton. One day Mr. Roberton, having nothing better to do, picked up Mr. Smith and threw him overboard into the sea from the poop of his own ship. He proposed to take the crew on, carry out his business—whatever it was—himself, and let Smith drown.

But the *Caledonia's* crew did not know what Mr. Roberton's business was and they did know that Mr. Smith paid them. They stopped the ship and picked up their half-drowned and cursing skipper.

After that relations between Messrs. Smith and Roberton were distinctly strained, but they both continued to occupy the same poop and to eat at the same table. Roberton confided to Smith that he had been fighting with Lord Cochrane—better known as Lord Dundonald—in the wars for the liberation of Chile and Peru. He allowed Smith to gather that they were after a very great treasure indeed, which had somehow passed into his possession from those days in Peru. They patched a sort of peace and the little schooner carried on, though still nobody but Roberton knew where she was supposed to be going.

Eventually they reached a spot in the Pacific somewhere close to the Ladrones. Here Roberton, fed up with Smith's grumbles and incessant threats to put back to Tasmania if he was not told the full purport of the expedition, calmly stole one of the schooner's boats, one night when Smith was asleep, took some of the men with him (the mention of gold was enough for that), and sneaked off to reach the goal on his own account.

Smith, waking up next morning to find his best boat and half his crew, together with that rascal Roberton upon whom he was depending for payment for the voyage, all cleared out, lost his head. He made for the Spanish island of Guam. If he had had any sense, he would have given anything Spanish the widest berth possible, since it was obvious that Roberton's dealings had not been on the side of Spain and, whatever he was after, it was nothing to Spain's profit.

The *Caledonia* reached Guam and anchored there. The Spanish governor came aboard and offered Smith warm welcome. Smith poured out his heart and told the governor all about the scoundrel Roberton, hinting that there was some story of treasure behind the scenes. The governor listened with polite interest. At the end of the recital he expressed deep sympathy for Señor Smith in the scurvy manner Señor Roberton had treated him, and said that anything upon earth that he could do he would most gladly set about. There was one slight matter, however, to which it desolated him to have to draw Señor Smith's attention. That was that no vessel whatever was allowed to come into Guam which had not previously been into the Philippines and got a license from the governor there.

Señor Smith suggested that he should put out again and go to the Philippines for the necessary license, but the governor, though declaring he would be delighted if such a suggestion were practicable, said that he would lose his position and his head if it were known that he had permitted any foreign ship to come into Guam and pass on to the Philippines afterward. There was no help for it; both Smith and his schooner would have to stay.

Señor Smith cursed and fumed but could do nothing. The governor, however, suggested that he might send out one of his own boats in search of the boorish ruffian Roberton, promising to do his best to apprehend the pirate. Probably he was much more interested in seeing what Señor Roberton was after in that locality: if it was anything to do with dollars he wanted some of them.

He sent out the boat, overlooking Smith's suggestion that he should be allowed to go with it. A gentleman named Miranda, a fiery son of Spain, was sent in charge.

Smith had to stay cooling his heels in Guam, while Señor Miranda set out to look for Roberton. Strangely enough, Miranda did find Roberton. And as soon as he saw him he recognized him. They had fought on opposite sides in the South American wars, Miranda for Spain and Roberton for Peru since the pay was better, and he didn't like Spain, anyway. In that encounter Roberton had once been unfortunate enough to capture Miranda, and had him soundly flogged for refusing to disclose information.

It must have been a tragic meeting, here in the South Seas, years afterwards.

Roberton was hopelessly outnumbered by Miranda and his boatful of well-fed Spaniards. He had only three men in his boat. Miranda took him easily, and immediately demanded of Roberton where the treasure was to be found. He knew very well that something of the kind was going on, for Roberton to be bringing strange schooners from Tasmania on quests of which even the captain was in ignorance.

Roberton admitted that there was a treasure, but told Miranda to go to hell and find it.

Miranda answered that he would send Roberton to hell, and that pretty quickly, if he didn't straightaway give all the information.

Roberton shut his mouth and kept it shut. Miranda had him taken ashore and lashed up to a tree. Then he placed a negro flagellator on each side of him, passing on the news that unless he spoke Roberton would have fifty of the best about his back.

Roberton said nothing.

Miranda smiled.

"Tear off his shirt!" he snarled to one of his men. "Now, dog of England, speak!"

Roberton proved that he was of England, but no dog. He did not speak.

"Carve him up!" Miranda yelled to the flagellators.

They immediately set about their duty, flailing the flesh from Roberton's bones, alternately bringing home great clouts on his bare back one of which would be enough to lay out a strong steer.

When it was over they rubbed in salt.

Again Miranda, with a curse, told Roberton when he regained consciousness, to disclose the whereabouts of the treasure. Roberton said not a word.

The next day they brought him out again, lashed him up, and gave him another fifty brutal lashes.

"Now, you bright pig! Speak!" hissed Miranda.

Roberton smiled.

Miranda nodded to the negroes, who, one each side, promptly began laying it on again.

But Roberton was flesh and blood. He could not stand much more. After a few more strokes he muttered, between clenched and bloody teeth, that he had something to say.

They removed his bonds, and took him out to the boat. He said there was not far to go.

As soon as he got to the boat he jumped over the side and promptly sank, making no slightest effort to swim.

Taken aback at this move, Miranda sent overboard a trained Manila diver who happened to be one of his crew, and this man soon reached Roberton and brought him again to the surface. In the excitement of passing him aboard the boat, however, he slipped out of their hands and, sinking, was seen no more.

That was the end of Roberton . . .

They found some of his papers afterwards, and amongst them was a sort of Treasure Island chart, complete with cross and directions, but so crudely done that not even the island was recognizable. Nobody but Roberton could have used that chart, and whatever the treasure was the chances are that it still lies hidden somewhere in the Pacific Islands. The papers showed, too, that some time in 1822 Roberton had sailed from Callao for Manila in a big Spanish galleon carrying 90,000 dollars. The galleon never arrived, and neither did Roberton. The probability is that, with accomplices among the crew, he led a mutiny aboard the galleon during the voyage, took her, murdered her officers and everybody else who opposed him, and then took her off to some out-of-the-way island where he buried the treasure and scuttled the ship.

Then he got rid of his accomplices, either by trapping

them into the hands of the savages who would promptly eat them, or by some other such means. Then he seems to have drifted down to Bass Strait where he picked up the hard bitten Captain Smith and decided that he and his schooner would be useful for the recovery of the treasure.

Eventually Smith drifted back to his old haunts of the Strait and listened no more to stories of strange gentlemen from Peru.

BOOK II

THE CONVICT SHIPS

CHAPTER V

THE STORY OF TRANSPORTATION

IN any survey of the history of Tasmania, from any angle, the transportation period cannot be overlooked. There are many who would prefer to forget that it ever came, and who have done their best already to make an authentic survey of it next to impossible; but it happened; it *was* an era—and a long and far-reaching one—it cannot be forgotten, and it should not be ignored. When the various convict stations of the island were abandoned, ship loads of priceless records were burned, or destroyed, or seized by private persons for their own ends; it is recorded that a boat load was taken and dumped into the sea. Everything was done that could be done to efface the records from memory and at least to remove them from the perusal of generations to come, but if many of the actual records are now lost the story goes on. There were still persons living in 1930 who had personal experience of something of the horror of these dark days, for the exportation of convicts from England to Tasmania did not cease until 1853, and for twenty years or so after that the penal settlement of Port Arthur was in existence.

From its very beginnings Tasmania was a convict island; it began as the "Botany Bay of Botany Bay," and the first settlers were convicts and their soldier guards. Afterwards free settlers came, of course, and took up land, but for many years the development was largely in the hands of the transported convicts and the place was little better than a penal settlement. At first they were sent from the earlier colony of New South Wales, and in the first years there were several occasions when the place was face to face with starvation. Before long things were on a better footing and the natural suitability of the soil to all forms of agriculture, coupled with the obvious potentialities of what really was a most beautiful and fertile island, led the English authorities to the belief—which they held for many years—that here was a penal settlement Nature-made.

There was another reason for that view. The island was a natural prison; even to-day, on the all-too-frequent occasions of Australian shipping strikes, one is forcibly struck at times by the difficulty of leaving it. A hundred years ago it was the very end of the world, a place to which one went giving up all hope; it lay at the end of a long and dangerous sea voyage; it was cut off completely from the sunnier and happier land of Australia by the waters of Bass Strait, across which no tiny craft would care to venture; beyond it to the south lay nothing but the continent of the Antarctic, and to east and west nothing but the great gray sea, windswept round the world. New Zealand's west coast, wild and forbidding, was 1,500 miles away and more, and that was the nearest land.

The island was encircled by an ocean noted with good cause for the fury of its storms, swept ceaselessly by the wild west winds of the Roaring Forties; the whole land lay in that windswept and hail-torn belt of Cape Horn winds. Along the west coast the west wind threw the long rollers of the ocean in ceaseless torment, for the gaunt cliffs here were the only stand against the wild wind and the wilder sea in the whole circle from Cape Horn upon the one side to Cape Horn upon the other; against this rock-bound island the sea leapt in fury, and the wind, so long used to undisputed kingdom, spent all the strength and all the bitter energy it had gathered in its world-circling whirl. From the latitudes of the Horn it came, fed upon the cold of the ice-drifts from the Antarctic, pampered by the submission of thousands upon thousands of miles of sea, and it lashed its servant hail and snow squalls before it upon the mountains of the south. Who could escape from an island such as that, surrounded by such seas?

To the east the sea was kinder, for a while, but all around its kindness was deceptive, and fierce and sudden storms awaited the trusting mariner. . . . And then where might the escapee go? Not to Australia, for there was nothing there; if he went to the haunts of man he would soon be apprehended, and if he did not he would soon die. Within the island of Tasmania itself there was little chance of successful escape; in the milder climate of the eastern shores an exile might live for a while, and some did, in friendship with the blacks. But for most of them escape was hopeless and the only way out was death.

It was a most excellent prison island, and the statesman who first appreciated that fact did his England a service indeed. But he cannot expect ever to be very gratefully remembered in Tasmania, for the discovery once made was not lightly to be forgotten and the story of the struggle for independence by the Tasmanians is not altogether a pleasant chapter of British history. They were not powerful enough to take up arms, and then they often had the knowledge that if they overthrew the government they themselves would be overthrown by the convicts, whom they could not hope to keep down. And then? It was better to go on. There were, indeed, many times in those early days when the authority of what government there was was very slender, and the safety of the whole island hung by a poor thread.

For half a century the convicts of England were poured into Tasmania, at the rate of thousands a year. In those bad old days the most ordinary thing to do with any person convicted of anything, speaking broadly, was to hang him; there was little thought of reform or any improved system of imprisonment. Life was cheap and also often nasty. The most paltry offense was often sufficient to reap ghastly punishment. Corpses swung by the English country roadsides, and women picnicked at the hangings. The prisons were over-crowded, for the simple psychological reason that brutality bred brutality and wanton murder by the state bred wanton murder by the people. Prisoners were housed in conditions that were indescribably appalling, and often their state was so low and their condition so terrible that nothing conceivable could have made it worse. It was a case of hanging them, letting them rot to death in their hell holes, or transporting them to Tasmania, New South Wales, Cape Colony, and those other places which would take them. The best thing was to transport them, for by that means they had a chance, and there were many who made good in after years who first became "pioneers" in that compulsory fashion.

As the years passed the condition of the prisons improved, as also did the condition of the people, and New South Wales, Cape Colony, Victoria, and other places which grew to power soon allowed it to be known that they would have no more of transportation. It had had its day, as far as they were concerned; something of the rough toil of pioneering had been done, and the future for these places was infinitely the brighter if the stigma of the broad arrow was removed from them. The free settlers did well; it was obvious that these places would develop into rich colonies of the Empire. But years after the clank of the chain gang and the sigh of the lash had disappeared from other colonies, the convict ships still set out for Tasmania. It was not that that lovely land would become any the less valuable a colony than those others. For it was a glorious place indeed, a God-made loveliness that was turned to hell by man. But it was small, and weak, and of little account in the eyes of the powers of the bigger lands; it was afar off and its voice was lowly. . . .

For years the people cried out against the yoke of English convictism and the stigma of the chains; self-government had not come then, and Downing Street was far re-

moved, unmoved, and hostile. Some of the earlier Governors were not strong men; the strongest was a martinet
who looked upon his charge as a penal settlement and a
penal settlement only. He had seen a good deal of the
foulest forms of slavery in Honduras, and was not to be
moved by what he saw in Tasmania. He ruled with an
iron hand; he suppressed the newspapers; he was a tyrant
in a land where tyranny held sway. After him came others
—the story has been told in many histories, and it is not
proposed to dwell upon it here—but steadily the voice of
the people arose until it was heard even in London.

"No people in this hemisphere will trust a British Minister until the history of Van Diemen's Land is forgotten!"
cried bitterly a newspaper of the day when for the thou-
sandth time it had to recount the intolerant attitude of the
British Government and to spread the news that yet another promise had been broken. "Shall the fairest isle in
the south be one huge jail? Shall the free inhabitants be
made the passive instruments of punishing English crimi-
nals? Is this the only capacity in which the British Gov-
ment will recognize free colonists?"

The cry of the people was loud and growing louder, and
there had to come a time when it could not pass unheard.
In 1846, Earl Grey said that he was "prepared to express
the opinion that transportation should be got rid of"—an
opinion that when published in Tasmania caused wild joy,—
and wilder sorrow, not very much later, when the same
Earl Grey launched out upon a grander and an even wider
scheme for the exportation of England's convicts. He sent
out a shipload of Irish convicts in the ship *Neptune* to the
Cape of Good Hope, with a pretty good idea that Good
Hope would not have them. The *Neptune* in the course
of time came to anchor in Table Bay, but not one of her
convicts ever set foot in Cape Town. The colonists were
stronger there, and in a mood not to be trifled with. They,
too, had had their experience of the futility of expecting

fair hearing of their case in Downing Street, and they too had long chafed under the yoke of convictism; the *Neptune* was the last straw and they chased her out of Table Bay forever. Feeling was high and the position ugly; no Cape colonist would supply food to the hated convict ship, and travelers ashore were issued with passes to prove that they were not from the *Neptune*. Every public body in Cape Town supported the resistance and was prepared to make it stronger, if the need arose.

But what did it matter? There was still Tasmania, and the *Neptune* was ordered on there. A settler of the Cape who had supplied her with food was given a knighthood that he probably did not enjoy; the people of the Cape came to the waterfront and cheered when she spread her sails to go. It was a victory for them, and none was more pleased than their fellow colonists of Tasmania, 6,000 miles away. But it was no victory for them. *They* could not chase the *Neptune* away, and she came to the Derwent with their convicts.

"The free inhabitants cannot expect that when they choose to call for the cessation of transportation, the Imperial policy is to be altered on their demand," said Earl Grey. The colonists burned his effigy and flung the ashes into the sea; they would have flung him in, too, had he been there. The colonists, he said, "have no right to refuse to receive any number of prisoners the Government may choose to send." The colonists thought otherwise and said so in no uncertain manner, but they were too weak to take up arms. The place *was* a penal settlement, a tyrannically governed Crown Colony; and they were not strong.

Immediately the *Neptune* came her shipload of convicts received pardons and was marched ashore, while the colonists looked grimly on. "This painful exhibition of Ministerial contempt stung more than it injured the people of Tasmania," said the newspapers, "and it was solemnly sworn that nothing but the want of power prevented them from taking up arms in their cause and chasing the vessel from these waters. . . . We are convinced that appeals to the justice and humanity of the English Ministry are utterly unavailing. The principles that have induced them to relieve armed or rebellious colonies lead only to the oppression and contemptuous disregard of those which are too feeble for effectual resistance. . . . We solemnly protest against the cruelty and the falsehood of the English Government." These and stronger statements were drawn up and signed by mass meetings of the free Tasmanians; but for three years after that the convicts still came. Influential colonists went to England and prayed to be heard at Downing Street; they *were* heard—sometimes, and with little grace, by insignificant officials; but the exportation of the vicious and the condemned went on unchecked and unrelieved.

"Are we doomed for ever, my God, to see the loveliness of our island stained with the refuse of the English jails; the fairness of our people tainted with the stigma of the broad arrow; the happiness of our children and our children's children saddened and embittered with the background of the triangles and the scourge?" cried a Hobart citizen of renown. But who answered? And who cared? The prisons of Old England were still crowded, and the gallows could not cope with all the fodder that was sent to them. "The question involved is more important than a single colony," said Lord Stanley; and transportation went on. . . . But there came a time when even Officialdom in all its glory had to fall before Justice, and at long last the fair name of Tasmania was cleared from the unsought and unmerited disgrace that had attached to it for half a century. On February 10th, 1853, transportation to Tasmania ceased.

In a way transportation was only a form of migration with the principal difference that the migrants had no choice in the matter, and the principal disadvantage that a pretty considerable proportion of them could scarcely be expected either to succeed in, or to develop into assets of, a new country. Many who came had committed little offense against the law; they were neither vicious nor criminal but had been forced into jail because the system under which they lived left few, if any, alternatives for such as they. They had poached a rabbit or a salmon when they were hungry; they had stolen a few pence from a master who should have paid them much more than they ever stole; they had infringed, in some unimportant manner, some one or two of the heterogeneous and largely incomprehensible laws under which they were governed and in the making of which they had no say. Some were political exiles; these were a different class and were for the most part treated well and gave no trouble. The important fact is that many were weak rather than criminal and had been beaten by life rather than by any inherent vice. But the fact that they were weak was no qualification for success in an Australian colony, and it would undoubtedly have been better for the colonies to have developed a free population slowly rather than to have had a comparatively large population that was not free thrust upon them. However, it is easy to look back. Convictism played its part in the growth of Australia, and the part was not wholly bad. It provided the rougher type of labor for the heavy pioneering work; it gave the farmers and the settlers labor to clear their land; it provided some colorful villains of bushrangers who have proved convenient for some compilers of "historical" fiction in later days. It must be remembered, too, that there were many officials and persons in high authority who honestly believed in this system of theirs, and did their best to make it succeed.

In the early days of Tasmania's settlement—between 1804 and, say, about 1810—the convicts worked under their military guards and were subject to strict discipline, although it was naturally impossible to jail them while they were engaged in wresting an outpost of civilization from the virgin bush. If it was futile for their guards to hope to jail them, it was equally futile for the convicts to hope to escape. Then later came the free settlers, and with them the place grew; Hobart Town began to take definite shape, and to provide other forms of employment than felling trees and making roads.

It was at this period that the convicts were of greatest use; the better of them were apportioned out to the settlers to work for them, under strict conditions, and if they behaved themselves they could work their sentences out in this fashion and later develop into more or less satisfactory members of the community, without the too close supervision of the red coats and the ever-present fear of a month or so in the chain gang or a day or two on the treadmill if they were found in some paltry wrong. Gradually the system developed until all the convicts who came were regarded as free labor, and as each vessel arrived her "manifest" was eagerly scanned and her skilled workmen picked out by those who wanted them.

The men were not prisoners so much as exiles, although there was a good smacking of slavery about the thing as well. If they behaved themselves and did not offend their masters, and did not stay out late at night or get drunk— a common habit of the time—and did not commit any breach of the multitudinous regulations drawn up for their benefit, then in the course of time they might become free men and look the world in the face once more.

This "assignment" became the very basis of the whole system, and only those who did grave wrong again after they had arrived in the colony were sent to the prison settlements of Port Arthur and Macquarie Harbour. The bulk of the convicts would better be termed slave migrants, for that was what they were. For minor offenses they were liable to serve varying terms in the road gangs, working out in the bush making roads through rough, inhospitable country. Here they were usually chained together and led a pretty wretched existence; they were housed in adobe huts the ruins of some of which still stand beside the roads the convicts built. But if they behaved, and if they were fortunate enough to secure good masters, the road to freedom was open to many of them. Tickets of leave were granted which carried many privileges, and in some ways the system was by no means so bad as it can be made now to appear. There were, of course, bad masters, who knew that they had only to lodge some frivolous complaint against their servants, when their time of service was nearly up, to have every hope of freedom torn from them and the period of their assignment lengthened indefinitely.

But, whatever may be said for it, in many ways the convict period was horror-filled and horrible. Anthony Trollope, who visited Tasmania in the early 70's, had something to say about it. "The period was a hanging period," he wrote. "The system was one to which flogging was necessary. Tenderness had no part in the thing as it was established. One of two events was certain to come about—either the Government must keep down the convicts or the convicts would put down the Government. There were times in which it almost seemed that the latter event might prevail . . . Of all crimes, murder and attempts to murder seem to have been most in excess. The hangings were frequent and gave rise to sharp expostulations.

"There is a story in the island that the jail chaplain at Hobart Town once remonstrated—not against hanging in general or the number that were hung—but as to the inconvenient celerity with which the ceremony was performed. Thirteen men, he said, could be comfortably hung at once, but no more . . . The hangman was a most important and well paid official. . . . There was much of murder and robbery, much of hanging and slavery. English settlers to whom convicts were assigned of course learned the sweets of slavery. Their servants were intelligent beasts of burden, who had only to be fed, coerced, and made to work. The slave, too, was not purchased, and if he died there was no loss . . ."

And what were the chances of escape in this convict island? Few, few indeed; although escape might have appeared, on the face of things, an easy enough business. . . . "The first preliminaries of escape were easy. A man could run into the bush, and be quit at any rate of the labor of the hour. If he were shepherding sheep, or building fences, or felling timber, during the greater part of the day, no eye, unless that of a brother convict, was upon him. He could go, and the chances of the world were open to him. But when these first preliminaries were so easy it was, of course, essential that they should ordinarily be rendered unsuccessful, and that the attempt should be followed by speedy and sharp punishment. The escaped convict was at once hunted, and generally tracked by the facilities which his starvation rendered to his pursuers. No one but an escaped convict would feed an escaped convict, and none but they who had established themselves as bushrangers had food either to eat or to give.

"Even the established bushrangers, who had homes of some sort in the mountain recesses, who were in league with the blacks, and who knew how to take the wild animals, the kangaroos and wallaby and opossums, were not infrequently driven by famine to surrender themselves . . ." The whole chances against real escape were so weighted, and the thing, from an island such as that, so impossible to the branded wretches who were sent there, that even when they were sent on errands to magistrates with notes requesting their own flogging, they knew it was hopeless to attempt to run away. They went, and were flogged; there was no trial and there was no appeal. The squatters did not have power themselves to punish their assigned servants, but that power was in the hands of the magistrate of the district—generally a squatter himself, to whom the word of any other squatter

was sufficient to bring a flogging on to the back of any
wretch sent to him.

It became so common that no interest was attached to it,
and nothing thought of it, for a convict, when he had done
something, or omitted to do it, or had displeased his master
or his master's mistress in any way, to be sent off to the
magistrate with a note like this: "Dear Sir, please give the
bearer three dozen hard and return him." The man would
take the note because there was nothing else for it, and
suffer the three dozen, too, because there was nothing else
for that. Flogging in Tasmania, in those dark old days,
was so common and so little thought of, that a Governor
of those days thought it so unusual as to merit inclusion
and special mention in his report that "only three-quarters
of the convicts had been flogged" in one year of his office.

Old residents speak to-day of having seen these convicts,
in the days of their youth, peel off their shirts to wash, and
their backs were cut and marked so that there was not a
piece of skin unscarred and scarcely a ridge of the flesh
left free of marks of the scourge. There was one old resident, dead not so very long since, who used to tell of having witnessed one of these floggings. The wretched convict
was lashed to the triangles so that he could not move, his
back was stripped and the flagellator—a fellow convict
who would be flogged himself if he refused to do the deed—
set about the business of carving pieces, literally, off his
back with a niceness and a skill that would have served him
well in the butchering business. There was no sound but
the swinging swish of the scourge and its dull impact on
the yielding flesh; it was handled "beautifully" and took
off the flesh and skin in long, regular pieces, which fell upon
the ground, and as fast as they fell crawling ants came and
fetched them away. When it was all over a bucket of salt
water was thrown over him, and he picked up his poor shirt
and, panting a little and drawn from the pain, was gone.

Of course, harrowing pictures may easily be drawn from

such incidents as that, and often are, nor is there—nor can there reasonably be—the slightest doubt that these days were brutal and terrible almost beyond comprehension to-day. But they were not so bad, in the eyes of the people who suffered them, as they appear in the eyes of those who only imagine them now. There was a different outlook towards pain in those days; everywhere there is evidence of that. Else why did not all wounded sailors die under the torture of the surgeon, after their battles were won? For they were tortured then in a way that would inspire horror now; and they stood it because it was necessary; it was accepted; it was part of their lives. If they were wounded they must suffer torture to be mended again; there were no anesthetics, and there was no escape from pain. They did not seek to escape because they never imagined that it could be done. They set their teeth and stood it. It was the same with the convicts, however base their mold. They expected hell from a world which had only hell to give such as they, and when it came they set their teeth and stood it while they could . . . But it was all horrible and terrible, for all the excuses and the reasonings one may bring forward in alleviation now.

The most terrible part of the transportation system was the penal settlements of Macquarie Harbour and Port Arthur. These were the prisons of a prison island, the places of torment of the damned again of the damned, the ghastly inner circles of a ghastly hell. Macquarie Harbour was the worst; it is doubtful if ever there was a worse man-made hell upon earth. Macquarie Harbour lies in the most inaccessible part of the west coast of Tasmania; the entrance is a narrow and dangerous one, with tide rips and shifting sands. To seaward there can be no escape; the land beyond is wild and inhospitable. It was 220 miles by sea from Hobart—220 of the worst sea-miles in the world. Overland it would not be so far, but nobody who set out to go that way ever came back to tell how it had been done;

wild mountain torrents, crevasse-distorted mountains, bush
so thickly entangled with undergrowth that it was utterly
impassable, combined with a severity of climate and an entire absence of all that would sustain life to make the overland route from Macquarie Harbour to Hobart an absolute
impossibility even to the stoutest expedition, and it was
not until the pioneering work of many years had thrown
roads out into the bush and built bridges and made tracks,
that any went that way.　To the north there was a belt of
country just as wild and equally hopeless to the desperate
men who escaped, and the choice of Macquarie Harbour as
a place of punishment for the convicts of a convict island
was a good one.　In 1821 the Government felt the need of
some place where these wretches could be sent, some place
of terror that would strike fear even into the bravest or
most callous convict soul, for many who were sent out were
desperate and dangerous men.　It was advisable, if any
good purpose were ever to be achieved with convictism, to
separate the worst from the merely bad.　It is obvious that
to discover some form of terror for wretches who had gone
through the English prisons, the hulks, and the miseries of
the convict voyages, called for a refinement of torture that
was difficult to achieve; or at least would have been difficult
of achievement had there been no Macquarie Harbour.
Perhaps it was because the wretched convicts thought there
could be no state worse than that in which they found themselves, landed into the chain gangs of old Hobart Town,
that they ventured further to incur the displeasure of their
masters by refusing to work, by impertinence to their over-
seers, and attempts to mutiny.

But they bargained without Macquarie Harbour.

Macquarie Harbour was chosen on the recommendation
of Captain Kelly, who had found it.　It was chosen because
it combined excellently three great advantages; it "afforded
means of employing the prisoners in such a manner as to
make them severely feel their punishment; it prevented by

its locality the chance of escape; and it rendered the prisoners' labor instrumental, in some measure, to the purposes of repaying the expenses of the establishment." It certainly possessed the first and the second advantage, but the third is doubtful. On December 12, 1821, the first lot of prisoners set out from Hobart Town for Macquarie Harbour, in two brigs, each strongly guarded. It was prophetic of the fate of many another vessel that was to set out upon that voyage that one of these brigs, so terrible was the weather and so dangerous the coast, fetched up on the coast of Australia instead of at Macquarie Harbour. The other did arrive there, on January 2, 1822, but even the heart of the officer in charge was chilled by the sight of the place, and a consultation was held to decide whether they should put back. But the Governor had ordered it, and they put their vessel's head through the tide rips of the entrance and anchored in the harbor.

For some curious reason—perhaps to make escape even more difficult although it was already almost impossible—the officer in charge, a Lieutenant Cuthbertson, decided to make the settlement on an island, called Sarah Island, in the harbor, instead of landing on the mainland. Sarah Island was small and without water; before long it was also without wood, and both wood and water had to be brought to it by gangs which were employed exclusively in that occupation.

From the first the place was hell. It rained every day, the only break in the weather being when it did not, by some chance, rain all day. South-west and westerly gales, with stinging hail squalls that swept in from the Southern Ocean, coupled with the cold and the exposed nature of the island, made the place a torment from which there was no respite. The soil was poor just there, and little would grow. All supplies had to be brought from Hobart, by sea, and so dangerous was the voyage that often the settlement was in a state of starvation before the supply ship arrived.　Often for weeks on end the westerly gale roared through the wet tree-tops and swept the sea upon the rocky shore with a warning fury, as if it were anxious that these mortals—no matter how bad they might be considered— should be gone from such a place as that; and nothing could live in such a sea.　The ships—little brigs and schooners, for the most part—that sailed round from Hobart had to stand on against that westerly wind along a particularly dangerous lee shore; and the natural result was that they spent the greater part of their voyagings at anchor in some one of the few sheltered spots along the coast.　It was not at all unusual for them to have to spend six or seven weeks at anchor in Recherché Bay or Port Davey until a slant in the gale enabled them to stand on; and all this time, of course, the settlement was waiting for the food they had aboard.

These supply ships brought convicts round, too, and sometimes there were mutinies and they never arrived. Wretches who had once been to Macquarie Harbour would dare anything to avoid the second visit, and it was better, in their view, to be shot down in cold blood rather than go back *there*.　Sometimes, too, the ships had so bad a reception from the sea that, after weeks of fruitless battling with gales and mountainous seas, they were forced to run back to Hobart in distress.　The south-west Cape of Tasmania enjoys a reputation as sinister as that of Cape Horn; and in winter time!　The lot of the unfortunate sailors of the little brigs was worse than that of the chained convicts battened down in the holds.

This inaccessibility that was so great an advantage from the point of view of preventing escapes was at the same time the greatest disadvantage in the successful carrying on of the settlement.　There were other disadvantages. Women had been sent there at first, but that soon had to stop.　It was an impossible business.　The plan had been that the women should be upon one island and the men

THE SEA IS WILD TO THE SOUTH OF TASMANIA, AND SHIPS
WERE SMALL

Photo courtesy of the Hobart "Mercury"

THE ELDERLY CUTTER *ROYAL WILLIAM*, A TOUGH LITTLE TAS-
MANIAN WHICH ONCE RAN THE MAILS TO THE MAINLAND AND
NEW ZEALAND

upon another, but from the first beginning of the long and hopeless war with Nature it was evident that there could be no separation, and morality had to go with the wind if life were to remain. There was soon no attempt to separate the women from the men, and in these circumstances, among such people—or any—the grossest immorality could not fail to reign. The attempt to separate the women on their own island was hopeless from the first and was soon abandoned; there is a record of four women having been sent to help a man who was lime burning near the Heads, and morality was so lax by then that there was not even the slightest attempt to cause any separation among the five of them. They shared the same hut. . . . It was apparent that the women must be sent elsewhere and gradually those who were there were sent back to Hobart and no more came.

The men were set to work felling timber with which the shores of the harbor abounded; a dockyard was made and shipbuilding was carried on. Around Macquarie Harbour Huon pine flourished—admittedly one of the finest of the world's shipbuilding timbers—and it was hoped that the sale of ships made by the convicts there would help to bear the cost of the settlement. Many ships were built and sold, and large quantities of the Huon pine were cut and sent to Hobart, but the excessive cost of keeping the place supplied with food made the extraction of any profit from it virtually impossible.

The conditions under which the convicts had to work were hellish. No attempt was even made to give them enough to eat; indeed there was very often not enough to give them. They had to work in all weathers. Felling timber in the bush, working up to their waists in water with the huge lumber rafts, toiling in the dockyard upon some barque or brig, slavishly carrying on the bitter attempt to produce something from the hopeless soil, they were forced to work the day long without food. They began in the cheerless mornings with half-a-pint of skilly, consisting of flour and water and a pinch of salt, each. They continued through the horrible days, wet through, miserable, and hungry beyond expression, with no further bite of food. The whole day long they were away from their island, but no man was permitted to have food; in the evenings they returned to the only real meal of the day—and that was often but a poor repast, irregularly and badly served. They had to return in their boats to the island for this food, and often the journey was made under conditions so terrible that it was well into the night before they could fall ravenously upon the day's rations.

For the paltriest thing they were flogged unmercifully, for they were looked upon as worse than brutes and treated accordingly. No beast of burden was allowed in the settlement, so that all the work had to be done by men. Men were harnessed like beasts to plows, and whipped in the harness as they stumbled and struggled over the uneven, muddy fields; men were forced to work up to their necks in the cold water of the harbor, battling with giant logs. Sometimes in utter dejection they suffered the water to close over their heads forever. If they attempted to escape they would die of exposure and starvation, if not from a soldier's shot before they had gone 20 yards. They saw others escape into the bush who were never again heard of because there was nothing further to hear; the bush swallowed them up like spirits, and gave them back no more. Once a skeleton was found, still with the chains lying rusted from ankle to ankle and the woodman's ax in the bony hands. Once six escaped and one only was recaptured; they had eaten each other until only he was left. He was hanged. They built poor coracles and fashioned logs, and put out to sea and were promptly drowned; they stayed in and were starved and flogged; they murdered and were hanged. They murdered each other, without excitement and without cause, merely in the hope of being hanged that they might be free of that terrible place.

"As I mentioned the names of those men who were to die, they one after another, as their names were pronounced, dropped on their knees and thanked God that they were to be delivered from that terrible place, whilst the others remained standing mute, weeping. It was the most horrible scene I have ever witnessed." So reads the evidence of a Macquarie Harbour chaplain before a Select Committee of the House of Commons that inquired into transportation in 1838; he was describing the scene following the announcement of the names of convicts sentenced to death for one of these murders.

"Why did you not drown yourself, for which there is plenty of opportunity, instead of taking life?" inquired another chaplain of a lad who had confessed that he had murdered only to be hanged. "Oh," the lad replied, "the case is quite different. If I killed myself I should immediately descend to the bottomless pit; but if I kill another I am sent to Hobart Town and tried for my life, and when I am found guilty the parson would attend me and I would be sure of going to heaven."

But he had, surely, a greater expectation of reaching heaven in that he had already suffered his share of hell. There were others who were not concerned with eternal life, nor with anything save escape from that hell upon earth. "Eternal life?" they cried. "Eternal life? Why should we want to go on? A Christ must die again to save such as us! Only let us rest. . . ." The place where they were buried was called Holiday Island, and it was the only holiday they knew.

In November, 1833, the Government decided that Macquarie Harbour should be abandoned, and without delay this was done. Through Hell's Gates—the appropriate name given the entrance of the harbor—the last of the convict ships was steered, and in the hearts of the miserable freight chained in her holds there was for the first time some hope.

Port Arthur, which in some ways was even worse than Macquarie Harbour, had had its birth before the older settlement was abandoned. It had the same object, the punishment of the re-convicted, although in addition large numbers of boys were sent direct from England to be "re-formed" at a station at Port Arthur known as Point Puer. Many of these boys, whose offenses were paltry in most cases, actually did reform, and developed in manhood into useful and orderly citizens of Tasmania and of the other Australian states. Port Arthur began as a convict settle-ment in September, 1830, and was continued as such until 1877, 47 years later. It was chosen by Governor Arthur whose name it bears; it was he who built up the convict system in Tasmania and at least made it workable. He certainly had excellent ideas as to what constituted an ideal convict settlement, and Port Arthur was an even better choice than Macquarie Harbour. It had all the advantages of the west-coast harbor, with the additional point that it was close to Hobart. The climate was not nearly so severe, however, and in natural beauty the peninsula was unsur-passed. Port Arthur lies upon the seaward side of a penin-sula which hangs suspended, upon the map of Tasmania, like an ear-ring into the Tasman Sea; the sea around is deep and stormy; a narrow neck of land which could easily be guarded gave the only access to the mainland. This was Eaglehawk Neck, and across here a chain of big dogs was posted, with about half a mile in front of them a chain of small, ill-tempered brutes which could be guaranteed to set up an unearthly din the instant any strange form came within smelling distance.

The idea—a cunning enough one—was that these small dogs should give warning of the proximity of a "bolter"— an escaping convict—and then the big dogs would be loosed and heaven help him! At first the big dogs were posted alone, but convicts sneaked past these on rare occasions and that could not be allowed. None ever got past the double row of yelping brutes and strong, biting enormous hounds. Escape was almost as difficult as from Macquarie Harbour, though it was tried frequently enough, mostly by sea. All manner of frail catamarans were bent together from wattle branches covered with shirts and in other precarious ways; canoes were hewn from boughs of trees, and cases were put together in the hope of forming something that would float away. But almost always the escapees were caught, or their corpses were washed upon the beach by the first storm that came.

Discipline was severe and life a wretched business. As at Macquarie Harbour no horse or beast of burden was allowed, and the most brutal and deadly work was done by men chained together in long lines. Everywhere was the clank of the chain and the sighing of the cat; and again there was this outcrop of murders committed solely in the hope of being hanged. For the torture of such of the ironed wretches who still managed to possess some independence of spirit in spite of the torments heaped upon them, all manner of fiendish practices were thought out and put into operation. There were dark cells, into which a man could be thrust sane and sound enough, and from which he would emerge, 24 hours later, a gibbering and hopeless idiot. One of these accursed things still stands amid the ruins of Port Arthur, and even to-day thrill-seeking tourists shudder to enter it. There were model prisons which seem to have been most efficient models of how to drive men insane; there was a madhouse which did not lack victims, and a hospital that did not have beds enough for all who should have occupied them. There was an island in the gloriously beautiful bay which was set aside for the dead; and upon a stormy night now a thousand tormented wraiths are said to rise from the cloddy earth. The scenery of this once so horrible peninsula is unexcelled in loveliness, and life to-day moves on quietly and with happiness amid the gaunt, blood-dripping ruins of the past. Upon a sunny day the blue water shimmers welcomingly along the sun-warmed sands and all the glory of Nature smiles entranc-ingly around. How charming is this lovely spot of Down-under Island, at the very end of the world! It is a tourist resort and famed beauty spot to-day; but not even a day-tripping pleasure-absorbed tourist could gaze upon those stones and, knowing something of what they have seen, re-main unmoved.

CHAPTER VI

THE VOYAGE OF THE "WOODMAN"

BUT it is with the convict ships and the actual conditions of the voyages that, in this book at least, one proposes more particularly to deal, and that is a phase most interesting. Did ever queerer ships put to sea than those old convict traffickers? It was a new land, and a new voyage—a long voyage, too, that early became known as the worst voyage in the world, and the worst trade.

Previously the men of the sail era had looked upon the Atlantic in winter—with good cause—as the most horrible field of their calling, but a taste of the long, stormy runs to Australia and back again convinced them that they had been wrong. It was so far, for one thing, and meant four, five, and even six months at sea—sometimes longer. No matter at what period of the year a ship might set out from the one end upon her voyage, or finish it at the other, she was sure to encounter, at some period, extremes both of hot and cold, belts of calms and tempestuous storms.

Setting out from England she had to cross the north-east and the south-east trades of the Atlantic; she had to make round Good Hope, and to cross from there 6,000 miles of stormy and gale-driven ocean that gave her no sight of land nor anything save ice—the sight she most dreaded—the whole bleak way; and in the end were the outposts of British colonization in Australia. Homeward bound the voyage was worse, for then there was no way save round the Horn. And Cape Horn never has been kind to sailing ships.

Setting out from Sydney or from Hobart Town there stretched before these tiny ships another 6,000 miles of west-wind-dominated ocean to Cape Horn, and their lonely

way through the greater part of it lay unavoidably well
within the ice line; it was of no use to stand against these
winds and make for Cape of Good Hope, the other way.
They had not then learned the trick of sneaking across the
Indian Ocean to Madagascar in the tail end of the south-
east trades, in 30° South or so, and slipping round the Cape
of Storms with the aid of the Agulhas current; and in any
case that kind of voyage was impossible from Sydney or
from old Hobart. It did not come until Adelaide and West
Australia came into the field, years later.

There was nothing for it but Cape Horn, and if the wind
was inclined pretty often to reach a strength that was ferocious it at least was fair; if they only drifted before it, in
the course of time they would run down their longitude and
come to the Horn. Then followed the long wander through
the full length of the South Atlantic, from beyond the ice
line to the horse latitudes and then the trades, and so to the
doldrums and through there, with as little delay as possible,
to the north-east trades of the North Atlantic. And then a
beat through these, making as much northing as possible
and as little westing; and so to the horse latitudes of the
north, with more calms and exasperating delays, and at last
the west winds of the high North Atlantic to blow them to
the Channel, the Dungeness pilot, and Home. If these little
ships circled the world in a year they were doing pretty
well, and every voyage to Van Diemen's Land meant encircling the globe. They were not clippers; the clipper had
not come then, and even if it had it would not have been used
in the transportation of convicts.

On the other hand these old sailing wagons which were
content to drift so placidly along did not possess the nasty
ease of losing people over the side which came to their low-
sided, sharp-bowed, long, iron and steel sisters of later
years; they did not drive like half-tide rocks through the
seas, wallowing heavily under a huge spread of canvas.
The sea did not hurl itself continually over their decks from

voyage beginning to voyage end, and sweep so exultantly over them in the great west winds that the oilskins were wrapped as constantly about their crews as scales upon fish, and were as needful. They were small, of two to four hundred tons, wooden, and rode buoyantly upon the ocean. They rose and fell with the seas: their full spread of canvas was not much, and the top speed of the fastest of them would probably be about eight knots. Their lines were cask-like and their sail plans slovenly; but they had a seat upon the water like swans and they were no killers. The day of the great steel windjammer, oversparred and undermanned, had not come then, and these homely old wagons might have leaked badly and have been possessed, pretty often, of a questionable seaworthiness. But for the most part they arrived.

Of course, in such a trade under such conditions it was only to be expected that the oldest and the most worn-out ships would be used, and there are frequent references to vessels which had to return to port because of their unseaworthiness. Some ships were lost and some were missing, but the percentage which successfully accomplished the voyage year after year was high.

In the very early days—for the first 20 years of last century especially—although the ships generally arrived, a good many of their convicts did not, and the mortality was unpardonably high. Ships came into Port Jackson and into Hobart Town with half their human cargoes down with scurvy, and the other half already dead. Sometimes this was directly attributable to the desire of the contractors to add to their profits by sending their ships to sea with so little food, and that of bad quality, that it was a wonder anybody arrived at all. The captains, too, were not above trading at the expense of the unfortunate convicts, who of course had no redress, and the most common means of extracting a miserable profit in this manner was by a combination with a rascally contractor ashore to send aboard inferior and insufficient stores. It was not unknown, either, that a captain should deliberately starve the convicts in order that he could sell their stores at the end of the voyage. When the ship arrived in port, of course, the convicts were lined on deck and asked if there were any complaints, and there was not often a response in the affirmative to that question. The explanation of that, however, as an officer sent to report to Lord Bathurst in 1822 discovered, was the fact that the captains were in the habit of assembling the convicts on deck a few days prior to making port and effecting the peace with them either by means of rum, tobacco, or money.

And even if the convicts did complain, there would only be their word against the captain's and his officers', and all the rest of his satellites. It was better to accept the rum or whatever else was offered, and say nothing. Their sufferings were nearly over then. Later it was the practice to carry a surgeon superintendent from the Royal Navy, in whose care the convicts were placed, and although this sometimes led to a conflict between the officer in charge of the convicts and the officer in charge of the ship which was no good for either the convicts or the ship, in the main it led to much improved conditions and a lessening of the loss of life. It was the job of the captain to deliver his ship with her cargo in safety; it was the duty of the surgeon superintendent to deliver the convicts alive.

The usual practice of most of the ships was to make a call either at Rio Janeiro or the Cape on the voyage out. At first they called more usually at the Cape, seeing that that was the natural and most convenient port of call on the voyage and all their wants could be well met there. For a hundred years and more before that the Cape had been a calling place for ships bound to India and on other voyages that meant a doubling of Good Hope, and the early maritime importance of Cape Town attached to this suitability as a port of call. Against Table Bay there was, of course, the poorness of the harbor; there were no docks then, and no breakwaters, and now and again a gale would arise and drive practically all the deepwatermen in Table Bay from their anchors. Even now the ribs of some of them lie deeply embedded in the sand around the shores of Cape Colony.

There began to be a greater inclination to put in at Rio rather than at the Cape, although this meant a lengthening of the voyage that should have been avoidable. A few days at the Cape would not have meant undue delay; it lay on the road to Van Diemen's Land and New South Wales, whereas Rio was off the track and necessitated a deviation. Rio was preferred for commercial purposes; it allowed the captain and the doctor, and everybody else in the ship except the convicts, greater chance of gain. They carried on private trading ventures. They made shortage of water, or any other thing they could think of, a pretext for putting in at Rio, because they knew that they could buy rum, tobacco, and silks there at rates absurdly cheap compared with the prices they could sell them for in Hobart Town and in Sydney. Some of the ship masters and surgeon superintendents were able to make more in this way than they would ever hope to receive in the way of pay for their services from the Government.

"The temptations to masters and surgeon superintendents to touch at Rio and to purchase sugar and tobacco there have at all times been very great. The proceeds from the sale of these adventures in New South Wales and Van Diemen's Land will always tempt them to create pretexts for the circuitous passage . . .", reported Bigges to Lord Bathurst in 1822. He recorded the fact that a Doctor Bromley, of the female convict ship *Wellington*, had brought from Rio 150 gallons of spirits, one hogshead and six dozen bottles of wine, and ten baskets of tobacco. All this he was permitted to land duty free, and his profits must have been extensive.

The detentions at Rio had a very bad effect upon the

convicts and upon discipline, and it was more generally in
the ships that called there that serious mutinies occurred;
an order was gazetted that all ships should proceed direct
upon the voyage if at all possible, and that if they called
anywhere it should be at the Cape.

"The attention of the captain and the surgeon, instead
of being devoted to the care of the ship and to the convicts,
is much interrupted by commercial speculations of their
own. . . . The Cape of Good Hope is a better place of
resort for our ships," said Bigges.

But Rio continued to be favored, and it was easy enough
to create pretexts for the call there. Some ships actually
set out with an insufficiency of water in order that they
might have a "legitimate" excuse for putting in at the
South American port. Bigges gives some interesting statistics comparing the voyages via Rio with those made direct
and via the Cape. In the period from 1810 to 1820, he
says, the average passage occupied on 44 direct voyages
from the Channel to Van Diemen's Land and New South
Wales was 127 days. For 38 voyages which included calls
at Rio, the average passage was 156 days; and for eleven
voyages which included calls at the Cape, the average passage was 146 days. More significant than that, however,
was the fact that of 7,657 convicts carried direct 71 died,
while of 6,470 carried via Rio 132 died on the voyage. Of
the 1,912 who came via the Cape, only nine died on the voyage. It is interesting to note that these statistics show that
only 212 convicts died at sea in ten years of sea carriage,
but this figure does not include the losses from wrecks and
from vessels which went missing.

Apart from the worst of them, conditions in most of the
convict transports to Tasmania were much the same, and
perhaps the best means of conveying a real impression of
what the voyage must have been like would be to attempt a
description—necessarily incomplete and not wholly authen-
ticated—of a passage in one of these ships—any of them,

the *Katherine Stewart Forbes, Mount Stewart Elphinstone,
Egyptian, Minerva, Lord Melville, Surry, George III,
Elizabeth, Phœnix, Prince Regent, Castle Forbes, Duke of
Northumberland, Earl Grey, Anna Maria, Midlothian,
Martin Luther, St. Vincent, Stately,* or any others of the
goodly list that came.

The prisoners were usually taken aboard from hulks
lying in the Thames off Woolwich and in other places.
These hulks were absolute breeding places for crime in the
worst sense. One quotes from the account of Jürgen Jürgensen, the "convict king" of Tasmania, as to his experiences in the convict hulk *Justitia* and on board the convict transport *Woodman.* Jürgensen was, of course, an
extraordinary man, and on any other subject one might
hesitate to quote too closely from him. But there is no
reason on earth why he should not have been perfectly
truthful at least as to these sections of his varied experiences, seeing that there was nothing—not even notoriety—
to be gained by the pursuit of any other course.

In October, 1825 (he says), I was removed from Newgate
to the hulk *Justitia,* which was lying at Woolwich. The moment a convict passes over the gangway of a hulk, he is
searched for money or other articles of value; he is then taken
below, and entirely stripped, is subjected to an ablution, has
his hair cut off, and a prison-dress put on; irons are placed
on his legs, and next morning he is sent to hard labour in
the dockyard. A very few, as a matter of great favour, are
permitted to wear a slight bezel on one leg and are exempted
from dockyard labour. I was one of those thus privileged.
All communication with the rest of the world is cut off, no
person is allowed on board, a visitor must stand on a platform by the side of the hulk, and can only speak to a prisoner
in the presence of an officer. Any money or articles given
to a prisoner must be handed over to the chief mate; all letters,
even from members of parliament, to a convict are opened,
and if the captain does not choose to deliver them, he need
not do so. In like manner, letters from convicts to friends,
relations and others are inspected, so should any one com-

plain, he only exposes himself to vengeance and punishment.

When a House of Commons committee of inspection visits the hulks, everything seems in admirable order, and when the unfortunate men are asked if they have any complaints to make, the reply is invariably in the negative, for woe betide him who should dare to open his lips except to say that the treatment on board was most humane and kind. The superintendent of a hulk is styled captain and the subordinate officers are called mates, although none of them are seafaring men, being simply promoted turnkeys. I have seen a captain knock a poor fellow down with one blow merely for not getting quickly out of his way when passing forward on the deck. Redress is impossible, for all is mystery and secrecy. I am bound to admit that I escaped any harsh treatment, and it is only a sense of truth and public utility that could impel me to state facts as they are.

I have long had by me several incidents of the hulks which I intended to have published, but a sense of shame prevented me from doing so, and I now feel happy that the hulk establishments are broken up, for hitherto they have proved nothing but schools of abominable pollution. Those who have been discharged from them have over-run England and spread vice and immorality everywhere in their track. I scarcely ever saw any signs of true repentance in any of them; on the contrary, most have, after their liberation, been again convicted, though by changing names they have succeeded in concealing the fact from the notice of the authorities. I am glad indeed that those establishments, those nuisances, those nurseries of deep crime, have been removed, for I should have felt reluctant to publish what I myself have seen in them. On board the hulks any one who should complain to the authorities concerning these heart-appalling scenes, would be destroyed by the other prisoners and would incur the resentment of the officers.

Should I be asked whether the whole, or at least the greater portion of the convicts on board the hulks really merited the punishments inflicted upon them, truth would compel me to answer in the affirmative, but the whole system tended unequivocally to make them sycophants, hypocrites, and ten times more the children of darkness than they were before. Only those amongst them were appointed to petty officers who would betray their fellow-convicts, not in matters of great crimes or attempts to escape, but in such little trivialities as the unwarrantable possession of an inch of tobacco, or a little tea or sugar, or half a loaf.

It was natural that, seeing myself surrounded with horrors such as I have indicated, I should make every interest to get away as speedily as possible from scenes which afflicted me more than any I had witnessed in the previous course of my life. I was therefore delighted to receive the permission of the Home Secretary to proceed to Van Diemen's Land in the *Woodman*, which had been chartered to convey convicts to that colony.

I found the *Woodman* in all the hurry and confusion of preparing for sea. The berths for the prisoners were not yet finished; friends had come from all parts to take a last farewell of those who were to be banished to a distant land; swearing, cursing, wrangling, lamentations and tears offended all within hearing, and one would fancy ten thousand demons had been let loose. The Surgeon-Superintendent had not arrived, and consequently there was no check on the prisoners, the other officers having quite enough to do without heeding them. One would imagine that prisoners sent to a penal settlement in expiation of crimes committed at home would, when starting on their voyage across the seas, show some signs of contrition, and cease their former evil practices, but it was not so. By daylight or by dark they did not scruple to steal all that came in their way. Boxes and parcels of tea and sugar were torn from under those who possessed them, and one's life would be endangered by resistance to these ruffians. I remember one day when I had occasion to open a trunk in the single berth allotted to me, a silk handkerchief was snatched by some one, and on looking round to see who it was, I was served in a similar manner by others. Having taken most of the articles out of the box, many of them were thus stolen before I could replace them in security. Those who were most active and daring in these exploits were looked up to with a great deal of respect by their less hardened fellow-convicts. It may seem strange how such stolen articles could be disposed of in a ship whose every hole and corner was liable to inspection and search. But the thieves easily found receivers, for wearing apparel and many other articles were sold to the soldiers, their wives, and the sailors in the half-deck.

The Surgeon-Superintendent now joined the ship. He was

of a meek and kind-hearted disposition, and well qualified for his work, having already made two voyages to the colonies with convicts and given general satisfaction. Mr. Leary, a lieutenant in the Navy, commanded the *Woodman*, and Mr. Nutting, the chief mate, was shrewd, honest and off-handed, with much of the gentleman about him. Order and regularity were soon established, and some of the prisoners, whose characters stood fair, were appointed to subordinate situations, such as boatswain's mates, cooks, sweepers, etc. As I had dabbled a little in medicine, I was placed in the hospital as dispenser and assistant. Those who were so selected enjoyed privileges to which the other convicts were strangers, and were entitled to go on deck nearly at all hours from sunrise to sunset. I had forwarded a letter to my friends to furnish me with some money, but our departure was so sudden that the one addressed to me in reply never reached me, although I have since been charged with it in account.

The *Woodman* having received her final orders, we sailed from Sheerness at the latter end of November, with 150 convicts on board and a detachment of military, the latter accompanied by their wives and children in some instances. We had not proceeded far down the Channel before we were overtaken by a storm, and the ship laboured exceedingly. Little care had been evinced in examining the ship before she was chartered, for the stem was so loose that an immense volume of water poured into the hospital and made sad havoc with all my arrangements. To those who had never been at sea before the situation was intensely disagreeable, a large number of persons cooped up in small berths, encumbered with irons, and dreadfully seasick, combining to make a scene of the most repellent description.

At length the weather abated, and we proceeded along with a fair breeze. The hour arrived when we gazed on the English shore for the last time. I now found myself torn from all that was dear to me on earth, from friends and relations whom I had not seen for years, but with whom I had held friendly intercourse. I stood in silent agony, taking a last and lingering view of those shores the sight of which had, on so many former occasions, afforded me keen delight when returning to them after long voyages to distant lands. I saw myself an exile and a captive on that element on which I had once been a commander. I felt the blow, and I felt it deeply. I

THE BARQUE *JAMES CRAIG* WAS A PACIFIC TRADER IN
WHICH ALAN VILLIERS SAILED TO TASMANIA

JOSEPH CONRAD ONCE COMMANDED THIS HULK, WHEN IT
WAS THE PROUD BARQUE *OTAGO*

OLD-TIME SAILORS REEFING A TOPS'L IN A GALE BETWEEN
HOBART AND CAPE HORN

THE SEA RAGES: THE SHIP IS SMALL – NORMAL GOING IN
THE WATERS SOUTH OF TASMANIA

could scarcely quell the emotions which swelled my unhappy breast without giving vent to tears, but a sense of manhood restrained me from any public exhibition of emotion. I then made a fervent appeal to Heaven, and I have not prayed in vain.

For the information of such as are not acquainted with the precise manner in which convicts are conveyed to the penal colonies, I will give a brief summary of the regulations. The British Government has hitherto regarded the transportation of prisoners as the chief mode of providing labour in the colonies. Punishment and utility have been connected so as to render convict labour alike beneficial to the colonists and conducive to the best interests of the parent state. All convicts sent out are newly clad, and ample rations of wholesome food are apportioned to them. Health is preserved by cleanliness, which is strictly attended to, and the ship-owners are bound by the terms of their charter to supply each prisoner with at least half-a-gallon of water per day. Care is also taken that they are not subjected to any oppressive or capricious treatment. Formerly, it frequently happened that brutal masters of convict ships would flog every prisoner on board. To prevent abuses of that sort, a surgeon of the Royal Navy has for some years past been attached to every convict-ship to superintend the prisoners on the passage out. This officer, in addition to his half-pay, is entitled to half-a-guinea per head for every prisoner he delivers safe and sound at the end of the voyage, on receiving a certificate from the governor of the colony that his conduct has merited such a gratuity.

Naturally under such a system surgeon-superintendents have every inducement to exercise the greatest attention and vigilance, and to see that every one receives his just allowance, which includes two pints of wine served every week, as well as a certain quantity of limejuice and sugar each day after arriving in the warmer latitudes. Canisters of preserved meat are supplied for the sick with rice, tea, sugar, sago, and extra wine, as well as an additional allowance of water. Should a convict be deemed deserving of corporal punishment, the superintendent and master must both concur before it can be inflicted and particular mention must be made in the ship's log-book of the nature of the offence and the amount of punishment awarded. During our passage from

England to the Cape of Good Hope, only two convicts were flogged, and they richly deserved it, having been caught in the act of robbing their comrades.

After Land's End had faded from our view, all the prisoners were called on deck and relieved of their irons. This relaxation threw an air of cheerfulness over the ship, and with happier countenances, we glided with gentle breezes over the swelling billows. As the prisoners conducted themselves extremely well, and were permitted to come on deck for a certain time every day, a general good-will prevailed on board, and the soldiers and sailors were alike very agreeable.

After crossing the tropic of Cancer, a number of the convicts were attacked by a species of brain fever, which speedily carried off four, who were buried in the deep. A considerable number had to be placed in the hospital. It certainly appeared to me that the surgeon was wrong in his treatment of the complaint. He sometimes gave in one dose from twenty to thirty grains of calomel, when the disease invariably terminated in madness. But, poor man! he was himself soon attacked with the fever, and one morning he suddenly dropped dead from his chair, to the grief of all on board. This sad event placed me in a position of great responsibility, for I was called upon to take sole charge of the hospital and to do the best I could. By following the simple practice I had learned from Dr. Box in Newgate, I succeeded in restoring all the afflicted to their usual health, and when the *Woodman* arrived at the Cape, there was not a single individual in the hospital.

The master and officers were not permitted to land by the Cape authorities, who supposed that some epidemic disease was lurking in the ship. But it was absolutely necessary according to the regulations that we should be supplied with a surgeon, and the Admiral on the station ordered Captain Auckland, commanding a sloop of war, to send his surgeon on board the *Woodman*. Mr. Kelly was this gentleman's name, and he was apparently glad to be removed to our ship. He was uncommonly skilful in his profession, and possessed great generosity. His history was rather singular. He had served with distinction in the Navy, and at the close of the war had settled down in a lucrative practice at Belfast. He had married a young wife and it is well-known how a young wife can manage a middle-aged husband. She was a Roman

Catholic and persuaded him on one occasion to attend an anti-
Orange demonstration. This was reported to the Lords of
the Admiralty, with the result that Mr. Kelly was immediately
ordered for active service. A refusal to comply with this
command would, of course, have entailed the forfeiture of
his half-pay. What with being appointed to a sloop, removed
from a profitable practice, and compelled to leave his wife
behind, his temper had become somewhat soured, and his
brother officers did not always find him an agreeable
companion.

When the *Woodman* put out to sea once more, it soon transpired that Mr. Kelly and the master, though both Irishmen,
were totally opposed to one another in political principles.
The convicts derived no small advantage from this conflict
of opinion, for if any one of them committed a breach of discipline and the surgeon desired to have him punished, the
master would not consent, and *vice versa*. However, the prisoners continued to conduct themselves very quietly on the
whole. A ludicrous incident occurred one evening when the
wind was blowing hard, and all hands were engaged reefing
and handing the sails. Mr. Kelly turned into his cot and
was in the act of pulling a garment over his head, but unfortunately he had forgotten to remove a pair of strong silver
sleeve-buttons, and the ship at that moment taking a lurch,
he tumbled out and remained perfectly helpless on the floor,
rolling to and fro for some time, the noise on deck being so
great that no one could hear his cries. The accident was
fortunately attended with no more serious consequences than
a broken nose and a black eye. It is but bare justice to Mr.
Kelly to say that his undoubted skill, and unremitting attention to the convicts, prevented any disease from spreading
amongst them, and only one died between the Cape and Van
Diemen's Land.

On May 4, 1826, we arrived in the Storm Bay passage and
sailed up the river with a fair wind. I, who had visited the
scene twenty-four years previously, when no white man occupied a single spot in Van Diemen's Land, and when all around
us was a wilderness, felt myself strongly moved by the changes
that time and colonial energy had brought about in my absence. Along the banks of the river I observed a long series
of farms and pleasant looking cottages, but it was when we
reached the harbour on the following morning that my aston-

ishment became truly great. It has fallen to my lot to visit
many colonies and settlements on this globe, and if I had not
witnessed the amazing transformation now disclosed to my
view on the site where Hobart Town reared its novel and
beautiful aspect, I could have formed no conception of it
from any published description, and I should have rejected
the truth as an exaggeration.

But Jürgensen's account, though interesting, cannot be
regarded as typical of the usual convict's lot when transported to Tasmania. He was a man who could wangle for
himself advantages anywhere, and it is pretty obvious that
he was more a passenger than a convict so far as his treatment aboard the *Woodman* was concerned. He was more
to be regarded as a political exile than a criminal outcast,
though he may have possessed excellent qualifications as
both. The lot of the ordinary convict was much worse than
his. Conditions in the ships generally were bad. It was
not always the case, as in the *Woodman*, that the irons were
struck off as soon as the ship was clear of the Channel.
Sometimes they were not removed at all. The surgeon usually wished them off in the interests of health, and the captain wished them to stop on in the interests of discipline and
the ship in general; frequently they were removed only for
the hottest part of the voyage, and even then the convicts
were allowed little on deck. Armed soldiers stood on constant guard over their hatchways—a guard which was very
necessary, as more than one mutiny and attempted mutiny
showed. The greatest difficulty which any organized gang
of convicts had to overcome in the perpetration of a successful mutiny was the distrust of their own kind; the mu-
tual suspicion among the felons was their own undoing, and
each knew that the fomentation of a scheme for the seizing
of the ship—if he gave too ready utterance to his plans—
was much more likely to find him on the triangles than on
the poop. There was always an informer, just as there
always will be when men of that class are banded together

as they were. But what an extraordinary world it was! For four and five months, often without a sight of land, two or three hundred branded and chained felons sweltered and fought, and lied and cursed and thieved, and idled and schemed and plotted, in the hold of a tiny wooden ship that drifted steadily on, with a handful of sailors in the fore part and a handful of soldiery aft, and a doctor and a ship master in command. It is not to be wondered at that queer things should happen on these voyages, and queer things often did. . . .

Arrived safely in Hobart Town the prisoners did not receive much of a welcome. But there were plenty of their kind there before them and—except in Governor Arthur's time—the place was pretty lawless. Sometimes, when some colonists wished to get ready labor to clear their land, they were welcome enough; always hordes of boats put out to see what was doing and who was aboard, and so on, the chief object of the occupants of most of them, of course, being to secure a journeyman in whatever skilled trade they happened to be concerned. This rush for skilled men had amusing consequences at times; assignments were supposed, of course, to be made by an assignment board, but if one waited for that all the skilled men would be gone. On one occasion the *Katherine Stewart Forbes* sailed up the Derwent with a likely lot of convicts on board, and just at the time the several newspapers published in Hobart Town were very short of compositors to set their type. Each was trying to steal from the other—feeling was pretty bitter between them—and things had reached an interesting stage in general. The representative of one of the papers was first aboard the *Katherine Stewart Forbes* and upon her manifest he was delighted to see, opposite one man's name, the glorious word "compositor." Without any further to-do or any more inquiries—the formalities could be adjusted later—the newspaper man swooped upon his compositor with a wild howl of joy, had his irons knocked off, and bore him in triumph ashore. After an adjournment at a hostelry at which the two of them celebrated the meeting they repaired to the press room, and it was not until the "compositor" had split two cases of type and upset a whole form of matter for the next day's issue that the awful discovery was made that he was really a Staffordshire composter! His specialty was pottery, and not a printing press; nevertheless, having once taken him, the newspaper had to keep him.

When the next convict ship came in one finds them gloomily writing:

"The prisoners by the *Mangles*, we regret to say, are to be numbered among the most miserable of mortals, and by far the worst sample of the human kind that has yet been brought to our shores. They consist for the most part of poor decrepit chimney sweepers thrown out of employment by the operation of the late Act, and those who do not belong to this unfortunate class of men are of a still uglier race, inasmuch as not being so black outside, they are yet blacker within. It is 'too bad,' as the late Lord Liverpool said, to father these poor creatures upon us, and attempt to make us pay for them into the bargain."

Obviously there were no compositors on her manifest.

Bad as conditions might generally have been in the male convict ships, how shall one describe those which usually existed aboard the vessels which conveyed females. *These* were queer ships; and hell ships, too, at times. For who could control the women? Who might control any woman? Not a man! For the most part there were no female supervisors, but in order to give some "tone" to the women ships it was the custom for a number of free women and children to take passage in them, usually occupying quarters between the prison in the hold and the officers' domain in the poop. But there was still the problem of the crew to be considered, and it was a matter of utter impossibility to prevent intercourse, during the whole of the long voyage, between the crew and the female prisoners. There was no escape from it; the women had to come on deck for exercise at some time of the day, and it was easy enough—unavoidable, indeed—for the men to make the acquaintance of those among them who were not averse to male friendships. In the nights, of course, the women were under lock and key below. But the crew had the forepart of the ship to themselves, and were able in most ships, if they wanted to, to find some form of entry into the women's quarters. They could get from the forepeak into the 'tween decks, and so to the prison; it was mostly easy enough. The officers, of course, knew that it was going on. But they were powerless, if once a thing like that took root in their ships; they would not face the risk of their crew mutinying if they attempted to stop this promiscuous intercourse, in which, indeed, very often they were themselves the ringleaders. For man is weak, and the voyage was a long one; it would be a pretty severe test for any man, to send him off to sea in a ship like that, with her cargo a hold full of depraved, vicious, and condemned women. They were not all bad, of course; but they were all women.

Often the female convict ships arrived with a good many of their charges in a state of pregnancy. "A very general intercourse took place between the crew and the female convicts," reported Bigges, and he made exhaustive recommendations as to ways and means of preventing access by the seamen to the women's quarters. Very often the officers were themselves the greatest offenders, which is not to be wondered at. The officers had the right to recommend women, on their arrival, for tickets-of-leave; with this power over a woman, what might they not do?

"From the evidence it appears that all the evils that unrestrained intercourse between the crew of the ship and a number of licentious women could produce existed to the full in the voyage of the *Janus* from the United Kingdom," said Bigges, who criticized the attempts of the captain to

bring about an improvement as "neither sincere nor effectual."

There is plenty of evidence of the same sort of thing in
the later-day female convict ships; how was it to be avoided?
No punishment was provided for either crew or master—or
surgeon either, for that matter—who shared in this evil
that only a strong man might overcome; it was a very serious evil that played no unimportant part in bringing
transportation to an end.

CHAPTER VII

THE LOSS OF THE "GEORGE III"

IN the whole sorry list of tragedies and wretched adventures with which the misery of the convict days of Tasmania is cursed, there is no tale so moving as that of the loss of the convict ship *George III*, which went down with 134 lives after striking an uncharted rock in D'Entrecasteaux Channel, quite close to the entrance of the Derwent River, in the blackness of the night of April 12, 1835. The whole voyage of the *George III* was one of sickness, death, and disaster, from the miserable beginning to the terrible end, and even if the ship had never torn herself to pieces, with 200 screaming convicts in her holds, her story would still have been one to move and to dismay in an era not given to being stirred to pity.

In the story of convictism in Tasmania there are many wrecks, and many strange ship losses, some of which have never been, and probably now never will be, explained. Many convict-laden ships set out from the Thames and from the Downs, and never put in anywhere, and never arrived at their destinations. The settlers of the far south island did not mind; they did not want the brand of the broad arrow imprinted upon their lovely land, and reviled the government which continued to think that in convictism lay the only way to populate the new colonies. The officials who shipped the convicts off did not mind; they were at least out of the way; and there were plenty more convicts. And certainly the convicts themselves would not care what became of them, for in their lives there was no room for such an abstract thing as hope. And the life without hope waits in despair for an end it does not fear to hasten.

Some of these convict ships were unseaworthy, which was more or less to be expected. It was a government job, in the first place; and a pretty miserable one, in the second place. The vessel that could carry free settlers would not look at the wretched prisoners, nor would any ship while there was hope of other cargo. The very nature of the "trade" was such that it would naturally attract to itself the worst, the weakest, the oldest, and the least seaworthy ships, and though there were scandals at times, followed by "inquiries" and "rigorous inspections," it is significant that while the *George III* was at sea two other ships that had set out laden with convicts from the Thames had had to struggle back in distress, and were condemned. Yet there does not appear at any time to have been any question raised about the seaworthiness of the *George III;* probably she was good enough. At the official inquiry afterwards nothing seems to have been asked upon this point, while it seems also to have been taken for granted that the ship would be so hopelessly provisioned that 50 of the convicts would die of scurvy. These things were, apparently, by no means untoward.

The *George III* was a full-rigged ship of 400 tons, which is not large but was big enough those days. She had previously been in the convict trade with Tasmania and had not had a good name in it. However, no ship *did* have a good name in such a business, nor could have. She lost some lives every voyage, but she arrived. On December 14, 1834—a wild and wretched winter's day with the wind whisking bitterly around the gray Thames waters and a wraith of rain in the dull and gloom-filled sky—the *George III* set out from Woolwich. She had taken 200 convicts on board, 40 of whom were boys, and with her soldiers and her people she had, in all, 308 souls on board. There were several women, mostly wives of the soldiers, and two births on board increased the number to 310.

Almost from the moment of setting out the voyage was a

terrible one. The English Channel in December is notoriously ill-favored, and all the torments of which it was capable it wreaked upon the unfortunate convict ship and its chained cargo. It would have been better had the ship been lost then, if lost she was to be, for the wretched human beings sufferings in her hold would have welcomed death, then, as an escape. They were cooped up in a great barricaded cage in the hold, where, with the constant rush of water across the decks above as the little vessel beat against the gale, there was no ventilation, and no purifying sea air came to bring life to the putrid hole or relief to the miserable sufferers. They were battened down, but even then armed soldiers stood always over them ready to shoot if they sought the outer air. For days the vessel lay at the mercy of the elements in the Channel, unable to progress against the howling westerly gales that swept in, one after the other, from the torment of the Western Ocean beyond; and when, after many days, she came free of the Channel, off the Bay of Biscay it was worse. Sails were blown away; the ship leaked. Even the officers and the surgeon, in the shelter of the poop, had a wretched time of it. If no air could get down into the sweltering hold, the water could. On sodden, sea-soaked straw the miserable convicts waited for the end, and the only hope they knew was that the ship might sink. But she did not sink, then, and she came on.

A month out from the Channel the first of the north-east trades was encountered, and—for the afterguard and the soldiers—life took on a kindlier face. But not for the dwellers of the hold. For their fare was scanty, and it had been found that much of what little they had they could not eat. It must have been beyond description to be too bad for such as they. Confined in a narrow, ill-lit, ill-ventilated space that would have been a gloomy hole even on the safety of the land; ill-fed, ill-nourished, ill-clad; unable to get sufficient exercise, hopeless, in utter despair, the lot of the convicts was a harrowing one. The bare allowance that was

supposed to be on board for them would just have kept them
alive, and little more; but much of even that was missing.
The natural consequence, which came and was accepted as
such, was scurvy in its most virulent form. It swept
through the emaciated wretches of the hold, and the tiny
hospital could not hold the dying, let alone the sick. Two
convicts died each day in the sweltering heat of the doldrums, where the *George III* lay for several weeks when she
was about two months on her road, and the sailmaker cursed
that so much of his canvas was going to be sewn around the
starved bodies. Then they flung them over as they were,
sometimes not even with a weight attached, to the scav-
enging sharks.

The two doctors with the ship, however, rose to the occasion splendidly, when there was no need—save humanity—
for them to do so. They need not have put themselves out;
it was only the convicts who were affected. Every one else
was in perfect health, although doubtless considerably bored
by the tardiness of the voyage. These physicians were Dr.
McGregor, of the 50th, and Dr. Wise, the surgeon superintendent of the convicts, and everything that they could do
to alleviate the convicts' sufferings in some way, they did.
But there was not much that they could do. Medical supplies were short, and after all the whole difficulty was the
scarcity of food for which they were not responsible and
could not remedy. Apparently there was no thought of
putting in anywhere, though that should not have been difficult. Pernambuco, Rio, the Cape—any of these places
would have been handy enough, at various stages of the
voyage; to be sure, the *George III* would have been only
one of the long line of distressed sailing ships that called
into Table Bay for provisions to resuscitate their wretched
human cargoes in the earlier half of last century, and the
fresh vegetables of old Cape Town put new heart into many
a sick mariner. Still, her people were not affected: it was
only the convicts who were dying. At the inquiry the pos-

sibility of a call anywhere to improve matters does not appear to have been mentioned.

While the ship lay in the doldrums fire broke out, and nearly destroyed her. A carelessness in drawing off spirits was blamed, but they must have been strong spirits indeed to cause a fire that nearly enveloped the ship. Possibly the carelessness was more concerned with the quantity consumed. At any rate there was a fire, and it spread to the magazine where a considerable quantity of powder was stored. In the dull and torpid heat of the enervating doldrums, fire is a curse indeed, and the prospect of saving the *George III* was remote. The convicts—those of whom who still could walk—were let free on deck to help save the ship, and with the sailors and the militia they must have worked heroically. It was two of the convicts who, hearing that the flames had spread to the magazine, rushed there undeterred by the flames and snatched the red hot kegs of powder out of the smoke and flung them over the side. They were burned severely. There were many kegs—fortunately they were of copper; had they been of the ordinary wood the ship would most certainly have been blown sky-high—but they stuck to their job and saved the ship. The copper kegs were so hot from the surrounding flames that they burnt into the flesh of these brave fellows' hands and arms. But they died of scurvy before the journey's end, just the same; perhaps that mercy was their reward.

Narrowly escaping this danger, the ship wandered on her way. Sixteen convicts had been left dead in the tropics; others died during the stormy passage from south of Good Hope to Tasmania—a stormy road. A desperate road, for the stoutest of steel sailing ships that fly, short-canvassed and with flooded decks, before the gloomy gale; a dangerous road indeed for the tiny *George III*, with her leaking wooden hull and her fettered cargo. Yet she sailed steadily on. Often the westerly gale shrieked through her rigging, and the great seas that swept round the world down there leapt round her, and swept exultantly over her, and threw her now high into the dull dome of the rain-soaked sky, whence her crew looked down upon the dull fury of the tortured sea; and now swept her deep into a trough between two huge seas, whence even from the rigging the watching sailors could see the horizon neither ahead nor astern— nothing all about them save boiling foam in a crater of furious water, that hissed, and roared, and snarled, and fumed about their little ship as if it were determined that she should not survive. Now ice came, and more gales; a following sea pooped the little vessel, and stove the hospital in, and flooded out the barricaded dungeon of the hold, and swept half the galley overboard, and all the pots. And yet the *George III* sailed on, if not in triumph then at least afloat; and her people were spared the knowledge that the sea spared them then because it knew a more frightful fate awaited them.

So there came at last a day when, 148 days out from the Thames, the welcome cry of "land," came from aloft. How sweet was that sound! Even the dying brightened a little at the cry, although the only thing the land could hold for them was the grave: the sick and tortured convicts permitted some ray of hope to penetrate to hearts that had grown almost to forget such a thing existed. They would have been better served to have forgotten entirely.

The land that was seen was the bleak and mountainous south-west coast of Tasmania—a wild and unwelcoming sight to most who come in from the sea, but madly joyous to these folks. The general aspect of Tasmania's south-western shores has nothing of gentleness about it, although something of wild and unwrought, untamed beauty for him who may see such things. Wild seas rush enraged upon the bases of gaunt cliffs that seem to answer rage with rage, and glower down threateningly upon the seas that hurl themselves upon them; the spray flings itself impotently high into the air, that it might reach high upon these gaunt precipices, and wreak on them the utmost damage possible; the precipices answer with a gloomy forbearance that maddens the cold sea to ever greater and greater effort. Here all Nature is at war. And puny man may look to all his wiles, if he will live; these long foaming seas have raced 10,000 miles unchecked from Cape Horn, and they will not suffer easily to be checked here. There is such a roaring of foam, and a crashing of great waters, and a rumbling defiance of gaunt mountainous cliffs that have flung their outpost rocks far into the sea the greater to enrage it, that the very sea fowl fly shy of these waters, and here nothing comes save the hail squalls and the rain that drive before the gale.

Such was the landfall the *George III* made; gloomy, melancholy, dispiriting, sad—yet welcome beyond expression to the people of the convict ship.

The breeze was strong and fair, and the ship made good progress. When night came she was not far from the entrance to D'Entrecasteaux Channel. There was a moon, but the sky was heavily clouded over and it could not be seen. The officers were in doubt as to whether they should proceed to Hobart by way of D'Entrecasteaux Channel, which was the shorter way, or stand on round Bruni Island and up through Storm Bay. If they headed up the channel they would be in smooth water almost immediately, and if the wind changed so that it would not allow them to proceed, their charts told them that there were plenty of good anchorages. Captain Moxey wished to use the channel way, if he could, for his ship had already been a long time on the road and he wished to get the sick and dying convicts ashore. When the landfall was made 60 convicts were down seriously with scurvy, and the chances of 50 of these were regarded as hopeless. They had to die in any case: even those who were not so seriously affected were weakened and ill. The anchors were cleared on the forecastle head and the deep-sea lead was set going. There were no lights round that shore, in those days, and navigation was a difficult business.

Captain Moxey called a conference of the officers, and it was decided to stand up the channel. This was done, and as soon as the ship was out of the stormy waters outside every one on board heaved a sigh of very real relief. The clouds had cleared a little then, and the moon shone, and generally the conditions for sailing through the channel were as good as they could well be. Captain Moxey would have preferred to wait for daylight, naturally, but his need was pressing and with the anchors cleared and a treble look-out he had taken all the precautions possible. He kept the lead going, and stayed on deck peering anxiously ahead. The convicts were below, a little cheered now that the dangers of the sea had passed, and looking forward hopefully to the morrow.

Sometimes the sky clouded again, and the captain was minded to anchor: he shortened her down to the reefed tops'ls, with the fores'l hanging clewed up in its gear that it might easily be set, or made fast, as it was wanted. The ship slipped on quietly into the night. In the hospital the surgeon could hear the monotonous droning voice of the leadsman in the chains.

Then suddenly this monotonous droning became louder, with a note of warning. The sea had swiftly shoaled, with no apparent cause.

"Heave quick!" called the captain.

"A quarter less four," came the leadsman's ill-omened answer. The water was shoaling fast. Yet the land was two miles away on the nearer side.

"Hard aport! Hard aport!" was the captain's next command.

"Hard a—", the helmsman began to answer as he feverishly leapt to swing around the spokes. He never completed that answer, for before he had the time to do so the ship, with a horrid, tearing sound of timbers torn into protesting pieces, was on the rocks.

"My God!" shrieked Captain Moxey. But no one heard him save the sea fowl and the convicts.

Until then the night, in the shelter of the channel, had been mild, and the moon shone frequently through rifts in the clouds to send a guiding light. Now the sky clouded heavily over and there was no trace of the moon; the wind set up a sighing in the doomed ship's rigging, and without apparent cause a heavy swell set suddenly in from nowhere.

There had been nothing to mark that rock—no broken water, no greasy swirling of the sea, nothing at all. Even now there is nothing there to distinguish this place of tragedy, and one may watch that spot for hours, knowing the rock is there, and see scarcely a sea break. It was not to be wondered that it had been missed by the early mariners who made a hasty survey of a coast that even now is ill charted and worse lit. The *George III* rock is on the charts now, known by the name of the ship that was lost there; but there might quite easily be other rocks equally dangerous which are still uncharted.

For a moment or two after the ship struck the position did not appear to be desperate, although it was bad enough. She had been going so quietly that she just slid upon the rock, swung to a little, and stayed there, and if the ocean swell had not come in all might still have been saved. There was no reason to expect a swell, when there had previously been no sign of one, and Captain Moxey set his gig in the water with an officer to take soundings, testing the possibility of refloating. No sooner was the gig in the water than the swell came, and grew with each succeeding roll, lifting the wooden ship and grinding her on the rocks with horrible, convulsive shudders that tore her timber from timber, and gave her no chance whatever.

Still the swell grew stronger, and the tortured ship ground upon the rocks. Her bottom was knocked right in,

and the water mounted swiftly upon the wretches imprisoned in the hold; with a crash the mainmast went over the
side, taking the mizzen top-mast with it. The foremast followed almost instantly, and these masts and spars, held to
the ship by their imprisoning rigging, remained foul alongside to be crashed into the ship with every lurch and every
movement of her. The grinding of the timbers in her bottom on the rocks, the gloomy crashing of these heavy spars
upon her sides, the swirl and eddy of the cold water round
and over the little vessel, combined to create a chaos that
could not be overcome. The rudder was wrenched off, and
the rudder post crushed up through the poop; the ever-
growing swell now swept aboard where the falling masts had
knocked the bulwarks down, and swirled about the wrecked
decks. Sea followed sea with murderous constancy, and
broke upon the hull, and leapt with mad exultancy over the
torn sides, and flooded the hold. The longboat was jammed
in the wreck on deck, and could not be cleared. The wind
took on an angrier moan, and the sea still rose.

The confusion on deck, with the officers and the sailors
trying to clear the boat that they might have some chance,
while the seas swept over them and the deck was crunching
to pieces beneath their feet, was peace and quiet to the
dreadful scenes in the hold. Here the convicts had been
asleep in greater peace of mind than they had known all
the voyage; they awoke to hear the awful crunch of rock-
torn timbers, and to see, by the dim light of the few lan-
terns by which the sentries kept their watch, little trickles
of water coming in that were the sea. Quickly the trickles
grew and the water rose; the ship, that had settled peace-
ably enough at first, began to drive, and to roll, and to
lurch madly, as if she was fighting for a life she knew she
had to lose; on deck above they could hear the roaring of
the water and the tumult of the crew. The convicts were
locked in their prison, securely barricaded against the
fiercest attempt at mutiny; what could they do? The

screams to be liberated, to be given some chance of saving their miserable lives, rose even above the snarling and the roaring of the sea. Quickly the water mounted upward in the hold; even where the convicts, a swaying, terrible, screaming, hopeless mass of terrified humanity, stood crying for their lives, the bottom was pierced on the rock and the sea swept them to their waists. Many were trampled under-foot in the hell there, and never rose again; many fell and were drowned. The sick, the aged, and the boys had little chance in that hell's chamber. They screamed for mercy, but death only smiled, and stretched out well filled arms. . . .

Meantime the crew continued their desperate endeavor to free the boat, which was entangled in the wreckage of the spars. The more desperate they became the angrier grew the sea, and several of them were swept overboard and drowned. So that there might be some hope of getting the boat away—and fearing that there would be none if the convicts came on deck, the soldiers were ordered to stand in a compact guard round the hatchway and allow none to ascend. But the maddening and desperate nature of their plight gave the emaciated wretches a strength that would have surprised them had they the time to think about it, and they tore at the solid iron bars of their cage with a power so ferocious that they broke down some of them, and a few of them crawled through the aperture. They rushed to the gangway that ascended to the hatchway and made to come up here, but the soldiers fired upon them and two, at least, were killed. About this there was much conflicting testimony afterwards, but it was true enough. In those terrible few moments while the soldiers stood over them with muskets pointed down, nearly a hundred of the convicts perished. All the sick save one, and all the boys, never came out of that hold. They never had a chance of life.

When the two were killed the others quietened a little, perhaps more with shock, and the doctor came down among them. They lifted pitiful arms to him, and cried to him not to desert them. "You have stood by us," they moaned, "don't desert us now!" He said that he would not, and there was no more shooting. After the longboat, which had at last been cleared, had got away, they were allowed on deck. In any case the grating of their cage had been broken down then, and they could not be kept below. When they came on deck they might have been expected, seeing what they had gone through, to behave like maddened wild beasts. But they accepted naturally that they should have last chance of life, and set to with those who were still on board to do what they could to clear the wreck, and prepare for the longboat's return. At the official enquiry afterwards the whole of the witnesses agreed that the conduct of the convicts was most praiseworthy.

When the longboat had got clear, the officer in the smaller boat who had been sent out to take soundings when the ship struck, set off for Hobart to bring help, but through some unpardonable oversight he does not appear to have been aware that Hobart was 50 miles away. He tried to find a landing place but could not, since the swell that had caused so much damage had set up too great a surf and there was no chance to land. The same difficulty was met by the people of the longboat when they tried to land, and hours were spent vainly looking for a landing place while the seas continued to sweep over what was left of the ship and to hurl more and more of the convicts over the broken sides. The sea now made a clean breach over the ship, the long swells sweeping steadily at her, throwing themselves upon her in a smother of cold, driving spray, descending on her torn decks in a thunderous cascade of cold water that flung everything before it. The decks were swept; there was no shelter there. Throughout the pitiless night—it was cold and bleak and raining—the wretches who had once been human beings clung where they could and prayed to be allowed to die. One man lashed himself to a ringbolt that he might be swept ashore with the wreckage when the ship broke up, as she seemed about to do at any moment. But the sea came and drowned him there, before he could free himself, and his body was found afterwards still lashed to the ringbolt.

It was after daybreak when the longboat came back, and 134 of those who had survived the scurvy and the terrors of the voyage had died then. Daylight brought a sail, and those who still lived were taken up to Hobart.

The doctor who had befriended the convicts was taken ashore with the longboat, and in the night he wandered into the bush and was lost. When he was found again he was so far gone that he died, and to-day, in a flowered square in Hobart where children play, there is a square of stone erected to his memory.

One statement by Dr. Wise, the surgeon superintendent, at the official enquiry, is of interest as indicative of the general conditions in the convict ship: "At the time the ship struck I had 60 patients, 50 of whom were totally unable to help themselves, being sick of scurvy in bed. Only two of these 60 have been saved. I attribute this inveterate fatal illness to the scantiness of provisions generally, but particularly to the withdrawal of the oatmeal, and cocoa being substituted for it. None on board but the prisoners who had this diet showed a symptom of this dreadful disease. All the others had at least one-third more rations. On mustering my list, I found that 115 convicts had never partaken of cocoa during the voyage. They loathed it so much it invariably made them sick. . . ."

Later the statements of convicts and soldiers were taken, mainly concerning the musket shots that were fired, ostensibly—so the inquiring officials were told—as signals, but perhaps really to prevent the convicts coming on deck. At any rate it was established that at least one convict was killed in this way, although all the soldiers swore there was no order to fire, and that when they did fire it was away from, and not at, the convicts. "I never ordered a shot to

be fired," said Lieutenant Minten, who admitted that he
heard some, however. The Corporal, who was in charge of
the guard over the hatch, said he heard cries for mercy from
the wretches below, but no cries of wounded. The prisoners
were positive in their declarations that two of them had
been killed by the soldiers. "I saw the soldiers level their
muskets against us," swore one prisoner, "and one shot was
fired. I saw one man, Robert Luker, fall. I heard a second
shot afterwards." Another prisoner swore to the death by
musket fire of a fellow convict named Yates. "I heard two
shots fired. I saw one man, Robert Luker, fall, and about
three or four minutes after that I heard another shot and
saw another man fall." "I am quite sure the two men were
killed in the hatchway," was the statement of yet another
convict witness. "When I was knocked down I fell across
the body of Robert Luker. There was another body there."

These shootings roused popular indignation to a high
pitch, and a coroner's jury was summoned to go to the scene
when it was reported there that bodies were coming ashore
which bore unmistakable evidence of death by gunshot.
Owing to some mistake, however, only eight of the jury
arrived and, since some fool Act or other demanded that
there should be twelve, they decided that they could do
nothing and the whole thing more or less appears to have
been allowed to slide over. The London *Times* commented
in strong terms on this later, and it is certain, looking back
now after nearly 100 years, that in the frightful chaos of
those first few moments after the vessel struck, nothing is
more likely than that the militia, acting in what they doubtless considered the best interests of the ship and all her
people, fired a shot or two down that crowded hatchway
which could not help but take fatal effect.

CHAPTER VIII

THE PIRATES OF OLD VAN DIEMEN'S LAND

IN such a place as Tasmania was in the convict period, with the only hope of escape by sea, it is not to be wondered at that seizings and attempted seizings of vessels were heard of quite frequently, and in this connection the place has some interesting stories to put forward. With ticket-of-leave men there was ever present the temptation to seize a boat and flee; with assigned servants—particularly if they were of the sea—the temptation was no less. It became not at all uncommon for boats and yachts to be seized in Hobart Harbor and taken hurriedly off to sea, but for the most part these were captured again and the offenders made to suffer pretty severely. The waters of Storm Bay were not kind to small craft, and escape by a small boat rarely meant getting quite clear of the island. One or two of the parties who decamped in this way, however, did manage at least to evade their pursuers, and although they may never have got clear away from those southern seas they remained to infest the islands of Bass Strait and to earn for one or two of the more outlandish of these the most unenviable reputation.

The number of wrecks around these islands is so great that it cannot be accurately stated; nor were all these vessels lost by act of God. There are queer old stories of the wreckers who once infested outlying rocks, and lured ships to destruction with false lights; the fate of more than one fine vessel remains unsatisfactorily explained until this day. There is at least one case in which it has been reasonably well established that the vessel fell a victim to piracy in Bass Strait. This was the ship *Britomart*, a well known trader both in Hobart and in Melbourne in the old days, which went mysteriously missing during a voyage from Melbourne to Hobart in 1840. It was at first thought that she had fallen a victim to one or other of the ill charted and worse lit islands of Bass Strait, but easy as that would have been, it was soon established that a worse fate had befallen her.

The *Britomart* was commanded by a Captain Gluas, and in addition to a fair crew, carried about 12 passengers. At the time of her disappearance several other vessels were also on the missing list, and nothing was ever heard of these. Nothing would have been heard of the *Britomart*, either, if the *Sir John Franklin*, detained by bad weather on a voyage from Melbourne to Hobart, had not happened to put in unexpectedly at Preservation Island, in Bass Strait. Here her captain reported to some sealers he found there (they said they were sealers), the loss of the *Britomart* and in response to all his questionings they expressed interest but no hint of knowledge. But, when his ship was held up for several days, the captain of the *Sir John Franklin*—a suspicious and inquisitive old gentleman with a notion in the back of his head that these Bass Strait sealers were not all they seemed—found, to his astonishment, that part of the *Britomart's* poop was serving as a covering for the sealers' pigsty. Then he found, hidden away in a cleft in the rocks, Captain Gluas' chest, his papers, and all his clothes; in a little creek he found a boat with *Britomart* plain on its stern, and among the sealers, now thoroughly aroused, he found other things. A significant fact about all these things was that none showed the slightest trace of having come from a vessel that had been wrecked and none bore any evidence of immersion in the sea.

The sealers, after the wreckage was discovered, said that a vessel had driven ashore on their island in the night but they did not know its name; they had seen nothing of it but the wreckage that had washed up, and they disclaimed all knowledge of the *Britomart's* boat. It was a curious fact, too, that at the time of the *Sir John Franklin's* visit most of the sealers were in Launceston, where it was noticed that they were spending a great many sovereigns and were in possession of considerably greater amounts of money than their profession might reasonably be expected to earn for them. Some of these gentlemen became intoxicated, when they freely boasted that they knew all that was to be known of the *Britomart* and "that no one else would find out." No significance was attached to this statement at the time, although it was remembered feelingly when the *Sir John Franklin* brought her story to port. The sealers had left then, naturally.

From the meager facts that have come down through the years, it certainly looks as if the *Britomart* was set upon suddenly, all her crew and passengers murdered, her valuables taken, and the ship stripped of all that could be taken and sunk. Nothing was ever heard of any of her people; the "sealers" would see to that. Nor is the *Britomart* the only vessel to disappear in circumstances of the gravest suspicion, and there can be little doubt that at that time, and for a good many years, nests of pirates infested some of the islands of Bass Strait. Some of these were escaped convicts who did not even pretend to seal, and as there were so many islands, literally hundreds of which were rarely even seen by any ship, it would have been a matter of no great difficulty for them to carry on their trade. . . .

The fact that some of the vessels which set out from Hobart with food and stores for the convict settlement at Macquarie Harbour never arrived at their destination has already been mentioned. One of these was the brig *Cyprus*, which was seized by the convicts she was transporting to the Harbour and carried off to sea. The *Cyprus* left Hobart on July 28, 1829, with 31 prisoners and guard for Hell's Gates, and because some of the convicts had been to Macquarie Harbour previously none of them looked forward either to the voyage or the end of it with any pleasure.

The *Cyprus* did not get very far on her voyage before the ceaseless westerly gales sent her flying for shelter with damage to her rigging, and for eight days she lay at anchor in Recherché Bay. When she weighed anchor again and stood out to sea, it was only to meet weather tenfold worse, and again she had to turn tail and race for shelter.

A second time the little *Cyprus* anchored in Recherché Bay. During the whole of this time a conspiracy to seize the ship had been carefully formulated by the worst of the convicts, but the dread of their fate gave them an especial cunning and they were able to hide all evidences of their intention so well that their irons were removed—which was exactly what they wanted—and the guard over them was not as strict as it might have been. When the brig was driven back the second time, every one was naturally relieved to reach the shelter of the Bay and there was not the slightest thought on the part of any of the officers or guard that the sullen-faced convicts might turn pirates at any moment.

On August 16—this was on the day after the brig had been driven back the second time—the mate, the doctor, and the officer of the guard left the vessel to fish a little distance off. They had not the slightest cause for suspicion. Towards the middle of the afternoon some of the convicts were lounging about the deck taking exercise, with two of the seven soldiers standing over them with loaded guns on the poop. The rest of the soldiers and the passengers were at tea in the saloon. Everything was quiet and orderly, except for the gale outside that sent the storm rack flying overhead. Without their strategy being noticed, the convicts on deck managed to work their way aft quite close to the soldiers, where they could hear the tinkle of teacups in the saloon and the gay laughter. They could also, at an opportune moment, draw the scuttle across and batten everybody down within about two seconds.

"By jiminy, soldier!" suddenly exclaimed one of the youngest of the convicts, "wotinallell's that over there!"

He pointed excitedly to the water astern of the brig.

Both soldiers, probably dreaming of home at the moment, were caught thoroughly unawares. They turned and bent over the poop rail, staring into the depths. At the same instant each of them received a crack over the back of the neck with belaying pins that put them out of action without a sound. They sprawled helplessly on the deck. The convicts seized their arms, and immediately drew the scuttle over the saloon, battened it down, and everybody below was a prisoner.

"Is it coming on to rain?" called a feminine voice from below. "They have pulled the scuttle over."

The ironic laughter of the convicts, now nicely in charge of the brig even easier than they had ever hoped to be, greeted the lady's question; immediately they knew they were trapped there came a volley of shots from the muskets of the soldiery in the cabin. One of the convicts had rushed for'ard to the forecastle hatch, where he stood over the crew with a musket taken from the guard. Another stood over aft and threatened to shoot everybody down in the cabin dead where they stood if they did not give in—a threat he was well able to carry out, seeing that he could take aim through the skylight and they could not take aim at him. He grazed the captain's cheek with a ball just to show that he meant what he said. The other convicts were now on deck and the brig was completely in their charge. They had got at the magazine and were well armed, and there was nothing for the people below but to choose between a miserable and useless death and surrender. They surrendered, hoping that the people away in the boat might, by some strategy, reverse the position.

But the convicts had allowed for that. The noise of the firing alarmed the fishers and before long their boat was seen hastily returning. The convicts dropped from view, all except two who remained standing aft, with the coats and helmets of the unconscious guards upon them. The boat came rapidly on, its occupants hailing repeatedly and getting no answer, and unable to fathom what was wrong. The convicts were afraid that they might have stood out into D'Entrecasteaux Channel and given the alarm to some ship if they had known that the brig was taken; therefore the strategy to lure them alongside.

The boat drew up to the *Cyprus*, and just as the mate was about to leap aboard the convict "guards" roared at him: "Now then, Mister, none o' that! You stop in that boat or we'll lead you!"

For the instant the mate—a Mr. Hurburgh—was so amazed he almost obeyed. Then he made a fight for it, but it was of no use; no one in the boat had any arms, and no one in the brig could help them. They were thoroughly beaten without the shedding of a drop of blood, and they had to admit it. When the convicts threatened that if they did not give in they would shoot every one in the cabin and the occupants of the boat as well in a voice and manner which showed only too plainly that they meant all they said, the boat's people were compelled to surrender. They were not allowed to come aboard, the convicts sending the boat ashore with the ship's people and some stores in five different parts of the big bay—a good move, since as they took the boat away with them when they went they left the marooned passengers, soldiers, and crew no small task even to get together. That done the convicts landed some thirteen of their own number who balked at setting out on so hazardous a cruise, and weighing the *Cyprus's* anchor, stood out to sea. The gale was as strong as ever and conditions very bad; it was winter then, and to set out against such weather looked like asking for a miserable death. However, they had no intention of beating up the west coast of Tasmania and, putting up the vessel's helm, allowed her to run before it well out of sight of the land.

The people who were left ashore were in a very bad state. The weather was cold, bitter, wet and tempestuous. There was no sun, and they could obtain no warmth. They had no shelter and no means of obtaining any. They had little food and no means of obtaining that either. They might not have been very far from Hobart as the crow flies, but to reach the capital they had either to make a long and difficult overland journey or a worse one by sea. They had no boat, and though they tried the venture by land flooded rivers and generally impossible conditions soon convinced them that all that was to be reached in that direction would be their graves. For weeks the luckless mariners and soldiers were marooned in this inhospitable spot, dragging out a wretched existence on mussel soup and such fish as they could find. They had not even a sail for shelter, and the lot of the one woman who was with them—the wife of the military officer—was a particularly bad one.

After some hopeless weeks of this a man named Morgan, one of the crew, said that he would build a coracle and sail to Hobart in it for help. He had seen coracles built, he said, and knew how to make and sail one. The captain said that he would most certainly be drowned if he ventured out of the bay, but Morgan said that they would all die if they remained there and the chance was good enough to take. To stay was death; to try the coracle was at least a chance. He made his coracle, which surely must be one of the strangest craft that ever took the water. "It was about 12 feet long, the keel, gunwales, stern and stem post were formed of the branches of the wattle tree, with smaller pieces for timbers; these composed the framework. It was covered with two hammocks, next painted or coated with boiled soap mixed with a little resin that one of the sailors had had with him in a pocket of his jacket."

Such was the craft, and when it set out no one expected ever to hear of it again. With Morgan went another sailor named Popjoy, and although their little craft struck bad weather immediately, it was not overwhelmed and came safely to D'Entrecasteaux Channel. Here it was lucky enough, before going very far, to fall in with the ships *Orelia* and *Georgiana*, bound to India, which took them aboard and went immediately to the relief of the people at Recherché, who were more amazed at the fact that the coracle had lived than at their own deliverance. Their sufferings were very bad; years later Lady Franklin, on a trip to Port Davey, records in a diary now in the possession of the Royal Society at Hobart the melancholy thoughts which came to her while meditating on the lot of the people cast ashore from the *Cyprus* in all the weary weeks that they spent down there, expecting no deliverance save death.

When the castaways were relieved, the *Cyprus* had got clear away and no one expected to hear more of her. Whenever she was mentioned both the hope and the belief were expressed that the pirates who had seized her would come to a bad end before they got very far, and it was generally expected, since few of them had the slightest knowledge of the sea, that they would lose the ship and themselves without even making a landfall. However, that did not prove the case, though their end was melancholy enough. After a most amazing cruise through the Pacific Islands, in the course of which several of the pirates cleared out in the Friendly Islands and lived there with native wives, and at other islands some of the ex-convicts were converted into soup, the *Cyprus* eventually finished her career in the China Sea. What exactly happened is not clear, but in any case seven of the convicts were found in different parts of China and sent to England from there. Thence they were shipped to Tasmania again and promptly hanged. . . .

Then there was the *Frederick*, another Macquarie Harbour brig, although in her case the circumstances were somewhat different. She was an easy capture and is more memorable because of the remarkable exploits and trials of her crew after they had escaped from Tasmania. When

the settlement at Macquarie Harbour was abandoned a brig
was still building there, and in order to finish her a party
of 12 convicts, four soldiers, Taw, a pilot, and Hoy, a master shipwright, were left behind with orders to rig the brig
and bring her round to Hobart as soon as possible.   The
brig, which was named the *Frederick*, was launched on December 16, 1833, and on January 10, 1834, was ready for
sea with all sails bent and provisions on board.   Up to that
time the convicts had behaved "splendidly" and there was
no sign of any approaching attempt at piracy or anything
else untoward.   The convicts were unironed, naturally, and
the severe discipline of the place was relaxed.   In the
course of time it became customary for the soldiers to go
about unarmed; there is also a possibility that they were
frequently in a state of intoxication, since a pretty good
supply of rum had been left behind and in those days a
teetotaler, among such men, would have been regarded with
graver suspicion than a convict.

In any case everything seems to have gone along smoothly,
with the convicts regarded more or less as ordinary crew,
until the brig was about to put to sea.   She dropped down
the harbor on January 11th but the wind was ahead to
cross the bar and she had to anchor.   The convicts obtained permission to go ashore to wash clothes, and later
in the afternoon returned in a cheerful frame of mind, proceeding to hold a vociferous sing-song on the fo'c'sle head.
Taw and Hoy retired below, to take "tea."   The two soldiers of the guard remained alone on deck, unarmed.   After
Messrs. Taw and Hoy had had some "tea" one of the convicts came along to ask permission to take the two soldiers
off guard fishing, saying that he knew of an excellent place
where they would be assured of a good haul.   The permission was granted readily enough, and they set off, although
two other convicts went in the boat and they saw that the
soldiers were without their arms.

They did not reach the fishing grounds.   They simply

pulled out of sight of the ship and laid the soldiers out, a matter quite easily accomplished, since they took them off their guard. Knowing from previous experience that Hoy and Taw would still be at their tea below, the boat now returned to the *Frederick*, while at the same time the convicts still on board took the other two soldiers unawares —which was again easily accomplished since neither of them had the slightest cause to suspect that anything was wrong, and both were taken leaning contentedly over the poop rail. The sing-song on the fo'c'sle head continued to drown any noise, and before Messrs. Hoy and Taw had the slightest idea that anything was amiss the poop scuttle was drawn upon them and they were battened down below. The four soldiers were bound and thrust into the hold, while the convicts had the arms and the magazine—and the decks—completely to themselves.

Seeing the scuttle hastily drawn and not realizing, for the moment, what had happened, Messrs. Hoy and Taw shouted loudly to know what the devil was up. In reply the ringleader of the convicts told them calmly that they had seized the ship, and if they gave in nothing would happen to them. Both Messrs. Hoy and Taw, now thoroughly aroused, used every curse they knew and swore that they would never give in to any such damned nonsense. They saw, however, that it was not quite "damned nonsense" when the convicts presented the soldiers' muskets at them through the skylight, but they still pleaded with the men to hand the ship back, saying that they would not report the occurrence in Hobart if that were done. The convicts had plotted well, however, and refused to listen to any appeal to reason. Having begun the mutiny they knew their only course was to keep it up.

Hoy and Taw, who were probably drunk, saw that the convicts were earnest enough. They retired into cabins opening off the saloon from which they proceeded to shoot at the convicts on deck, but as they could not see them

AFTER SAILING IN BALLAST FROM EUROPE TO HOBART,
A BIG FRENCH BARQUE IN BALLAST SAILS FOR SAN FRANCISCO.
HER VOYAGE WAS FOR THAT PORT IN THE FIRST PLACE,
BUT THE CONSIDERABLE MILEAGE TO TASMANIA ADDED TO
HER "BOUNTY" EARNINGS. THESE WERE PAID ON MILEAGE.
WHEN THE BOUNTY ACT WAS REPEALED,
HOBART SAW NO MORE SUCH SHIPS

HOBART IN THE NINETEENTH CENTURY: SLOOP-OF-WAR IN FOREGROUND

properly to take aim that was not of much use. Their
position was hopeless from the beginning, but it was not
until the crowd of grinning convicts came along the poop
with a pot of molten pitch which they threatened to pour
down on top of the pilot and shipmaster—a threat they
most certainly would have carried out—that Hoy and Taw
surrendered. Until this time they had been expecting some
help from the soldiers, of whose fate they had been unaware, but when they came on deck and saw that they, too,
had been overpowered they knew that the *Frederick* would
not be delivered to the representative of His Majesty the
King in Hobart Town that voyage. The convicts gave
them both the chance of throwing in their lot with them,
but Hoy said he would sooner go with the blacks. Taw
said he would sooner go to hell.

"Very well, then," replied the ringleader of the convicts
to that. "We may give you a hand."

They then marooned the officers and the soldiers, together with one of their own number who refused to join
them, on the shores of Macquarie Harbour, leaving them
little stores and the reflection that it would probably be a
long time before any vessel came round from Hobart to
discover why the *Frederick* had not appeared.

The next day the wind changed and the captured brig
put to sea. Hoy, Taw and the others eventually escaped
from Macquarie Harbour after a most wretched experience,
walking through the almost impenetrable bush to Circular
Head, in the north-west, where they arrived months later
more dead than alive.

But fate did not smile kindly upon the pirates of the
Frederick, either.

The convicts who seized the brig were, of course, either
seafaring men or shipwrights, or they would not have been
chosen to remain behind at the Harbour. One of them,
named John Barker, had been a deep-sea mate and had
once, indeed, been a master; another named John Fair had

also executive experience of the management of sailing ships, and quite half the little vessel's complement consisted of experienced sailors. The first thing they did, when they safely negotiated Hell's Gates, was to elect Barker master and Fair mate. Barker decided to stand to the south of Tasmania and New Zealand and to run the ship on until she came to South America. Fair thought the South Seas better, but Barker and some of the others referred to the *Cyprus's* people who had gone that way and been caught. South America, too, he said, was the most lawless place they could find and the most suitable in every way for such as they; nor was he far wrong. Accordingly the brig shaped a course to the south'ard to clear the south of Tasmania, and the first night out a westerly gale came down that was nearly the end of everything. Fearing capture, although there was not even the slightest need to fear pursuit, the pirates would not take in sail and drove their brig before the gale more than she could stand. They kept the fores'l and the full tops'ls on her; she was a sweet lined little thing and ran gamely at a steady eleven knots through the tempestuous night and the following day and night, so that when the gale abated she was somewhere out in the Tasman Sea safe from all pursuit and all fear of capture. But she was strained badly by the effort of driving so furiously before the gale; she was a new ship, and should have had better care than that. She had not had time to take up properly before she put to sea, so that even under the best conditions she might have been expected to leak a good deal. That hard driving the first night out never gave her a chance, and from the first day at sea it was a case of pump all the time to keep her afloat.

There was four feet of water in the well and she settled down sluggishly; to make matters worse the rigging, which was of rope, slackened badly, causing the masts to jolt as if they would come out with the laboring of the ship, and her top-gallant masts had to be struck while the lower rig-

ging was set up.   From the very first it was evident that
the mutineers were to have a heavy time of it, and many
times in the course of the long run across the stormy South
Pacific they wished that they were back in Tasmania.   The
only relief from the pumps was the helm; for many days
some of them were violently seasick, and to make things
worse Barker, the master, developed a serious illness which
kept him to his bunk for nine days, during which the ship
raced on blindly before almost incessant gales.   Fair, the
mate, was not much of a sailor, and in spite of the water
that the little ship made from her previous straining he
persisted in driving her—a course that was totally unneces-
sary, since the fact that the *Frederick* had been seized was
not discovered in Hobart until after she had reached South
America.

The leaks became worse and worse; some of the provisions in the hold became unfit for use, and the crew were in
a bad state through the incessant pumping.   They had to
pump so much that the flesh was literally worn from their
hands, and with hands in such a terrible state they had to
haul on wet ropes and fist rain-sodden canvas, while the
westerly gales shrieked round them and hail squalls hissed
about them every day.   During his illness Barker took no
sights and ship's position was never known; the crew became alarmed and said that they would be lost.   How did
they know, they asked, that they would come to South
America; Barker answered that they need have no worries
about that; if they kept a straight course before the wind
they would arrive somewhere on the coast of Chile.   That
was true enough.

More gales came, the whole passage was one constant
fight to keep the vessel afloat while she raced before the
westerly wind.   The pumps were in the waist of the ship
which was very wet, and one of the convicts was sent sprawl-
ing by a sea that swept her decks and left him with a broken
arm.   Barker set it without ceremony; the lot of them, by

then, had suffered so much that one injury the more did
not matter.

Then a white squall threw her on her beam ends and they
gave up hope altogether; the *Frederick* had been beautifully built, however, and she lived even through this. At
this stage things were in a desperate way and the crew
were pretty near the end. To add to all their other worries they had the greater worry of the doubtful reception
which awaited them at the end of the voyage—if it were
to have an end. They knew that along the Patagonian
coast they would most probably be murdered; they knew
that if they fell in with any other vessel there would be
awkward questions to answer, and if they could not show a
clean pair of heels it would be a sorry day for them. Along
the Chilean coast, too, they had reason to expect a chance
of meeting with an English frigate; that was a fate they
feared worst of all. But they saw nothing on the whole
long voyage save a French whaler which took no notice of
them, being too busily occupied in its own pursuits, and
after a stormy passage of 43 days, during which no one in
the ship had a proper rest nor a proper meal, land was
made out from the fore topgallant yard.

At this time the ship was practically in a sinking state,
and although her wearied crew did what they could at the
pumps it was evident that they could not keep by her very
much longer. In readiness for the day when they would
have to abandon the *Frederick*, they had decked over the
longboat and had made it as seaworthy as they could.

On the day they sighted land Barker was still ill; they
went below and told him the news which he refused flatly
to believe, saying that according to his reckoning they were
still 500 miles from the South American coast. His reckoning must have been 500 miles out, however, for the coast
was there plainly enough. Barker figured that it was somewhere "between Chili and Valdivia," and that night they
abandoned the *Frederick* to her fate. She was leaking so

badly then that during the few hours that they left the pumps to swing out the longboat—stoving in some of its planks in the process—the little brig settled down to her chain plates, and when the pirates left her her decks were almost level with the water. There was a heavy swell running, and round the brig the seas broke with a peculiar greasiness in their swell; they gurgled with "a kind of satisfaction," and lapped the decks with a caress. Before the longboat was out of sight the *Frederick* was gone.

The convicts now had the vaguest of ideas regarding both where they were and what they intended to do with themselves. They at first proposed to land anywhere where life was supportable, and to go on satisfied only with their liberty. But before they set foot on land they had given up that idea; they had suffered a lot, and craved human companionship and human sympathy. They set off for the land and found an uninhabited bay, after a long search along the coast for a suitable place to land, but as that part of the coast was uninhabitable as well as uninhabited, they could not remain there. They rested a little, keeping constant watch for Indians and wild beasts, and then put off to sea again. For a week or more they wandered about the coast in their boat, hoping to find some port, and at length, in a starving and utterly worn-out condition, came to Valdivia.

Here they had at first intended to tell a "ship-wrecked" story, which would be true enough, except that that sort of thing always led to complications. The inhabitants would receive them kindly, and so on, but in the course of time would come to wonder that they had no home to go to; the story would drift about, and be reported, as like as not, to some English consul, with the consequent end of everything. The wreck would be reported, if nothing else, and that must lead to a revelation. If they were shipwrecked mariners they would be expected to move on, and the mutineers of the *Frederick* did not want that. Moving

on was dangerous for them and would be for a year or two
after the loss of their ship became known; what they wanted
was some place where they could remain, happily out of
the world and without fear of sudden arrest and the cer-
tainty of the hangman. Valdivia was just the place, if it
would stand for them. They decided to tell the governor—
a picturesque and kind-hearted Spaniard named Don Fernando Martelle—the plain truth, seeing that they had murdered nobody and had done nothing wrong beyond seizing
the brig. They looked in the last stages of starvation and
exhaustion, and Don Fernando listened to them sympathetically. They were imprisoned but soon let free and
allowed to work. Their first job was to put the finishing
touches to a ship that had already been three years on the
stocks; they finished it in a day and launched it the next,
and Valdivia was en fête in their honor. The governor said
that they might marry and settle down, if they chose, and
five of them chose wives for themselves from the Spanish
maidens of the populace. Everything went well for a
while; they were hard workers and knew their craft. They
had suffered so much, at Macquarie Harbour and then in
the *Frederick*, that for a long time they were prepared to
ask nothing of life than that it should forget them, and
allow them to go quietly on. Those who were married were
good husbands, and all of them were well spoken of.

Then one day the British frigate *Blonde*, Commodore
Mason, hove-to outside Valdivia and the ex-pirates were in
fear of their lives. The governor clapped them in the jail
where no inquiring British naval officer was likely to look
for them, and after a few hours the *Blonde* moved on, to
the intense relief of everybody. Mason was ashore but
noticed nothing of interest; he would never have dreamed
of looking for the *Frederick's* pirates there, even if he had
known they were still living. If he had heard of the seizing
of that vessel in far off Van Diemen's Land he would probably have concluded that the lot of the convicts had been

promptly drowned without reaching any port. He knew something of the seas of the South Pacific.

After the visit of the *Blonde* some of the pirates became restless, fearing that one day she might return and take them. The decent life, too, began to pall on them. Three of them—Fair, Jones, and Reilly—cleared out of Valdivia in a brig bound up the coast and never came back again. The governor might have had reasonable excuse then to clap the others under lock and key and deliver them to the English consul at Valparaiso, but he still allowed them to go free.

Then, a year after her first visit, the *Blonde* was back again at Valdivia, this time in avowed search of "several Englishmen who had come upon the coast in a clandestine manner." Commodore Mason sent a brusque demand to the governor to send these men on board his frigate for interrogation, but the governor, after consulting the nine who remained and learning that they would sooner be killed on the spot than sent aboard the frigate, sent a reply that the Commodore could interview them if he came ashore alone. The Commodore sent in an armed boat at that but the Spanish battery repulsed it, and again the *Blonde* made off. It was certain, now, however, that she would not be very long.

It was discovered afterwards that the three who had cleared out from Valdivia in the brig had, while on a drunken spree in Callao, boasted openly to some bluejackets from the *Blonde* that they were pirates from the *Frederick* who had come from Valdivia and before that from Van Diemen's Land. They were promptly arrested and taken aboard the *Blonde*, when one of them told Commodore Mason of the others who still remained at Valdivia.

However, the *Blonde* did not return to Valdivia. There was much more important work for her to do on that coast. Don Fernando Martelle was removed from his governorship, being succeeded by a gentleman of evil name who

boded no good to the ex-convicts, all of whom were still
in the place, leading good and useful enough lives, for
the Chile of those days. The new governor promptly imposed all manner of restrictions upon the Englishmen, and
life ceased to be as pleasant for them as it had been under
the old régime. Four of them, under the pretense of making a boat for the governor, obtained his permission to
build a substantial whale boat. Their movements in the
harbor had been closely watched since the three deserted
in the brig, and the new governor never lost sight of the
fact that, if at any time he wished to curry favor with the
English consul at Valparaiso or Callao, he had only to
hand over the renegades, and he did not intend that the
Englishmen should slip through his fingers. Despairing of
escape by sea, four of them conceived the plan of building
the whale boat and clearing off in it. It was a clever trick
to do it openly, with the governor's permission and with
his funds, but when the boat was finally completed and they
promptly cleared off in it the position of the others who
remained was pretty bad. The men who had escaped in the
whale boat plotted well and got clear away; they took their
newly launched craft to sea one Saturday evening, presum-
ably to test it and so on, and the next day being Sunday
they were not missed until the following morning. They
were clear by then and were never afterwards heard of.
The governor was in a towering rage when he learnt how
he had been tricked and promptly threw the remaining four
into prison. They had not been in the plot, apparently,
although they were made to suffer for it. They were sent
in irons to Valparaiso and thence to the *Blonde* at Callao,
where Commodore Mason greeted them with the cheerful
announcement that he knew he would have them aboard
sooner or later. He had not forgotten the repulse of his
armed boat from Valdivia, and swore that he would run
down the other miscreants who cleared away in the whale
boat. These he never captured, however, and he had to

be satisfied to send the four back to England round Cape Horn. Returned to England they were bundled into the hulk *Leviathan*, to await the first convict transport for Tasmania.

These four—Shires, Connor, Lyon and Cheshire—were sent out to Hobart Town again by the convict ship *Sarah*, along with 253 other prisoners, to stand their trial, and after a passage of 96 days from London, arrived on March 28, 1837. On the way out the four pirates conceived a plan for the taking of the ship, but a sailor in whom they confided gave them away and the mutiny did not come off. They were tried at the Supreme Court, Hobart Town, before the Chief Justice and a military jury. They were charged on three counts, the first with piracy, the second with breaking their trust as sworn mariners, and the third with having absconded while being prisoners of the Crown in Van Diemen's Land. The principal witness against them was Hoy. Hoy narrated the circumstances of the capture at great length. Taw was drunk at the launching, he said, and had been so drunk since then that one day he had to be placed under restraint. James Tait, the acting mate of the vessel, had more to say about Taw's drunkenness. He said that he drank with the soldiers, and that the lower rigging was all spoilt because Taw cut it badly when he was drunk. In their defense the prisoners said that they were compelled to join the mutiny and that they had not instigated it. They added that the hardships they had endured on the way to South America were indescribable, and avowed that they had given themselves up to the Government there. They concluded by throwing themselves upon the mercy of the court, but the court had no mercy and they were found guilty and duly hanged. . . .

Towards the end of January or early in February, 1819, the schooner *Young Lachlan* came up the Derwent River and anchored opposite Government House. The port regulations relating to the safety of vessels in harbor were then

very strict, as they had to be in what was little more than
a penal settlement pure and simple. With the bands of
assigned servants and ticket-of-leave men roaming round,
whose only hope of escape was the sea, it was only to be expected that the utmost precautions would be taken with
such vessels as came into the Derwent from the sea. The
Governor of the day had drawn up a long and imposing
list of orders which were to be obeyed, but as usual with
orders that are overdone they were not properly obeyed.
Every vessel upon making the harbor was required to un-
bend all her sails, and stow them away under lock and key
below; to unship her rudder and send it ashore; to keep a
vigilant armed watch on deck, lest there should be any attempt on the part of marauding convicts to seize the vessel,
and to keep the small arms loaded and in readiness. The
town battery was ordered to fire into any vessel leaving the
harbor after nightfall—if it were seen, of course. A Governor of those days in Tasmania had large powers, at least
in theory, but as he was not able always to command the
means of carrying out his orders, they sometimes did not
mean too much. It was not unknown, indeed, that a vessel
would come into port, sell her cargo, and then suddenly, at
a propitious moment, clear off to sea again without bother-
ing about the formality of parting with port dues, pilotage
fees, and so on.

The *Young Lachlan* had not been long in the port before
a party of convicts, with an eye out for such a handy vessel,
conceived the plan of seizing her. They saw that her sails
were not unbent and her rudder had not been sent ashore,
and had reason to believe that her watch might not be found
to possess any extraordinary vigilance. They knew, too,
that her master had gone inland to buy wheat and other
crops to form a cargo for the schooner, and in the early
hours of the morning of February 28, 1819, they slipped
out in a waterman's boat they had stolen and climbed cautiously aboard, prepared to clout the guard on deck across

the head with half an oar if the need existed. The need did
not exist, for the simple reason that everybody on board
was below and sound asleep. The convicts clapped the
hatch over them and battened it there so that no noise could
escape to awaken the slumbering town. The rudder had
been unshipped, in accordance with the Governor's orders,
but that was as far as his orders had been obeyed, and it
was lying on deck instead of having been sent ashore. The
whole of the thirteen escaped men were sailors and they
soon reshipped the rudder. The sails were bent, and within
ten minutes of their first coming on board they had slipped
the cable, spread some canvas, shipped the rudder, and were
standing down the Derwent out to sea. No one from the
fort fired upon them because nobody there saw them, and
no one else was awake to see the deed. A stiff land breeze
was blowing down the river and conditions for the daring
escape were ideal. At the northern end of Bruni they put
the crew ashore, first giving them the chance to throw in
their lot with them, which the crew all refused. After this
delay they packed on all the sail the schooner would stand
and headed her for the open sea, nor was the *Young Lachlan*
ever seen there again.

In the morning the absence of the schooner was noticed,
and later the absence of the convicts as well. The Government vessels set off in chase but the *Young Lachlan* had
too good a start. It was reported that she had no water
on board, and for a time it was hoped that she would be
taken when she was forced to put in somewhere to take
water. But she did not touch at any place where she might
have been reported, and with water or without her piratical
captors made good their escape. The Governor, knocked
unceremoniously out of his bed before six o'clock in the
morning, could not believe at first that the schooner had
really gone. But gone it had, and he was most perturbed.
He was hampered in his endeavors to chase the runaway
because of the fact that the only other vessels in the harbor

at the time—the brig *Sophia* and a sloop—*had* obeyed all
his instructions to the last letter and were little better than
rigged-down hulks. The Governor bit his lip, cursed himself a little, and set off in boats.

For two years after that nothing more was heard of the
Young Lachlan, and all hope of ever hearing anything of
her or the fate of her captors was given up. Then one day
a full-rigged ship came up the river, the *St. Michael,* from
Calcutta, and the little town buzzed with excitement when
it was known that she had the survivors from the *Young
Lachlan* on board. This was on September 28, 1820, and
the survivors she brought with her—five of them—later
told a court appointed to try them that, after many vicis-
situdes and a great deal of suffering, they had brought the
Young Lachlan to the coast of Batavia. Here they intended to sell her and purchase a passage to England with
the money, but the Dutch official launches which were pok-
ing about were too inquisitive and they became alarmed.
Putting into a bay one day a launch came off demanding
to see the papers; the pirates had no papers, and repulsed
the launch, which set off hurriedly to the nearest town for
reënforcements. As soon as the Dutchmen had gone the
pirates stood out to sea, sailed out of sight of land, manned
the boat and fully provisioned it, and set fire to the schooner,
which they watched burn to the water's edge. They then
set off in their boats to make for whatever place they might
reach, but a storm came up and cast them ashore at the
very town to which the repulsed launch had returned for
reënforcements to seize them. They had intended to tell a
harrowing tale of shipwreck and so on, and to move the
inhabitants with the story of their sufferings—they had
suffered something, too—but they were recognized and
flung into jail.

Here most of the thirteen died from fever, and eventually
the five survivors were sent to Calcutta. There they made
a clean breast of their real story, so sick were they of the

horrors of the Batavian jails and the terrors of their life, and were shipped by the *St. Michael* back to Hobart Town. They were tried at that place on January 19, 1821, but so emaciated were they from their dreadful experiences and so pitiful was their aspect that even the judge took pity on them and they were not hanged. The owner of the schooner, a Captain Howard, whose life was a singular procession of misfortunes, had been lost at sea, and there was no public irritation against the prisoners, according to the press of the time. They were sentenced to die, of course, but there is no record of their execution.

CHAPTER IX

THE "CONVICT KING"

FROM the host of petty thieves, forgers, burglars, tricksters, and unfortunates whose only "wrong" had been that they were hungry and ill clad, who were sent out during the years of transportation to Tasmania, there arises one gallant figure of stirring romance and interesting adventure who compels attention. A mariner he was, of course, and his name was Jürgen Jürgensen. If Jürgen Jürgensen had never lived and somebody had written a book in which the hero went through that man's adventures, no one would have published it. It would have been described as far-fetched to the point of impossibility, if not of idiocy; there would have been endeavors to commit the author to the care of a Board of Guardians. Sailor, whaler, explorer, privateer, naval officer, spy, author, dramatist, preacher, revolutionist, gambler, prisoner, convict doctor, police constable, editor, exile, prospector, vagabond and King of Iceland—what a list!

And yet Jürgen Jürgensen was all these things, and others into the bargain. He was at the discovery of Bass Strait and the founding of Tasmania; as a privateer he fought for Denmark against England, and as a spy later on carried out dangerous work on the Continent for that same England; he was a prisoner in Newgate and Tothill Fields; he voyaged round the world in whaling ships, convict ships, tiny sloops of discovery; he wrote voluminous "works" the manuscripts of which are still preserved in the British Museum; he edited a newspaper and he stole Iceland.

One of the best things Jürgensen ever did was to write something of the story of his life in the Van Diemen's Land

128

Annual for 1835 and 1838. There one learns that he was
born in Copenhagen in 1780. His father was watch and
clock maker to the Court of Denmark. From his earliest
boyhood he always wanted to go to sea. "When I beheld
a Danish India-man set sail with its officers on deck, dressed
in their attractive uniforms, my heart burned with envy,
and it appeared to my susceptible imagination that there
could be no enjoyment greater than that of gliding over
the smooth waters in an immense ship"—and to sicken him
of these imaginative longings his father had him bound
'prentice in an English collier brig. He served there four
years, trading in the Baltic in summer and the North Sea
in winter, and if that did not sicken him of the sea then
he was meant for it. He had here "little of the cream of
life" and did no "gliding over the smooth waters in an immense ship"; yet he stuck to it and had a thorough training in a hard school.

As soon as his apprenticeship was up he left that collier
brig and never served in another in his life. He tried deep-
water next, in a South Seas whaler, and in her went to the
Cape of Good Hope. Here he left the whaler and shipped
in a vessel called the *Harbinger*, bound with stores "for
the forces stationed at Algoa Bay to defend the settlers
from the attacks of the Kaffirs." In Algoa Bay the *Harbinger* engaged a French 44-gunner, and with the help of
an English sloop of war drove her from the African shores.
Next we find Jürgensen again at the Cape, this time shipping in the tiny brig *Lady Nelson*,* which he describes as
"a small surveying vessel of 65 tons appointed as a tender
to Captain Flinders, of the *Investigator*, . . . under orders
to proceed to the south of Australia to ascertain definitely
whether the straits now called Bass's, separating Australia
from Van Diemen's Land, really existed." In the *Lady
Nelson*, in which Jürgensen appears to have been mate—

---

* There is reason to believe that the authorities of Table Bay were
glad to see him go; it is not unlikely that for some misdemeanor he was
shipped away in the *Lady Nelson*.

he doesn't say himself what he was—King Island was discovered and the little brig sailed through Bass Strait to
Sydney, afterwards returning to that neighborhood to complete the survey of Port Phillip (where Melbourne now
stands), Western Port, Port Dalrymple, and the Derwent.
After that Jürgensen was still in the *Lady Nelson* when she
accompanied Flinders, in the *Investigator*, on a cruise to
Northern Australia.   Here the brig lost her anchors and
had to return to Sydney with an anchor of wood, which
had so dried on her decks that when it was dropped overboard on arrival in Port Jackson it floated instead of sinking, and the *Lady Nelson* drifted ashore.

Jürgensen was in the *Lady Nelson* for a considerable
period, and was still on board when in 1803 she set out
from Sydney to establish a new settlement on the banks of
the River Derwent in Tasmania.   This settlement later
grew into the city of Hobart, to which this same Jürgensen
was fated to return, over 20 years later, as a prisoner transported for life.   However, much was to happen before that.
He was in the *Lady Nelson* on a visit to Newcastle, too—
a place he describes as "rich in coals, cedar, and fish."
After that he left the *Lady Nelson* and went as master of
a sealer to New Zealand.   From there he joined the *Alexander*, southern whaler, as chief mate; here he says that he
could "boast of having struck the first whale ever taken
in the Derwent River." *   The *Alexander* cruised round
Tasmania and to Norfolk Island and New Zealand, where
her crew engaged in battle with some warlike Maoris at
the Bay of Islands.   With a full cargo of sperm oil she set
out at last for England, but, the future king's autobiog-
raphy goes on, "whilst rounding Cape Horn we encountered
a tremendous gale which compelled us to run nearly 3,000
miles out of our course," fetching up at Tahiti.   It must
have been indeed a tremendous gale.   The story of the
Alexander's meanderings towards England is a good illus-

* A typical statement. Jürgensen never held any brief for modesty.

SOUTH TASMANIAN KETCHES RACE ON A HOBART REGATTA DAY IN THE EARLY
TWENTIETH CENTURY

PART OF THE SOUTH PACIFIC SQUADRON AT ANCHOR
IN THE DERWENT RIVER OFF HOBART

tration of the leisurely manner in which long sea voyages were often made in those days. She was 15 months on the voyage, although, of course, not all that time at sea. She was over half of it in port—Tahiti, Brazil, St. Helena. The *Alexander's* idea of sailing must have been to make a fair wind of every breeze that blew. No matter how bad a Cape Horn hurricane might be, there was no excuse for running to Tahiti; and then Cape Horn blows are notoriously from the west'ard. It is more than likely that before she put in at Tahiti the *Alexander* had never been anywhere near Cape Horn; it was difficult to say just where those old whalers might have got to, at times, or what they might have been up to. At any rate she had no excuse for running her easting down in the South East Trades of the Pacific, nor need she have sailed across the South Atlantic to St. Helena after her call at Brazil. That wasn't making much headway towards England.

However, in the long run the *Alexander* did arrive at London, and Jürgensen brought to an end his first series of colonial adventures. Returned to his native Copenhagen he found it being bombarded by the English, under Lord Cathcart, and his next move was to take command of a Danish privateer of 28 guns to give to English ships some of the medicine they had been giving to the Danes. In this vessel, Jürgensen, always a man of courage and resource, cut through the ice a month before it was supposed that any ship could get out, and was able to sink eight or nine English vessels before being engaged in fatal encounter with two English men-o'-war off Flamborough Head. Jürgensen had no need to be near Flamborough Head, and if he had kept away from the English coast he might have continued in his career of destruction. However, he had to strike his flag, with most of his men killed and his guns out of action, to the two Englishmen. He was taken prisoner and landed at Yarmouth.

Exactly what Jürgensen's position was in England after

that is not quite clear. He says himself that he gave no parole, and apparently he was allowed to roam round London unsupervised and at his leisure. At any rate we next find him setting off on the expedition to Iceland which was to end in his usurpation of the government of that country and abrupt assumption of a monarchy as absolute and single-handed as any in history.

At that time the people in Iceland, cut off from their usual supplies from Denmark because of the war between that country and England, were in a very bad state. In the general unsettled condition of affairs in Europe then no one appeared worried over the fate of Iceland, and the Icelanders would probably have been left to starve had not a London merchant named Phelp sought the permission of the English government to send a shipload of foodstuffs there. The permission was granted, and Jürgensen went in command. The ship set out from Liverpool at the end of the year, at a time when it was most dangerous for small sailing vessels to attempt the passage to Iceland; in Jürgensen's care she arrived safely enough, only to find that the Danish authorities of the island were so hostile to all things English that they would not even allow their starving people to secure relief from the foodstuffs brought by an English ship. Smoothing over this trouble for the time being, Jürgensen landed his cargo and hurried back to England for more. On his return the second time to Iceland, he found that the Danish authorities had gone a good deal further, rigorously prohibiting all intercourse with the English in any way, although the Icelanders were in serious distress because of the shortage of provisions. In effect, Jürgensen was peremptorily told to get out of it, and to take his ship and his cargo with him. He didn't go. Instead, he arrested, kidnaped and deposed the Danish governor, engineered one of the most interesting little revolutions in history, and assumed the throne of Iceland.

Here is Jürgensen's own account of his rise to the
Monarchy:

I resolutely refused to go back after a fruitless errand, and
to see a whole population deprived of the support which Providence had brought to their doors in a time of need. I formed
my plan without taking any one into my confidence, and the
day after my arrival, being Sunday, I went on shore with 12
of my sailors as soon as I saw that the people had gone to
church. I went straight to the Governor's house, and divid-
ing my little troop into two bodies, I stationed six before and
six behind the building, with orders to fire upon anybody that
should attempt to interrupt me. I then opened the door and
walked in with a brace of pistols. His Lordship, Count
Tramp, was reposing upon a sofa, all unsuspicious of what
was in progress, and was completely surprised by my abrupt
appearance. With the exception of the cook, who was busy
preparing dinner, one or two domestics, and a Danish lady,
he was alone in the house. Had he been religiously disposed
and gone to church with his people, I would not have been
able to effect my purpose so easily. But as it happened, I
had no difficulty whatever in arresting the Count and escort-
ing him to a place of security on board my ship. I am not
aware, unless some more deeply-read historian than myself
can cite an instance, that any revolution in the annals of
nations was ever more adroitly, more harmlessly or more
decisively effected than this. The whole government of the
island was changed in a moment without the firing of a shot
or the shedding of a drop of human blood. I was pretty well
aware of the sentiments of the people before I planned my
scheme, and had a shrewd suspicion that all would be well;
nevertheless, to make assurance doubly sure, I carefully secured the iron chest of state. When the people emerged from
church they soon heard the news, and gathered in astonished
groups to discuss the arrest and deposition of their erstwhile
governor, but feeling that I would never have taken so bold
and decisive a step without the sanction and approval of the
British Government, they cheerfully submitted to the new
order of things and gradually dispersed to their homes.

After that King Jürgensen "had no hesitation in issuing
a proclamation to the effect that the people of Iceland had

thrown off the intolerable yoke of the Danish oppression,"
and had "unanimously called me to the head of the government." Although the "unanimous call" to occupy it had
come only from himself, he found the throne of Iceland
comfortable enough and straightway set about making a
proper job of his kingship. He had had "no experience
of that sort of thing," he admits himself, but that did not
trouble him. He commanded that no debts due to Danes
were to be paid, increased the stipends of the clergy, and
made a royal progress throughout the land. He set about
reducing the Danish influence in Iceland to hopeless im-
potency with a ruthlessness that made him many enemies
among the Danes, but many friends among the Icelanders.
The truth of the whole extraordinary story probably is
that the Danes had so oppressed the struggling poor of
Iceland that they were glad of deliverance from any quarter. One Sigrid Schulesen, a native of Iceland, afterwards
declared that the fact that Jürgensen's ship's guns covered
the houses of Rejkjavik during the period of his monarchy,
was the principal reason why the usurper was suffered.
Rejkjavik, said Schulesen, was of wood, and could easily
be destroyed. But there were 50,000 people in Iceland,
descendants of a race noteworthy for anything but peaceful
inclinations, and surely if they had wanted to they would
soon have cast out Jürgen Jürgensen for all his ship's guns.
But they suffered proclamations from him headed "We,
Jürgen Jürgensen," and seemed content enough to carry
on.

Jürgensen appears to have been something of a born
statesman, as well as a strategist. He was a gigantic bluff,
of course, and that was an infinitely valuable qualification
in both callings. The increase in the stipends of the clergy
was a master move; it looks as if Count Tramp, who would
not have been deposed so easily had he gone to church, was
not the man to notice the Icelandic clerics' want, and that
move must have gained Jürgensen considerable popularity

with the people. For would not the clergy regard the raiser of their stipends as a leader sent by Providence? They would say so from their pulpits, and the good propaganda would be spread. But the order to cease payments of Danish debts was the greatest stroke; the only trouble was that many of the populace took it to mean that they had no need to pay any debts at all, not even to the State. That belief King Jürgensen soon put down.

Here is a typical proclamation of Jürgensen's:

Rejkjavik, July 11th, 1809.

In our proclamation, dated the 26th of June, 1809, it was requested that the nearest districts should within a fortnight, and the more distant within a certain limited time, send in representatives to consult as to what was best to be done in the present exigency. We find, however, that the public officers have far from facilitated such a meeting; and we are therefore under the necessity of no longer resisting the wish of the people, who have earnestly solicited us to manage the administration of public affairs, and who have in hundreds offered to serve in the defence of their country. It is therefore declared, that we Jürgen Jürgensen, have undertaken the management of public affairs, under the name of PROTECTOR, with full power to make war or conclude peace with foreign powers.

That the military have nominated us their commander by land and sea, and to regulate the whole military department in the country.

That the great seal of the island shall no longer be respected, but that all public documents of consequence, shall be signed by my own hand, and my seal (J.J.) fixed thereunto.

That the Icelandic flag shall be blue, with three white stock-fish thereon, and the honour of it we promise to defend at the risk of our life and blood . . . and so on.

Everything would have gone well if it had not been for the arrival of a British warship commanded by a person named Jones. Jones interfered. He wanted to know who made Jürgensen King of Iceland, and refused to salute the flag of blue, with the three white stock-fish thereon. Count

Tramp, waiting for such a chance as this, contrived to get aboard Mr. Jones' warship and poured such a tale of persecution and woe into the British naval officer's ears that something had to be done about it; and in the end, Jürgensen was, in his turn, summarily deposed and taken back to London to explain just what he had been doing.

In London he held his end up pretty well, all things considered, and made a better showing of it than Count Tramp, but authority ruled that such things as peremptory depositions of foreign governors could not be countenanced in England and the reign of King Jürgen I of Iceland was at an end. Then he was arrested and thrown into Tothill Fields Prison, not for his Royal wrong, but "for being an alien enemy at large without the King's license" and for having broken his parole, although he said he never gave one.

It was at Tothill Fields that he learnt to become an habitual gambler, and the vice never left him.

Then followed adventures in Spain and Portugal, where he was arrested on suspicion of being a spy. He might have been one, too; he is not explicit as to what he was up to in the peninsula. He got out of it at last by shipping as a seaman in a gunboat that was going to London with the mail, but at the last moment another faster vessel took it and Jürgensen found that he had to remain in the navy longer than he expected. In the end, returned at last to England from a long Mediterranean cruise, he got out of the naval service by feigning illness. Then he took to gambling again, and the upshot of that was arrest for debt and incarceration in the Fleet Prison. He was there two years, occupying the time with the writing of books and "a tragedy suggested by the cruel execution of the Duc d' Enghien by order of Napoleon," as well as a statistical essay on the Russian Empire.

It was while he was in the Fleet that Jürgensen was chosen by the Foreign Office for an important secret mission to the Continent. What it was exactly no one can say now; he describes it himself merely as a "diplomatic mission to the seat of war." He was discharged from the Fleet, his debts paid, and he was given funds to get across to the Continent to begin the mission. But as soon as he was out of the prison he took to the gaming tables again, lost every penny he had, sold his clothes and lost the proceeds, sold his ticket to France and lost the money from that—and emerged once more into the sunlit streets penniless, coatless, and desperate. But he was not yet disgraced. He managed to secure a sailor's jacket, and stowed away in a vessel bound for Antwerp. Once in Antwerp, he had an order from the British Foreign Office to draw upon some bankers for a considerable amount. He drew the lot, went to Paris, and lost it all in gambling. His mission had nothing to do with Paris and he was not supposed to go there, but a trifle like that did not worry Jürgensen.

Again penniless and absolutely destitute, he at last set out on his mission, and instead of traveling comfortably about the Continent had to walk begging, from place to place; as a homeless vagabond he strolled through Europe, now and again drawing more money from the Foreign Office and promptly gambling away every penny of it. Perhaps because of the very fact that he had to travel as a vagabond, and therefore would have means of finding out things not known to officials of state—even secret ones— Jürgensen's mission appears to have been most successful, and when he returned to London it was to be warmly welcomed by a Foreign Office which had no faintest idea of the manner in which he had carried out his duties. He didn't inform them; he took the money offered him, gambled it away to the last cent, got into debt heavily, and was flung into Newgate to await transportation to the colonies. In Newgate he preached, wrote, acted as assistant to the surgeon, schemed, and sought the intervention of great persons in his favor. The upshot of it all was that he was released from Newgate, after a year or so, and told to get out of England within a month. As soon as he was out of jail he took to gambling again and overstayed his month; he was at last hurrying to the docks to ship away from England forever when an acquaintance, chancing to see him there, betrayed him to the police, and again he was flung into prison. This time he stayed there until the convict ship *Woodman* carried him to Tasmania. The story of the voyage in the *Woodman* appears elsewhere in these pages.

In most of the biographies that mention him, Jürgensen is summarily dismissed upon his transportation and is usually regarded as having died obscurely not long afterwards in New South Wales. But Jürgensen never did anything obscurely; neither did he die shortly afterwards in New South Wales. He never went there; the remainder of his life he spent in Tasmania. There he was Government clerk, newspaper editor—leaving that engagement because "the worthy proprietor insisted on every one in the house attending prayers three times a day," the said prayers being "unusually long and delivered in a tone and dialect that were extremely disagreeable"—ticket-of-leave man, colonial constable, prospector, explorer, ranger for the Van Diemen's Land Company, and happy enough exile.

And in Tasmania he went through the greatest adventure of even his life. He was married—to an elderly woman, stout and thirsty, who is usually described as chasing ex-King Jürgen through the streets of Hobart with a weapon variously stated to be a pot-stick, a rolling-pin, and a broom-handle. At the age of 65 he died, a broken down and unknown old man, in a bed in the Hobart Public Hospital, and no one now has any idea where his grave lies.

CHAPTER X

THE GIRL SHIPS

AT different stages of its history various schemes were put forward for the migration of single women from the United Kingdom to Tasmania, and the story of these efforts makes an interesting chapter in the maritime history of the colony. In the very early days Hobart Town suffered severely because of the gross disproportion between the sexes, and the morals of the place were deplorably low. There is an actual record of the public sale by a man of his wife, for a purchase price—not very high—that included some rum; there were probably other cases but this one, at least, may definitely be traced. For many years drunkenness, debauchery, profligacy, and prostitution were thriving and the last at least was for years a leading industry.

Nothing else was to be expected. Few women came of their own accord, and most who did were married; the majority of the single women were convicts. Quite early in its history the port assumed a considerable importance in the South Sea whaling, and for many years it was resorted to by whaling ships in to refit and "refresh their crews." At times there would be as many as thirty and forty whalers in port together, each of them manned by a husky band of derelicts, ne'er-do-wells, and tough-living sailors, and few of these ships came in without having been six or seven months at sea—sometimes it was 17 months, and more than that. Grog was plentiful, and cheap enough, and a public house stood at every corner. The convicts who formed a goodly proportion of the population of the place were scarcely to be depended upon to raise its moral tone, and it was natural that old Hobart, through those colorful years, was painted a permanent shade of violent red.

In order to bring about something of a better balance between the sexes and thereby improve the morals of at least the permanent section of the population, in the early 30's—or perhaps before that—the idea of a general migration of desirable, free and single young women (referred to always merely as "females") to Tasmania was brought forward and committees were formed both in London and in Hobart Town, the former to select the girls and the latter to look after them on their arrival. Neither was as successful as it might have been, although the idea—in theory—may have been an excellent one. In practice it was rather the reverse, and some of these "free females" who were brought out proved worse than the convicts. Conditions in the ships which brought them defy description, or at any rate are better not described. They may be imagined readily enough. The trouble was that no proper measure of control could be exercised over the girls, particularly at night. In the convict ships the women were under lock and key at night, and closely guarded; in the girl ships they were free, of course, and could do what they liked. There was ample opportunity for doing anything. The whole trouble—or at any rate the substantial cause of it—lay in the selection of the girls in London. The committee there did its best, one supposes, to select desirable girls of good character, but it appears that, if it had chartered a ship and then, at the last moment, found that it could not be filled with satisfactory girls, it was prepared to fill it anyhow. And fill it anyhow it did.

The first ship to come out from London to Hobart Town under this scheme appears to have been the *Princess Royal*, in 1832, and here immorality prevailed to such an extent that upon her arrival off the Derwent after a passage of some five months, the crew was in such a state that the ship drifted ashore and pretty nearly developed into a total wreck right in the Derwent harbor. There were about 150 girls in this ship, and their arrival was naturally an event of the first importance in the colony. For weeks the young bloods of the place—and the old rakes—had been looking out for the girls, and when the news was spread that the ship had gone ashore and was hard and fast, boats set off without delay for the scene. The news was slow drifting up to the town, and when Governor Arthur arrived with his yacht and two vessels to bring the girls up, he found them all camped happily ashore, enjoying the smell of the bush after the long voyage.

The first thing that came to his ears was a bitter complaint about the voyage, and it was not long before he heard a good deal more about it. The girl ship scheme was a failure from the start, and the decent girls who shipped in the *Princess Royal* had to suffer for it. These told Arthur a pitiful story of their long fight against the gross immorality of persons with whom the only thing they had in common was sex, of the breaking down of the sailors by the looseness of these women, of the drunkenness of the surgeon who was supposed to look after them and developed instead into the biggest rake on board, of the hopeless task that confronted the master and the very young minister, who was making his first essay into the serious business of real life. Arthur—a strict moralist himself, and for that very reason unpopular with many of his subjects—was shocked at the tales that were told to him, and scant enquiry was necessary to establish their truth. He immediately took the matter up with the Colonial Office, and implored the English Authorities, if they were to continue sending these girls, to exercise proper care in the selection of them and to endeavor, at least, to see that there was some proper supervision in the ships that brought them. A despatch of his in the vaults of the Tasmanian Government underneath the public buildings in Hobart, on this very subject—one of many that he sent—contains much that is of interest, throwing a strong light on the conditions that prevailed in these shiploads of girls.

"A great proportion of the women by the *Princess Royal* remaining undisposed of," he writes, "consists, I lament to say, of females of the very worst character, and many of them I fear it will be wholly impossible to provide for in the families of respectable persons, but the Ladies' Committee are continuing to exert themselves with undiminished anxiety, watching over and admonishing those who are so utterly regardless of themselves . . . No person appears to be even responsible for these women . . ." Arthur goes on to point out, at length, that it had been definitely promised that none but the "most respectable females" would be sent, but the females who came he divided into three sharply differentiating classes. Firstly, there were those who were "quite respectable" and there was no fault with these. They were even respectable after the voyage in the *Princess Royal*, than which there could not have been designed a severer test for any young woman. Then there came the second division, those who were useful as domestics but possessed no other qualifications, and the third class was "composed of the most abandoned creatures that could have disgraced the streets of the metropolis . . . and the indecent conduct, the profane language, and the licentious proceedings of these women in connection with the sailors had the most baneful influence upon those less depraved than themselves . . ." The actions of these abandoned women, Arthur goes on, "filled the minds of those who were really of the class from which the committee should have selected the whole shipload with greatest distress and anguish, being for so long a period the daily witnesses of such extreme moral depravity. Many of these respectable girls, indeed, still feel deeply humiliated and cannot dispossess themselves of the idea that their own characters have suffered from the lamentable association.

Arthur pointed out that no one in the ship appeared to be responsible and there was no way of satisfactorily controlling either the women or the sailors, from the moral point of view. "No distinct instructions appear to have been given either to the master, the surgeon, minister or matron," and it was due to the very high moral tone of the very able master, Mr. Greenwood, that things did not become even worse than they were, and the whole ship develop into a floating bedlam. The master does not appear to have had much support. "His officers acted in the most drunken and insubordinate manner, after having, with the seamen, been seduced from their duty by some of the most abandoned of the females . . . Women of known respectable character only are wanted," he concludes his long despatch, and insisted that the "selection be confided to persons *officially* responsible."

The same despatch contains a printed report of the formation of the Ladies' Committee in Hobart, consisting of six sub-committees of seven each, giving a total membership of forty-two—a number that might have been somewhat unwieldy. In a communication a little later he laments the fact that some forty of the *Princess Royal's* girls had "entirely and defiantly withdrawn themselves from the protection of the Government and the attentions of the Committee, and have either engaged themselves in disreputable unions or are leading a vicious course of life." At the end of the despatch is a full list of the young women, their names, their characters, whence they came and what they did on arrival in Hobart. It is sordid reading. Most of them came from homes for the destitute or other questionable sources in London, and in the column marked "Character" the entry opposite most of the names is "none." The majority of them had gone into the public houses or the houses of ill-fame in the city.

The newspapers of the time had a good deal to say on

the subject, naturally. The *Colonial Times* held forth as follows:

The present selection of female emigrants was made by a ladies' committee in London, one of the principal leaders of which committee was the celebrated Mrs. Fry, well known to be both a praiseworthy and humane woman. Mrs. Fry's practice has always been to keep the depraved and guilty separate from the innocent; and yet, in this present instance, the lady committee in question seems to have cared very little upon this point . . . Could it be believed that any conscientious females of the saintly school would first entice respectable individuals to place themselves on board such a vessel as the *Princess Royal*, under the express understanding that only respectable individuals were to join them, and that then, in open defiance to all promises, that a lady committee should fill up the number required for the despatching of the vessel, from the Workhouse at St. Giles, the Penitentiary, and the Magdalen, and other similar sinks of the Refuge for the Destitute? . . . Of the two hundred and odd females who have now arrived, about one fourth are really respectable . . . The respectable part of the passengers cry out most grievously and with reason; they affirm that they were imposed upon; that promises upon promises were held out to them— that no female of suspicious character should be allowed to take her passage, otherwise they would never have left their respectable, though poverty-stricken homes. Mrs. Fry and her coadjutants well know in what manner the lady committee kept those promises, when on the eve of the vessel's sailing, the outcasts of society, the dregs of the lowest quarters of the metropolis, were huddled on board, leaving a passage of five months to settle matters between the different classes.

Quite the worst feature of these ships must have been, of course, their terrible effect upon quiet girls from decent homes, who were setting out upon an adventure to which, probably, the forces of circumstances had largely driven them. There was no way, perhaps, of preventing loose living aboard the ships to a certain extent, no matter how carefully the girls might have been chosen, for amongst 200 or more of them on such a long voyage, there would

THE GIRL SHIPS — 145

have been some who would not have kept a straight line. It was too much to expect. But deliberately to freight the ships with women rescued from the streets—half-rescued would be a better description—appears to have been one of the best methods for the creation of a hell-ship that could be conceived. They were certainly most extraordinary vessels, these quaint old girl ships that sailed to Tasmania.

The experience of the first does not appear to have deterred the committee chiefly responsible for it, and other ships were sent. The *Sarah, Amelia Thompson, Bussorah Merchant, Edward Coulson, Lady East,* and *Strathfieldsaye* each brought out more. Not long after the *Princess Royal* had arrived one finds the old *Colonial Times* holding forth again:

Two vessels, it is stated, are on their way for this Colony, with 600 free unmarried females on board—what the plague shall we do with them?—inundated with petticoats all at once! And then, to keep them out of mischief, where shall we put them until they become, as it were, settled? The Factory is, of course, out of the question! Thank goodness we shall have nothing to do with them.

The next girl ships, to make things worse, received an absolutely, inexcusably boorish reception. In such a place as Hobart was in the thirties a refinement of morals was not to be expected, but the manner in which some of these unfortunate girls were met would have reflected disgrace upon a gang of Chinese pirates. Men flocked to the quayside when a girl ship was coming up the harbor, and long before the anchor was free from the cathead boats swarmed round with men shouting and gesticulating. That was not so bad; what was a thousandfold worse was the reception they received when they came ashore. All kinds of men, except apparently decent ones, would gather round the waterfront and form an almost impassable mob, through which the girls had to make their way, the while insults, lewd suggestions, and all kind of horrible offers were hurled at

them to the intense amusement of the crowd and the horror
of those who were good among the girls—and these were
many, for even a very small proportion of loose women in
a ship could make it a hell.   In this connection, there is a
ghastly record of the landing of the girls from the *Strathfieldsaye* at Hobart Town in August, 1834.   The account
reads:

On Saturday the free females were landed from the *Strathfieldsaye*.   Of all the disgusting, abominable sights we ever
witnessed, nothing ever equalled the scene which took place
on that occasion.   It is well known that the females of the
Strathfieldsaye are of a far superior order to those hitherto
sent us by the Home Government, poverty being the greatest
crime of the greatest part of the number.   It is true that a
small portion of them are not of that description which ought
to have been allowed to associate with the innocent; but that
indiscriminate mixture of virtue and vice is not, at present,
the subject before us.   Early on Saturday morning, it was
known all over the town that the free women were to be landed
at mid-day.   The *Strathfieldsaye* was bedecked with all the
colours on board, and great was the preparation.   About
eleven o'clock some of the women were stowed in one of the
ship's boats, and then another boat went alongside and was
filled, and others followed in succession.   Those who had first
left the vessel had to remain on the water upwards of an
hour before all the boats were stowed, when they were all
towed together towards the New Jetty.   At this time the mob
waiting to witness the landing of the women could not have
been much less in number than a couple of thousand.   As soon
as the first boat reached the shore there was a regular rush
towards the spot, and the half dozen constables present could
scarcely open a passage sufficient to allow the females to pass
from the boats; and now the most unheard of, disgusting
scenes ensued.   The avenue opened through the crowd was
of considerable length, and as each female passed on, she was
jeered by the blackguards who stationed themselves, as it
were, purposely to insult.   The most vile and brutal language
was addressed to almost every woman as she passed along—
some brutes, more brutal than others even took still further
liberties, and stopped the women by force, and addressed them

pointedly in the most obscene manner. Any woman with one spark of the feeling of modesty must have felt this degradation of the most terrible kind, and the consequence was that by far the greater portion could bear the insults no longer. Scarcely a female was there but who wept, and that most bitterly; but this, again, was made the subject of mirth by the brutes that were present. One of the poor creatures was so overcome that she absolutely fainted, but there was no hand to assist—no one present who appeared to have any power in preventing these disgraceful scenes. After the females had passed through the long passage the ordeal was not over, for men singled out the girls they fancied and went in pursuit of them, annoying them until they arrived at the door of the house wherein these friendless beings expected to find security. The greater portion of the more insulting of the men were those apparently prisoners; indeed, it appeared as if the whole town had been picked to select the lowest ruffians expressly for the purpose of insulting these helpless females. It is true there were one or two young men present who ought to have known better—one in particular, a clerk belonging to a Government department, who will do well to take advice in time, otherwise it will be to his cost.

On arriving at Bellevue, the house said to be prepared for their reception, the rabble still loitered about as if still further to insult. There had been plenty of time to prepare everything for the reception of the women, and yet, we understand, the poor creatures did not have any dinner till half-past six in the evening; and as to their bedding, we are credibly informed that at five o'clock a few dozen blankets were provided, and as many bed ticks, in which the girls were set to put straw so that they might have something better than the bare boards to lie down upon. During the whole of the night the neighbourhood was in complete confusion. The most disorderly scenes were witnessed; men were seen pestering the purlieus of the place. Nor did the Sabbath allow a peaceable moment—on the contrary, during nearly the whole of Sunday, a mob somewhat similar to that seen the day before at the New Jetty, surrounded the house, and scarcely could a girl stir herself, but the most obscene language was addressed to her. Those who strolled about the town shared no better fate, for at every step and at every turning, knots of blackguards were assembled, whose only pleasure seemed to be in trying to be more disgusting in their conversation than their companions. Sunday evening and Sunday night were spent in a similar manner with additional increase of noise and disorder, nor was it till Monday that a female could leave her temporary lodging without having the most disgusting language applied to her by some of the bystanders, who considered it all very fine sport.

Never was there a worse managed affair, nor, in any civilised society, such outrages on common decency. Where were the scrupulous, conscientious psalm singers? Could none of these stand forth and protect innocent females from insult, contamination, and ruin? Talk of squeamish-minded men not receiving money for the support of a public institution because it was raised by innocent theatrical representations, are there such conscientious men in Van Diemen's Land? Will it be believed, none of them were present to protect, to save, virtuous females from insult, infamy and destruction? Shame on all those concerned—we know not who they are, nor does it matter. Mrs. Arthur and one or two more ladies assisted all in their power, but so soon as these ladies left so soon did the scenes of infamy re-commence. Why was not a different time chosen for their disembarking, and different arrangements made? Contrast the landing of these free females with the landing of three hundred and twenty convicts the same morning. At seven the prisoners were landed. They were in an orderly manner marched up to the prisoners' barracks. They were immediately supplied with rations; their clothing was good. His Excellency arrived and addressed them a useful lesson. Sleeping berths were provided, they received no insult. We cannot conclude these remarks without repeating that the whole affair was improperly managed, and no one can say what misery and distress may ensue in consequence. We do sincerely hope that should another increase be made to our population some degree of caution will be manifested and that scenes like these, partly only described, may never again disgrace the Colony.

There is another record of the *Strathfieldsaye*, however, which while serving to throw some light upon the conditions of these ships is not so depressing reading as the terrible account of the landing of the unfortunate young women. It appears in a newspaper of the day—September, 1834—as part of a report of police court proceedings, and in those days the courts and all that transpired in them were written up in a light, humorous kind of mood, as if writing about such things was extremely congenial to the reporters. As far as that goes, a good many of the paragraphs give rather strong evidence of having been written by persons in a state of more or less permanent intoxication, which was probably the case. This paragraph relates the prosecution of a sailor from the *Strathfieldsaye* for having caused a disturbance.

Joseph Bowden, an absentee seaman from the *Strathfieldsaye*, was charged by Constable Stevens with disorderly conduct in the streets, and threatening to assault Miss Rudelhoff, one of the newly arrived actresses. It appeared that the defendant had been permitted to enjoy the conversation of the lady on board, and, therefore, made sure of a good reception on shore. The lady, however, thought fit to give him the cut direct, and an order to march at the same time, as she had some other friends with her. At this, Jack never having received an order of this kind before, and hearing the sound of the harmony within, winced a little, letting fly a volley of sea lingo, which the lady returned in her own style, until the storm raged high, which Jack threatened to end by giving little Dinah a broadside, when the Constable, attracted by the row, interfered, and removed him, slightly wounded, to the Bathurst Street cockpit. Reprimanded and discharged.

The whole scheme was doomed from the beginning and should have been hastily scrapped. But it dragged on over years; one or two of the governors after Arthur had returned to England were not such strict moralists as he had been, and probably did not bother to urge so strongly as he had done, that improvements should be effected. They just let the thing go on. One of them, indeed, thought so little of the conventions that the lady he installed at Government House was, by some oversight, not his wife. In the course of time the impossibility of the girl ships scheme must have been impressed upon some one in authority in England, and it stopped.

In later years various schemes for the wholesale migration of young women to the Colony were promulgated by persons who had not learned much from history, but the success of any of them was questionable and they soon came to an abrupt end. It *was* a desirable thing to increase the numbers of the young women in the island and thus to give the young men the chance of marrying, but no scheme was ever devised which would accomplish that object without carrying in its train disadvantages that absolutely damned it.*

And quite probably, none ever will be.

* The appendix contains an advertisement from a London newspaper of the thirties, calling for "single women and widows of good character from 15 to 30 years of age" to go to Tasmania.

BOOK III

THE WHALERS

CHAPTER XI

THE WHALERS

WHEN the Hobart Gas Company was first incorporated in the fifties, a hesitant council of citizens stipulated that the illumination it provided should come up to the standard of the sperm oil lamps which had then been in use for half a century and more. That was the natural standard of comparison in a seaport which had for so long, and to such a great extent, been mixed up with the development of whaling. Indeed, skeptics were not wanting who declared that the newfangled gas contraption was more likely to blow Hobart and every one in it sky-high than to provide a better illumination than the good old whale oil lamps, and there was some opposition to the establishment of the gas company.

A whaler brought the first settlers to Hobart, and the first Governor. This was the little *Albion*, which left Sydney, together with the much smaller *Lady Nelson*, on August 31, 1803. The *Lady Nelson* was either a very good sailor or the *Albion* a very bad one, for it was not until five days after the *Lady Nelson* had anchored in the Derwent that the *Albion* put in an appearance. The *Albion* brought live stock, convicts, and soldiers, and at the time was commanded by one Captain Ebor Bunker, an interesting pioneer who was probably the first Australian whaler. Bunker had been master of a convict transport named the *William and Ann*, in which he brought a couple of hundred prisoners to New South Wales in 1791. He had been whaling before that, and on his arrival in Port Jackson he reported to Governor Phillip that during the vessel's progress up the coast from the south of Tasmania to her destination, she had literally gone through a sea of whales. The *William and Ann* appears to have been whaling previously, too, as well as her master, and as soon as her convicts were discharged she set off on the chase. She was not successful, then, but later on his return to London Bunker talked again of the whales he had seen in Tasmania and Australian waters, to such an extent that a big firm—Messrs. Campion —rigged out the *Albion* especially for an Australian cruise, and gave her to him. The *Albion* was of 362 tons, which was a good size for those days, and carried 29 sailors and ten guns.

The *Albion* was successful this second time on the whaling grounds and appears then to have remained in Australian waters; what happened to her after taking part in the founding of Tasmania one cannot say. On the return voyage from the Derwent to Port Jackson, Captain Bunker took three sperms in her "without looking," as he said, so easy was it to get them in those waters. Other convict transport captains had noticed the great number of whales around the shores of the new colony, and it was not long before enterprising firms in London were sending out ships, and enterprising masters from New Bedford and from London were including the Tasmanian and the New South Wales coasts in their cruises. It was in 1803 that the *Albion* took her sperms along the coast of Tasmania; the following year the ship *Alexander* (Jürgensen's ship) took several right whales in the estuary of the Derwent. In 1816 the *Adamant*, English whaler, put in at Hobart— then a small village—to land her oil and refit, and she probably was the first deep-water whaler to call at the far southern port which was to see so many of them.

Throughout the great whaling years of the 19th century Hobart steadily rose in importance: the capital of a State peculiarly situated to breed seafarers, surrounded by waters rich in blubbery wealth, it was natural that its enterprising spirits should turn to the difficult but adventurous business of whaling for the big prizes that it offered. At first Hobart looked on while English and American whalers reaped the harvest; in later years it took a hand itself.

First there was the era of bay whaling—the hunting of black whales in the rivers and bays round the island. Whales were so plentiful and so easily secured that there was no need, in the early days, to fit out ships to go hunting for them. There was no sense in rigging out a ship to go to look for the whales when they came to look for you, and for many years the only whaling in which the Tasmanians engaged was this hunting of black whales and right whales which came into the Derwent and far up the river past the capital—there is a record that they blew so much they disturbed the Governor's sleep, and that irascible old gentleman wanted to know why "the damned blubber-hunters couldn't kill a few more of them"—and into most of the sheltered bays and estuaries round Tasmania's eastern and south-eastern coasts. Probably it had been the practice for the black whales to visit these waters in the breeding season for countless centuries, and at first they were easy prey.

It would be about 1815, as far as the records available indicate, that the business properly began, and in the 40's bay whaling was still being carried on. The boats' crews lived ashore and a constant lookout was kept for spouts from some high vantage point: the sighting of a spout was the immediate signal for a hurried launching of the sharp-lined boats and a race for the quarry, and in not very long the whale would be killed and towed back to the rough slipways leading to the flensing stage. Whales were so plentiful that there is a record of a boat taking four big ones in one day: for the most part they were easily enough killed, although it was always a dangerous business, and there were not as many fatalities as there might have been. The manner of hunting was exactly the same as that used by the deep-water ships—the chase in the boat, the hand-thrown harpoon, the playing of the amazed whale, and at last the lancing to death when it came exhausted to the surface; with the difference that instead of having to flense the carcass as it lay on the blood-stained water by the side of the ship it was towed to a landing stage and hauled up on the beach. There the blubber was stripped off and boiled down in try-works similar to those on shipboard, and the unrefined oil shipped as freight to London.

It was easier to whale with a station ashore than with one's only headquarters and working place a ship subject to all weathers and all the troubles of sail navigation of stormy waters; the practice was that application was made to the governor or the government—mostly the same person—for a bay whaling lease, just as one might ask for a section to take up as a farm. In 1841, quite late in the story of bay whaling, as many as thirty-five of these leases were granted. Three acres of land were given, with a sea frontage of three chains, and the rental was five shillings a year. Of course this was only to serve as headquarters for the crews and the flensing plant, and so on, and the wide waters were open to all of the boats. They were not confined to the capture of only such whales as chanced to enter the territorial waters of their lease. Indeed, as the whales became scarcer competition became very fierce, and on one occasion twenty-one whaleboats started in chase of one spout at Recherché Bay.

In those times, of course, the lookout who shouted the news of a blow was more likely to be rewarded with a kick than with any expression of gratitude, and great measures were taken—or tried—to steal a march on competitors. When the moon was full the whalers were at work, and the weather was bad indeed when they would not launch their boats. Nor did they scruple at following whales out to the open sea, if they could not take them in more sheltered waters. For the most part they agreed well enough together; they were rough men, in a rough calling, and if they were wont to make rough and ready laws for themselves they were also prone to obey them. They had little to do with signed agreements and legal phraseology and all that sort of thing—the man who could read and write was a rarity—but their word was good enough. If it wasn't, then there were ways of seeing that an improvement was effected in the shortest period possible. If ever one boat were fast to a whale and found that it could not kill it, then the steerer might call to another boat near by and offer half-shares if they would help in the kill. There would only be a few shouted words, more likely than not punctuated by sundry oaths, but those agreements were never broken.

In 1825 there was a Derwent Whaling Club formed at Hobart—incidentally this must have been one of the first clubs founded in Tasmania—by the leading spirits of the bay whaling era, Captain Kelly, William Wilson, Angus Bethune, Ross Nairne, and their confreres. Besides being the first to sample the various brands of rum brought in by arriving convict transports and all other vessels which visited the port, the club members gave a prize of eight dollars for the first person giving information of a whale in the river.

As the whales became more and more chary of the narrow waters, small brigs were fitted out as headquarters for the boats. At first these brigs worked the waters of Frederick Henry Bay, quite close to Hobart, where whales swarmed in the winter months. In 1834 there were seven ships and twenty-four boats out of Hobart alone in the whaling business, and that season they took 207 whales. To-day 207 whales would scarcely make a day's work at South Georgia or the South Shetland Islands, but at that time they were worth a good many thousands of pounds. The value of the whale oil and bone secured by the Hobart whalers for the 1838 season, for instance, was £137,000, so there must have been money in the business. The total value of wool exported by Tasmania that year was £172,000, which was not so much more than the oil; before long the oil and bone actually became of far greater importance in the wealth of the State than the wool. From the first Tasmanians took up the business of whaling as their own; at the zenith of its fame, Tasmania ranked second only to the United States in the prosecution of the sperm whale fisheries.

In 1840 bay whaling began to decline rapidly. It was only to be expected that in the course of time the whales would either be killed out or would cease to visit such destructive waters, and their capture became more and more difficult. It was the same old story of all rises and declines in whaling or any other hunting upon great waters; at first fortunes were made by a few. Others, seeing these fortunes made, rushed into the business and made something. Others still came, and steadily made it more and more difficult for any one to gain a livelihood; then came swift and final decline with ruination for many and loss for all. From 1840 onwards, for the next eighteen years, only thirteen bay whaling leaseholds were granted, and few of these were profitable. Of course, long before that the deep-water whalers had come and the sperm was being hunted almost over the face of the globe, so that there was still a very good outlet for capital and enterprising spirits in the whaling business.

Not many fatalities are recorded from the bay whaling era, although it is likely that there were far more than the records now indicate. Now and then a boat was overturned and somebody drowned; it was a winter calling, and the waters of Southern Tasmania are pretty cold at any time. One of the earliest and best of the Tasmanian headsmen, one James Foley, was killed while fighting a lone whale off Brown's River, in the Derwent, at the close of one of the earliest of the seasons. His wife, whom he had told to watch the fun, was standing on the cliffs near by, looking on.

Even until recently, bay whaling has been carried on in Australian and South African waters. Cape Town, of

course, is famous for its whaling history—in the Southern
Hemisphere the greatest whaling ports, through years of
importance in the sperm whale fishery, were always Cape
Town, Hobart, and Valparaiso, in Chile. In 1926 there
was still one of the Cape Town whaleboats afloat—a long,
green-painted double-ender, with fine lines, sharp ends, and
a light frame. It lay in disuse, then, outside a shed in Table
Bay Docks, but not long ago many of its kind were ready
for constant use at Woodstock Beach, Rogge Bay, and
Mouille Point; even to-day one might still find a harpooner
and boat's crew of experienced and able men from Simon's
Town and the Cape Town waterfront, and there still lingers
something of a blubbery flavor about the old houses and
shops of Bree Street. The try-pots and the harpoons have
gone, of course, but here and there a man remains and his
yarns are always interesting. There is a yarn at the Cape
about a whale that overturned a boat and went off with a
hunter in its mouth; there is another of a whale capsizing
a boat in its last death struggles and the harpooner, seizing
a lance from the sinking boat, leapt upon its back and killed
it. As late as 1896 three Woodstock fishermen were
drowned in the pursuit of a whale.

At Norfolk Island, in the Pacific, whales are still hunted
from open boats in the time-honored fashion; round Java
and in a few other places, they are still sometimes taken by
these means, although now it is not their blubber or their
bone that is wanted, but their flesh. Whale meat is very
good meat, cooked properly, especially in a cold climate.
Upon a whaling cruise in the Antarctic a few years ago,
beef from the blue whale was the best food we had. Whale
beef and onions! The memory of it arouses pangs around
one's belt even now—although the circumstance that this is
being written in the fo'c'sle of a full-rigged ship seventy-two
days at sea, where the staple item of diet in the meat line is
salt horse (very salt and very horse!) may have something

to do with that.　But it was very good stuff down there beyond the ice line.

The most interesting of all instances of modern bay whaling that one has come across is the Eden Bay, New South Wales, whaling station.　Here the unbelievable has been achieved; a school of killer whales, the natural enemy of the big chaps, was taught to drive whatever big whales might be lolling about in the Pacific outside into the narrow waters of the bay, where the whalers were able to kill them easily enough and flense them for their blubber.　On first hearing of this one is naturally skeptical, but it is true enough.　The killers had learnt from former days, when deep-sea whalers put into the bay to try out, that bits of whale tongue and other great delicacies were to be found there; they are credited with intelligence sufficient to combine their driving of whales into the bay with the receipt of the tongues thereof, and certainly the tongues *were* always given to them.　Season after season these killers returned to Eden and brought in their whales, but then—I think it was in 1926—the headsman died and when they hunted in their whales they were killed no more.　Unable to comprehend the reason for the change, the killers have departed, although now-and-again one still looks in to see if by any chance a piece of whale tongue may be floating by.

This story is on a par with that of Pelorus Jack, the famous dolphin, porpoise, or killer whale—the accounts seem to vary—which for years piloted ships through Pelorus Sound, in New Zealand.　Each might qualify easily as the world's best fish story, but the queerest circumstance about them is that both happen to be true.　Of course, Pelorus Jack might have swum backwards and forwards through Pelorus Sound because there was plenty to eat there and may have had no idea he was assisting in the navigation of divers vessels, and the killer whales of Eden might have been driving whales to that bay for countless years before any one came to whale there.　In the narrow, shallower waters, they would naturally be at a greater advantage in the contest with the giant sperms, and they were probably most surprised and indignant when man first took a hand.

At any rate no killer whales came to assist the Tasmanian industry, although many came to harass it by tearing pieces from the dead whales while they were being towed ashore.

Long before bay whaling declined, sperm whaling had become of greater importance. Seeing the money that was to be made from bay whaling, and knowing that English and American ships were doing even better out in the Tasman Sea, round New Zealand, and off the coasts of Tasmania and New South Wales, the more enterprising of the Hobart whalers early turned their attention to the deep-sea voyages. It was an easy step from the bay whaling brigs to a deep-water barque, and in 1829 the *Caroline*, the first of the Hobart barques to set off on deep-sea whaling, dropped down the Derwent on her way to the sea. This was on January 4, 1829; Smith was the master's name and John Lord the owner's. Seeing that she was the first Hobart ship to set out for the sperm whale grounds, the *Caroline* fired a salute of 15 guns as she tripped her anchor and gathered way.

"We trust the enterprise of Mr. Lord upon this occasion," said the *Colonial Times*, "will be an inducement to other merchants to fit out vessels for the sperm fishery." And that it certainly was.

Early in the following year the brig *Deveron* came in from New Zealand with 200 tons of oil and 20 tons of bone. She had been out only six months and her cargo was worth £5,000. The following year—1831—the ship *Dragon* also returned from a smart New Zealand cruise a full ship, while the *Marianne* was almost as lucky. From then onwards for the next forty years the sperm whale fishery flourished, and almost up to the end of last century whaling was one of the

most important of Tasmanian maritime enterprises. A
circumstance which helped materially in the early days was
the heavy duty against American oil charged by the British
Government. In an endeavor to wrest something of its whaling supremacy from America and also to encourage British
whalers, Britain levied a duty of £26. 12s. a ton on whale
oil taken under the American flag. Taken under the British
flag, the charge was only one shilling a ton. Practically the
whole of the oil taken by Hobart whalers was shipped to
England and sold there, so that this concession was a big
factor.

In 1850 Sir Andrew Clark, then private secretary to the
Governor of Tasmania, Sir William Denison, wrote: "Van
Diemen's Land is now second only to the United States in
whale fisheries. We have thirty-five square-rigged vessels
out of the port, besides smaller ones." Long before the discovery of gold in Australia—that upsetting influence that
did a lot of harm as well as some good—a newspaper
states that the Tasmanian whaling fleet "consisted of 40
large sailing vessels, carrying 200 boats, casks for 2,000
tuns of oil, and maintained, in the aggregate, crews of about
1,000 men." The deep-sea whalers of this period were as
successful as the bay whalers of the earlier years had been;
phenomenally successful voyages were made, and fortunes
came to the merchants of old Hobart Town. In short four-
five- six- and seven-month cruises—nothing at all in those
days, when a passage to England took anything from three
to eight months—tiny 200- and 300-ton barques and brigs
brought in cargoes worth thousands of pounds, practically
the whole of which was clear profit. The expenses of fitting
out were infinitesimal, compared with the gains; wood and
water, and a good deal of food, were to be had merely for
the taking round many of New Zealand's lovely bays and
among the South Sea Islands. The crew did not receive so
great a share, although naturally it paid to treat a good
master liberally.

ROALD AMUNDSEN ABOARD THE *FRAM* AT
HOBART, BACK FROM THE SOUTH POLE

AMUNDSEN'S *FRAM* IN THE DERWENT, WITH MOUNT
WELLINGTON IN THE BACKGROUND

Photo courtesy of the Hobart "Mercury"

ONE OF THE LAST TASMANIAN KETCHES ALONGSIDE THE HULK
OF THE BARQUE *JAMES CRAIG*, ONE OF THE LAST TASMAN SEA
TRADERS

Inside three days once the barque *Grecian*, commanded by Captain John Watson, took 39 tons of oil worth over £90 a ton—£3,500 in three days.

But these times could not last. The discovery of gold in 1851 had a bad effect upon the Tasmanian whalers, since nothing would satisfy 99 per cent of the adventurous spirits who manned them but that they should join in the quest for gold. From that blow the industry never properly recovered. Whaling was open to all, of course, but only the most adventurous would sign before the mast in a cachalot chaser, and in every ship, no matter how great a proportion of green hands she might carry, there had to be a leaven of old hands who knew the business if anything was to be done. The boat-steerers, above all else, must be skilled and thoroughly experienced men; a cruise, with everything else in its favor, might be completely spoilt because the boat-steerers were not properly competent. But the boat-steerers were the first to join the quest for gold, and it became more and more difficult—and more and more expensive—to obtain good ones.

At the same time the value of sperm oil was declining, and substitutes were being found to do most of the work it had done. In 1862 there were 25 whalers owned in Hobart cruising on the deep-sea grounds; after that they steadily declined. The ships which had previously been able to fill up round New Zealand and the Tasman Sea—at first they scarcely required to leave the Tasmanian coast, and the odor (pretty strong) of an anchored barque trying out a whale was familiarly met with by traders coming down the coast from New South Wales—had to cruise now further and further afield. Around the Pacific Islands, into the China Sea, through the Behring Straits into the Arctic, beyond the Antarctic circle, and around the ice-capped islands there, to north-west Australia and the Indian Ocean, to Kerguelen Land, Campbell Island, Table Bay, the Chilean coast—wherever there might be a sperm whale spout the little barques went, taking sometimes years upon their voyages now and yielding less and less return, meeting more and greater dangers, losing more men, encountering greater difficulty in getting a full complement each time they came back to port. In the grand old times every merchant in Hobart who had the slightest trace of the speculative in his soul had a good part of his savings in the whaling business; as time went by, however, it became more difficult to secure capital, and many of those who made fortunes "on the whale's back" lost them again.

In the 50's there were seven Hobart Town whalers at work regularly in Behring Straits, hunting whales from tiny boats. Some of the cruises which the ships had to make, as the whales became scarcer and scarcer, are almost incredible. They would set out from Hobart and try New Zealand first; doing no good there, they would bear away for the Pacific Islands and spend, perhaps, five months there for a few tons of oil. Thence they would cruise, maybe, to the Behring Straits, spending a season there; when the ice forced them out they would come down through the Pacific to the East Indian archipelago and fetch up for a few months around the north-west of Australia and round King George's Sound. Then, as like as not, they would dip down into the ice-rim of the Antarctic and spend a summer in that frigid and unpleasant neighborhood before returning, at long last, to their home port, perhaps still a half empty ship with a heavy bill for repairs. In the 70's and later the ships came back with reports that became increasingly pessimistic, and more and more of them, as they came back to port, were withdrawn from whaling and either sold to be broken up or put into general trading.

As far as the ships themselves are concerned, one cannot do better than quote from the excellent account given by Mr. J. E. Philp, a recognized authority on all things maritime in the history of Tasmania.

The ships employed from the port of Hobart ranged from 200 to 400 tons register [writes Mr. Philp]. They had to be specially fitted for blubber hunting. Speed was not an essential factor, and craft which had completed long years of service as men of war (in the good old sailing days), or homely cargo waggons, were taken into this other avenue of seaways, and ended their careers amid the grime and "gurry" attendant on the chase of the Cachelot. The last but one of the old Hobart whalers, was the *Waterwitch,* a successful ship in her later calling. She was launched from Pembroke dockyard in 1820 as H.M.S. *Falcon,* and finished her seafaring at the hands of shipbreakers after her last whaling cruise in 1895. And there were many others with a romantic past. The vessels were, as a rule, fitted out for an eighteen months' voyage. With the exception of the afterguard, or expert officers, consisting of the master, first, second, third and fourth mates, boat steerers, shipkeeper, cooper and sailmaker, the calling was open to all and sundry, and, as a rule, the crews were studies in mixed humanity. Country youths who had heard adventure whispering, and who, perhaps, had never before set feet on a vessel's deck, found an easy channel for their desire to view the sights and scenes revealed to those who "go down to the sea in ships." The "green" hands were soon licked into shape, introduced in a pulling thwart in a boat, and taught to handle the easy canvas carried on the cruising grounds. Many of these youths, abandoning the chase and capture of greasy spoil, followed the more legitimate (if one may so term it) profession of the sea, and attained high grades in the merchant service. Whaling was a rough apprenticeship. In the selection of crews there was no color bar drawn, and Kanakas, Maoris, Portuguese half-breeds, and the varied human flotsam of any seaport could be found in any whaler's fo'c'sle. A native of Samoa who sailed in Hobart ships rose to a command and proved himself a successful whaler.

The masters of whaling vessels usually graduated from the lower ranks, successively, as boat steerer, fourth mate, and so upward. A certificate of competency as a master mariner was not necessary, though, naturally, these hardy skippers had to possess, or acquire, a knowledge of navigation to enable them to undertake the sometime protracted cruises, following the whales to the various grounds frequented at different seasons. Occasionally a man who ranked as master, though an excellent whaler, was no navigator, and therefore, had to carry an officer for that duty. A successful skipper was a veritable encyclopœdia of the habits and habitat of his prey, and could always command the best talent in his cabin officers and "half-deck" executive. The half-deck, so called, was the usual quarters of the boat-steerers, cooper and ship-keeper.

The crews were engaged on the "lay" or share principle, in which they participated proportionately, in the amount of oil taken. I have before me the articles of agreement of the schooner *Friends,* dated 25th April, 1856, in which the chief mate is set down to receive a 14th share of sperm oil at £65 per tun; a 12th share of black at £25 per tun; whilst for bone his share was 15th at £80. The bo'sun and ship-keeper figure thus: A 30th sperm at £50; 25th black at £14; 30th bone at £50. The seamen's lay was on a lower scale, viz., 50th share of sperm at £40; 20th for black at £14, and for bone a 50th at £40 per tun.*

The last active whaling master out of Hobart gave me figures showing that on one voyage as mate he earned £360, plus a bonus of £40. As master his best voyage returned him £570. The second mate of the *Eliza Adams* was offered, when signing on, £12 per month, but declined this in favor of the lay system. When the ship paid off his earnings amounted to £22. 10. 0. per month. She was a lucky ship, for fourteen days out from port she had stowed away 38 tuns. There was money in the game in the good old days. Another prominent skipper earned £30 per month for two years, and, in addition, made an extra £50 "bone faking."

The *Runnymede* was "out" nine months securing 100 tuns, which sold on Hobart wharf at £110 per tun. The barque *Othello* in thirteen months took 100 tuns, which realised £90 per tun. The *Derwent Hunter* some time in 1860 was cruising for five months and twenty days. Her catch realised £8,500.

Covering a period of 60 years, records give the total value of whale products as amounting to £2,245,450. These figures will serve to show the money put into circulation from such a greasy source. It slipped easily through the fingers of the rank and file, and the lights burned brightly after a good "pay off."

Considering the hazardous nature of the calling, it says

* A copy of an old agreement is contained in the appendix.

much for the skill of those engaged that fatalities were comparatively few. The actual killing of the whale was effected from a lightly built boat, and it should be remembered that the sperm whale is probably the most powerful sea mammal—a fighter, an aggressor at times—quite unlike the more placid rorqual of the Arctic, or the big blue whale of the far southern seas. The modus operandi is briefly described. At sea a whaler's mastheads were always manned by lookouts from sunrise to sundown. When a spout was sighted a lusty voice roused the ship's company into activity. The sharp ended boats, always ready, with their crews, were lowered away without delay, and the lookout, having given the direction, the boat's crew, pulling five oars, with an officer in charge handling a nineteen-foot steering sweep, bent to their task. If the whale, having had his breathing time, sounded, then the judgment of the officer was called upon to estimate where the chase must rise again. The cetacean, after his submergence, must come to the surface to breathe. This gives the hunters their chance, as the whale must take a specified time to get his spoutings over before he can again seek the depths. When nearing the monster the bow-oarsman, at the instruction of the officer, relinquished his oar and stood, firmly braced against the "thigh-board" in the bow of the boat, with his harpoon ready for action. At the order "Give it to him!" he hove his weapon with all his skill and strength. Attached to the harpoon was a specially prepared pliable line of great strength, which was neatly coiled in tubs in the boat, so as to run out freely through the groove in the stem head as the whale madly dashed from his assailants.

The harpooning was only the preliminary step towards the actual killing, being the means by which the boat could be hauled up to the whale, when the latter, partly exhausted by his strenuous efforts to escape, and by the weight of the towing boat and line to which drogues were often affixed to offer still more resistance, quietened down. The harpooner, whose rating, really that of boat-steerer, now changed ends with the officer, the latter doing the killing, which was effected by means of keen lances attached to a long pole, which were thrust again and again into the known vital parts. Sometimes a gun, fired from the shoulder, and charged with a lance-tipped explosive bomb, was used. Hours sometimes passed before the coup de grace could be administered, and the whale went into its "flurry." The parent ship endeavoured to sail as close as she could to the carcase, which was towed alongside, and secured for the "cutting in." This, the operation of removing the oleaginous covering which sheaths the whale, was an expert's job. The head was first disconnected, and the blubber removed in long strips, the carcase turning as the crew hove away on the windlass. The head of a whale contains about one-third of the oil it returns, and from the portion known as the "case" it could be baled in a fluid state into barrels set for the purpose. The long strips of blubber were lowered into the blubber-room below deck, where it was cut up into sizes suitable for boiling down or "trying out."

Each ship had what was known as the try works fixed on deck. These were big cauldrons, bricked in, with furnaces beneath. In these the blubber was rendered down, baled into cooling tanks, and from these transferred to the casks, which formed a necessary part of the equipment. Sperm oil was a more valuable product than black. In 1843 the former sold at from £82. 5. 0. to £83. 15. 0.; black oil at £31. 10. 0. to £33 per tun; whale bone bringing up to £210 per ton, according to quality. In 1870 the last boom in oil took place, sperm touching £120. This price brought new owners into the field, and led to the refitting of vessels which had for various reasons been withdrawn or otherwise employed. This revival was of short duration, and the business languished; the firm of Alex. McGregor & Co. keeping a couple of ships going, and finally working only the *Waterwitch*, which old-timer made her last cruise from August, 1894 to February, 1895, when she landed 63 tuns.

The *Helen* was the last of the Hobart Town whalers. In 1894 she was fitted out as a four-boat ship and continued to make voyages with varying success until 1900. Then she was withdrawn from whaling and sent into the merchant service, in which she remained to the end of her days. She is now, I believe, a coal hulk in the port of Melbourne.

CHAPTER XII

THE WHALERS (*Continued*)

SEVERAL books could be filled with stories of adventure of the old whaling days. When whaling was at its height, a whaler called the *Betsy*—quite an ordinary little barque with four boats swung out from her sturdy davits, and no yards crossed on her royal poles in the whaler's style—set out from Hobart on a cruise of the South Seas. She never returned, and for years her fate was a mystery—one of the many in which the fate of Hobart barques was surrounded. Then, years later, a privateer lay dying on the deck of a vessel in the Gulf of Mexico, fatally wounded in an unsuccessful engagement. He said there was something he would like to say before he died; there was the fate of a vessel which he could clear up.

It turned out that he was from the *Betsy,* and the story he had to tell was an interesting one. The *Betsy's* cruise, he said, had been very unsuccessful. For months they saw nothing of whales. They tried the Solander and the Three Kings, the Middle Grounds and the Pacific Islands, and never saw the spout of a whale. The ship had been badly provided with stores, and it was not very long before even the tough stomachs of the whalers were in trouble. Scurvy broke out; bad weather came, and head winds, and they could not hope to make any island at which they could secure fresh food. The scurvy became worse and worse, until everybody in the ship was down to it more or less seriously, and the ship could not be worked. The look-outs at the mastheads had long since been abandoned, and the only face that was raised above the decks was the pain-twisted, hopeless countenance of some member of the crew, looking desperately for land. He never saw any; there was none to see. The *Betsy's* best speed was about four knots, and light winds and headwinds would not allow her to do that. She began to leak badly, to make an already desperate position tenfold worse. The pumps were manned, but the crew were so far gone that it was quite impossible for them to cope with the water that was coming in, or even to pump at all with any continued effort.

At the time, the ship was not very far from New Zealand, then a questionable haven because of the uncertain welcome to be met with from the Maoris. With ordinary luck she should have been able to make some quiet bay where she could anchor and, if all hands were not promptly murdered, the crew could rest awhile and recover something of their health. But the position became worse and worse; the *Betsy* did not sink, but the lower she got in the water the slower she sailed, and it was only too plain that to stay in her meant death for everybody.

So she was abandoned. Two boats were used. In one all who still had strength to pull an oar—not many—went, while the dying and the very sick went in the other. There were not enough of the "healthy" ones to pull both of the boats, and it was thought that the best course was for a division to be made, the healthy ones in one boat taking the invalids in tow in the other. They set off, leaving the old *Betsy* wallowing in a stagnant calm, her scuppers not very far from the level of the sea.

But the calm did not last. Pulling the boat, easy enough when the crew were sound, became an agonizing, pain-tortured process, from which there was no relief and in which there appeared no hope. The calm changed to a light wind from the land; light enough as it was, it was more than the rowers could stand. After eight hours they still had the masts of the *Betsy* in sight; the boats fell uneasily into the troughs of a rising sea, and rose on oily crests that brought no sight of land. Overhead screaming seagulls wheeled in a gray and gloomy sky; astern the invalids lay in the second boat, hunched together, hopelessly in the bottom, waiting for whatever end might come, and careless how it found them. The old mate, fifty years a whaler, struggled now and then with the steering oar but did not achieve much. The boat yawed, and made the task of the rowers more difficult; it fell in a trough, at times, while the other boat rose on a swell, and the towrope of harpoon line all but parted.

So the first day passed, and the night, with rain and dull cold. One of the invalids died and the body was dropped into the sea; the screaming seagulls screamed the more as they fought but wheeled by overhead no more.

The second day was hot. Two of the healthy oarsmen broke down, and lay helpless in the bottom of their boat. The others struggled on sullenly, too hopeless even to despair. Schooled by long years to the backbreaking, hellish task of rowing countless miles on the open ocean, they kept on where others would have given up long before. No one said anything. There wasn't anything to say. No one did anything, except to row; no one looked for land.

They made so little progress that the second boat ranged alongside at times. On one of these occasions the boat-steerer in charge of the towing boat looked up, and caught the face of the mate in charge of the invalids. He didn't say anything.

"All right," said the mate. "I guess there's naught else to do."

"You take all the grub," said the boat steerer. "If we make it we'll come back."

"It ain't far," said the mate. "You ought to make it if you go on. If we stay no one'll get anywhere except pretty quick to hell."

After a silence: "I guess you'd better take the grub, too."

The boat steerer looked. Sullen, despairing, hopeless, emaciated faces followed the look, waited for what he might say.

"We won't need it," the mate went on. "An' we don't care. Quicker the better," he concluded.

He himself let the towrope go. . . .

The erstwhile towing boat did reach New Zealand, but the invalids and their boat were never seen again. Their shipmates shared a fate a little better, for the Maoris where they landed, incensed by repeated outrages against them and their women, murdered them as they came helplessly to the beach. One escaped, to wander among unfriendly Maoris in an unfriendly land; after almost incredible sufferings lasting over five months he was rescued by an American whaling brig which took him to Tahiti, and thence he made his way to the Panama Isthmus, and shipped in a privateer for a pirate cruise in the Gulf of Mexico. It was he who cleared up the *Betsy's* fate, and there he was killed. . . .

Some time in February, 1832, a little vessel of curious rig came into the port of Hobart, and beat about as if she were not able to anchor. Sturdily enough built, she looked somehow strange, she was rigged queerly, and had unusual lines. No one could recognize her as she came up; no one had seen her, or anything like her, before. She looked, in some curious way, out of the common run of ships altogether. And so she was. A boat that went out to meet her read that her name was *Liberty*, and her port of registry Desolation Island; she was manned by fourteen of the toughest looking ruffians who had ever been seen in Tasmania. Long, unkempt beards straggled down their chests and spread shaggily over their big faces; their clothes were in pieces, torn in all directions, poorly mended together again with old canvas, the *Liberty* herself was the more curious the closer she was seen.

Then the unkempt ones told their story. *They* had built the *Liberty*, at Desolation Island, because they were wrecked there, and likely to die there, if they did not resort to some such desperate means of that kind. They were members of the crew of the whaler *Betsy and Sophia*, belonging to

Messrs. Barkworth & Co. of London, and on June 6th, 1830, they had set out from London on a whaling voyage. They were to do some sealing, too, and for that purpose made their way to the subantarctic islands that stretch from below Good Hope, in the roaring winds and biting cold down there, to below Australia. Here, at the cost of terrible toil, they managed to secure some 150 sealskins and about 100 tons of oil. Then the *Betsy and Sophia* was dismasted in a furious gale, and before she could be properly rigged again she drifted ashore on the Island of Desolation and became a total wreck.

She carried a crew of 19, and all of these were able to get ashore. There was nothing on the well-named Island of Desolation to support life, and though they were able to salvage some stores from the wreck before she went to pieces, they knew that they could not hope to live for long. They secured some sails from the *Betsy and Sophia* before she broke up, and tools, and being handy men it was not very long before they set about the construction of a little vessel. They laid down a keel hewn laboriously from one of their lost vessel's ribs, and roughly sketched out a plan of what they proposed the new craft to be, with a chisel on a stone, since they had neither papers nor pen, and that was the only way.

So was the little *Liberty* born.

For six months they worked. They had to cross one of the stormiest seas in the world if they were to reach any sanctuary, and their vessel could not be too small. They made her a 20-ton sloop, high-sided and high in the stern, round-bowed and full-lined. For sails they cut out something from what they had saved of the *Betsy and Sophia's* canvas, and for rigging they used the whaler's rope. They had had experience enough of boatbuilding and at rigging jobs in the course of the long voyage, but the building of the *Liberty* with the tools and the materials at their command was a long job. They had to calk her with seaweed because there was nothing else to use, and almost constant bad weather came to harass them at their work.

Some said it was all useless; she would never get anywhere, and it was better to stay in the comparative security of the island in the hope, they said, that some other whaler would call there, since there were few rocks and islands round which some whaler did not nose sooner or later. But the others went on preferring to try to save themselves rather than wait in idleness and hope deferred.

So at last the *Liberty* was fit for launching, and slid down her rough slipways into a sheltered spot in the wild Southern Indian Ocean to the accompaniment of cheers more deeply meant than many which welcomed the birth of ships ten times her size. She sat upon the water well, although she looked very small.

Now five of the nineteen definitely refused to go in her.

"We stay here," they said. "If the storms down here can wreck the *Betsy*, then what'll they do with a rough-built cockleshell like that?"

But the fourteen took no notice of their pessimism and went aboard. They halved the provisions, leaving the full half with the five who would not come in the little *Liberty*, and taking the other half themselves, though there were nearly three times as many men in the sloop as on the island. They had lost all the oil from the whaler, but the sealskins they still had, and these, like good whalers, they loaded into the sloop.

Then the *Liberty* set out and shaped a course for Tasmania, which although it was not the nearest land, was the most easily reached, lying directly in the west wind belt in which lay the Rock of Desolation. The voyage was a terrible one, but the little vessel stuck it out; the provisions ran short, and much of them was spoilt; constant gales shrieked around and great seas did their best, since they could not sink the tiny sloop, to roll her over and over in the thunder of their foam. But she kept on, and came to Macquarie

Harbour on February 3, 1832, "in great distress," according to the Hobart Town *Courier* of February 15th of that year. At Macquarie Harbour they secured further stores and put out again for Hobart, arriving in the Derwent after a passage of a little more than two months, including the delay at Macquarie Harbour.

The sealskins were sold and the men shipped in other whalers out of the port; the strangely built *Liberty* was trading for many years on the River Derwent where she looked, loaded with firewood, insignificant enough, without standing out into the great seas outside. The other five who remained behind were picked up from the island, some months later, by the French whaler *Ocean*, Captain Distant, and brought into Hobart. There they were amazed to find that their 14 ex-shipmates had arrived long before them and had since gone whaling again.

They were certainly wonderful hardy men, these whalers. No one appears to have thought much of the *Betsy and Sophia* and the *Liberty* that came out of her ribs; that was all part of the game, and if there was anything to cause comment in it, it was the remarkable fact that every one was saved. Whaling was a dangerous and risky business, and whole boats full of men were sometimes lost. Whalers set out, too, on their lonely cruises and never returned to port, nor was ever the slightest trace of tidings found of them. The whaler *Grecian* lost a boat within sight of the South West Cape of Tasmania; they were seen to fasten a sperm whale which made off with the boat in tow, and although the *Grecian* did her best to sail down towards the boat she had other boats to look after, and darkness was coming on. The boat was never seen again, although the *Grecian* searched for it for days and another whaler—the *Briton's Queen*—was specially chartered, because there happened to be some one of importance in the crew, to help in the search. Incidents of that kind were not uncommon,

and such of the old whaling log-books that still survive—a
sad, sad few—make thrilling reading.

In one such log there is the record of the death of a very
brave man.   Cracknell was his name, and he was one of the
real old Hobart Town whalers.   He was in charge of a boat
getting ready for lowering to go in chase.   His boat-steerer
had just charged and loaded a bomb gun and was easing the
hammer down on to the nipple when the charge exploded.
The bomb caught Cracknell in the stomach, and some of the
crew rushed instantly to him to do what they might to help.

Cracknell saw that nothing could help.

"Stand back, lads," he quickly said, "else you'll go where
I'm going.   An' one's enough there for to-day."

He was suffering the most horrible agony with the pain
of the heavy pointed bomb in his stomach; he knew that at
any instant it would explode, hurling him from frightful
pain to more frightful death.   Yet he calmly bade his shipmates to stand back. . . . Then the bomb exploded, and he
was dead.

A pretty easy guess could be made as to the fate of at
least some of the whalers which set out from old Hobart
never to return, New Bedford whalers as well as those belonging to the port.   They were surprised at some one of
their wood and water islands in the Pacific, the ships burnt
and all hands murdered.   It is known that several whalers
met their end in that way, and for that there certainly was
a reason.   At first there were no better, quieter, nor more
peaceful havens than the beautiful islands of the sunny Pacific, and for years the whalers were accustomed to seek
peace and rest along some one of the countless bays of these
beautiful islands.   Some they avoided, of course, since the
inhabitants were cannibals and would eat them if they had
half a chance, but generally the natives were interested and
friendly.   When they became otherwise it was the fault of
the white man himself, for some hellish things were done
among those lovely islands.   Whalers did some of them—

carrying off women, and the like—but they were not the worst. The blackbirders were the real scions of hell who tormented the natives into treacherous murderers, who spread woe and murder, and terror and affliction, agony and assassination broadcast through the Islands.

Some of the things they did are now almost unbelievable.

Their object was the recruiting of black labor, to be sold in the best market, and some of them were careless enough of how they achieved it.

There is the notorious case of the *Carl*, a blackbirding brig which set out on a "labor" cruise from Melbourne on June 8th, 1871, chartered to a fiend named Murray, who called himself a doctor but might better be described as a malignant and diabolical murderer. The *Carl* took her recruits from the Sandwich Islands and the Solomons, by the simple and inexpensive means of luring them alongside by posing as a missionary ship and by other means, and then dropping pig iron into their canoes and seizing them from the water. Once, with a hold full of natives who disturbed his sleep, Murray gave himself some "sport" with them by firing into the hold all night, shining a spotlight into the miserable darkness, and soddening the wooden ribs of the brig with their blood.

Later there were murder charges out of this, of course, but Murray did not figure in them, except to give evidence. He turned Queen's evidence, and sent to the gallows the murderers he had hired for the deeds he had done. Two sailors, Henry Mount and William Morris, stood their trial for murder arising out of the *Carl's* voyage at the City Police Court, Melbourne, in December, 1872. The charge was that they had willfully murdered certain natives of the Solomon Islands, on the high seas on September 17th, 1871, on board the brig *Carl*. The evidence according to the opening address of the Crown Prosecutor, "would detail fully how the brig was put under easy sail, and the canoes were lured to the ship's side; the manner in which these

canoes were sunk, by pig iron and small cannon attached to
rope being lowered precipitously down the ship's sides into
the canoes, upsetting them; how while in the water the natives were seized, and if any resistance was offered, how they
were knocked on the head with oars, or slingshot, or clubs,
or whatever else was handy; how at Bouka some 80 natives
were seized and put into the vessel, and how they resisted
their captivity and made efforts to regain their liberty; how
those on board the *Carl* fired at intervals during the whole
night into the hold of the vessel until in the morning it was
found that about seventy natives were killed or wounded;
how in the morning the dead were brought on deck with the
dying, some of them tied, and thrown overboard; all of
them, those that were dead with those that were dying. . . ."

From the evidence of George Heath, a seaman in the
Carl, the following may be extracted:

We went cruising to several islands until we came to
Bougainville, where canoes came off in great numbers. The
canoes were capsized by means of cannon and pig iron dropped
into them, and the natives seized. There was a good deal of
resistance every time at Bougainville. Somewhere about
eighty-five natives were taken and they were all put into the
hold. The hold was then very crowded, and there was just
room for the natives to lie down. After filling the hold we
put to sea, and the first night the natives were noisy. They
were told to be quiet, but no shot was fired this night. The
next night there was more noise. The natives had armed
themselves with poles which were got in Apia to lay fore and
aft as bunks for sleeping in. They had broken these up and
were trying to force the hatchway. All hands then commenced firing down the hatchway. No natives came out.
They could not. This firing continued on and off during the
night from half-past ten till daylight. Mount shone a bull's
eye through the hatch and the others shot. In the morning
Mr. Scott tried to go down the hatchway but was repulsed
by the natives with poles. He came up, went aft, and with
Dr. Murray—the charterer of the ship—went down the fore
cabin. Here they bored holes with augers in the bulkhead
and fired at the natives again through these. This was in

THE *VELOCITY*, A SMALL WHALER, ON A HOBART SLIP

LOCAL BARQUE ON THE SLIP, HOBART

the morning, and went on for about half-an-hour. Then a ladder was lowered into the hold, and those of the natives who could walk came up it. They did not offer to do anything then. They were all wounded, and blood covered. Only about 10 would come up. They were more dead than alive. Dr. Murray picked out a few who would recover quickly and ordered them to be kept, and ordered the other natives to be thrown overboard. They were thrown overboard. Some of those who were thrown overboard were alive. Some could stand and some could talk. Some were tied. Some of the natives crawled to the side when they saw the others thrown overboard, and jumped over themselves. . . .

In the course of his evidence Heath describes Murray's attempt at making the *Carl* a missionary ship:

. . . At one of the islands, about seven miles from Apii, the captain wanted the natives to come off but they would not, and while they were laughing and chaffing in the cabin Murray said "This is a big ship; I think the best thing we can do is to dress up as missionaries." They were to disguise the ship as if she had been a missionary ship. They did disguise her, and the captain put on the mate's monkey jacket turned inside out, the inside being red, and took a book under his arm. The mate was disguised and did not have his usual ship rig. Dr. Murray got a rug and put it over Wilson's shoulders and pinned it behind. Mount put on a red dressing gown, a smoking cap, and a chinese umbrella and Chinese slippers, and was knocking about the decks that way with a book under his arm. A seaman named Mick disguised himself with white duck trousers and a blue serge shirt which he had got from some one. Then two Kanakas who had shipped at Fiji as part of the regular crew pulled them all ashore, where they went to the natives, giving out leaves from the books as tracts. . . .

And then God help the real missionary ship that came there!

The *Carl* was not alone in these depredations, nor were all who shared her ill fame brought to book. After such ships had been cruising round the Islands, it was not to be wondered at that the natives were in a state fit to murder all

white men on sight, and to burn their ships and all that
belonged to them.

It was the whalers who suffered most heavily, although
some splendid missionaries also were murdered, and trading
vessels lost.   The Islands always had been most popular
with the whalers for the balminess of their climate, for the
fruit that could so easily be obtained there, and the pleasure
of a romp ashore among the woods after the long, unrelieved monotony of the voyage; for the most part the whale
ship men agreed well enough with the natives, and did not
treat them badly even if they did not set them always a very
high standard of white man's conduct.   But after such hell
ships as the *Carl* and her evil consorts had been cruising
round, the Islands became safe only to heavily armed men-
of-war.   Then after a murder or two and perhaps a massacre, the men-of-war went among the natives and taught
them a "lesson," by murdering them by the hundred and
burning down their villages.

The old Hobart whaling barques did not confine themselves to cruising the sea-lanes after whales.   Seals they
hunted, if they could get them; sea elephants, which were
good for oil; sea lions and even penguins, in later days.
From all of these a blubbery and blood-stained wealth was
to be obtained, if one secured enough of them, and the enterprising old owners of the whaling barques were ready
enough to send them anywhere.   Uncharted waters meant
nothing to them, when they spent the greater part of their
voyages in them; many of the masters for that matter, could
scarcely read a chart.   One remarkable cruise, worthy of
inclusion in any story of whaling, was that of the barque
Offley to Kerguelen Land in the fifties.   The *Offley* was one
of the fleet owned by Dr. W. L. Crowther, one of the most
prominent and enterprising of the old Hobart Town whaling owners, and when in 1857 he fitted her out for the Kerguelen Land voyage he little guessed what an epitome of
misfortune was to follow.

At Kerguelen Land sea elephants abound—big, fat hairy seals with ugly snouts and thick blubber—and the *Offley* was to land a shore party to kill as many of these as possible, boil down their blubber, and ship the oil for the return voyage to Hobart. The plan was that a smaller vessel should set out first and make the necessary preparations for the shore party so that it could go straight on with its work, and the *Elizabeth Jane* left Hobart some months ahead of the *Offley* for this purpose.

But she never arrived at her destination. She was a small vessel for such stormy seas—against the west winds from Hobart to Kerguelen. There was no way to avoid the storminess of the wild ocean down there; if she stood away before the wind, she would have to turn round the Horn and Good Hope. If she tried to beat against the westerlies she was in for a pretty bad time. She was sure of that, anyway. After months of endless battling with the seas and vain searching for Kerguelen she put in in distress at Mauritius, and here she was condemned as unseaworthy. She had been seaworthy enough when she set out from Hobart, and there is a suspicion that her master, sick of the constant fighting with the west winds and the sea they made, and the long, desperate effort to reach Kerguelen, had some influence in the condemnation of his schooner. At any rate, not long afterwards she was sailing again in the cattle trade with Madagascar, so she could not have been so bad.

In the meantime, while the *Elizabeth Jane* was fooling around the Southern Indian Ocean and getting condemned in Mauritius, the *Offley* left Hobart and was making for Kerguelen in full confidence that the tender would have arrived long since, and there would be no obstacle in getting on with the work as soon as the anchor was down. It was not until, after a five-month passage, she eventually arrived at the far southern island that it was found the tender had failed. Five months was a long time to take on that voyage, even though it had to be made in the face of the wildest

winds in the world at the worst time of the year. But there
was no need for hurry if the tender ahead had done her job,
and the *Offley* couldn't hurry much anyway.

It was a long time before Dr. Crowther heard of the non-
arrival of his tender. News of any kind was not distributed
very quickly in those days, being dependent upon the slow
passages of the old sailing ships for the most part, and the
doctor, carrying on with his practice in Hobart Town the
while he looked forward to a successful issue of his cruise,
had to wait until some vessel from Mauritius chanced to put
in at the port. When he heard the bad news, however, he
was not beaten. He immediately made ready another of his
schooners, the *Flying Squirrel,* for the voyage, to take the
place of the *Elizabeth Jane,* but the crew of the second
tender mutinied before the *Flying Squirrel* had got very far
and she was forced to return to Hobart.

The *Offley's* people, of course, neither knew that the
Elizabeth Jane had put in at Mauritius nor that the *Flying
Squirrel* had been ineffectually ordered to help them. They
concluded, when they arrived at Kerguelen to find that they
were alone, that the tender had been lost. Since it was impossible for them to communicate with Hobart by any other
means than returning there, they decided to make the best
of a bad job and carry on. Tents, huts, and tools for the
shore party were all with the tender. Other shelters had to
be made from oars, sealskins, tarpaulins, and old sails. The
climate of Kerguelen Land is severe, and in the rough shelters that were made for them the members of the shore party
suffered badly. The carpenter was so badly frost-bitten
that all of his fingers had to be amputated, and since there
were no proper surgical instruments aboard the *Offley* this
had to be done with an ax. Captain J. W. Robinson, who
had the *Offley* that voyage, performed the operation, and
when months later the ship was at last back at Hobart and
medical men examined the carpenter's hands, they could not
find anything to criticize.

For three months the *Offley* carried on with the sea elephant hunting at Herd Island, some 300 miles to the south'ard of Kerguelen, the ship herself lying practically rigged down and abandoned in a bay while all hands toiled with the blubber. The sea elephants were easily enough killed and gave no trouble, as long as they remained at the island. The modus operandi seems to have consisted, according to the story of a survivor, of the simple process of touching the elephant on the snout with a stick. Then it opened its mouth to roar, and was immediately shot in the roof of the mouth. The blubber was boiled down in pots improvised from the *Offley's* whaling gear, and stored in barrels for removal to the ship. Despite constant bad weather and the handicap of the non-arrival of the tender, good progress was made that season.

Then the sea elephants went, and the *Offley*, rigged again, took to whaling in the locality until they returned. She entered into partnership with an American sealer named the *Mary Powell*, which acted as tender in the continued absence of the *Elizabeth Jane*, and in the off-season the two vessels whaled together, the Americans and Tasmanians sharing alike in all they secured.

Captain Robinson was accompanied by his wife, and while the *Offley* was at Kerguelen she gave birth to a son, who was given Kerguelen for his middle name in honor of the land of his birth—James Kerguelen Robinson he was christened, and through life was known as Kerguelen Jim. He died of thirst, years afterwards, while prospecting for gold in Western Australia.

So the time passed until the next elephant season arrived, and in the meantime a fair quantity of whale oil had been stored in the *Offley's* hold. But the ill-luck of the expedition still held. With the return of the season the *Mary Powell* was almost immediately wrecked, losing a fair quantity of both her own and the *Offley's* hard-won oil. An iceberg looming up out of the mist in a heavy squall caused her end, and her people were fortunate to escape with their lives.

The loss of the *Mary Powell* was a further serious blow to the *Offley*, which was pretty helpless by herself. She then went into partnership with another American sealer called the *Axford*, but after two trips to Herd Island the *Axford* also was wrecked and became a total loss. Still Captain Robinson struggled on as best he could to retrieve something of the capital embarked in the expedition, but when, after 20 months, the *Offley* returned to Hobart she had little over 100 tons of oil in her hold—black whale, sperm and sea elephant. The expedition was a bad failure, as far as the financial side was concerned, but it may be considered rich enough in heroism.

This same Dr. Crowther who fitted the *Offley* out, a big owner of whalers in his day, was Premier of the State of Tasmania for some time and figured actively in the story of the development of that lovely island in more ways than one. A bold and enterprising spirit, he did not hesitate to fit out his ships for all kinds of expeditions which sometimes succeeded and sometimes lost. He owned six whalers—the *Offley, Elizabeth Jane, Sapphire, Velocity, Flying Squirrel* and *Isabella*—had guano interests in the South Seas, a medical practice in Hobart, the chairmanship of the Tasmanian Cabinet, and an energy and enterprise which still left him looking for further fields. At the time of the Californian gold rush he sent some of his vessels there, and would have gone himself had he not happened to be Premier of Tasmania at the time. At first he sent his ships across the Pacific freighted with stores and housing material and the like, and on the way back they whaled. Then he shipped ready-made houses across; the houses (such as they were) were assembled in Hobart, rigged down, and shipped in neatly stacked numbered parts to be put together again on the diggings in California. Things went well enough; the ship arrived at San Francisco and landed the houses. Then they were all neatly erected in readiness for diggers' occupation, and should have returned something like a 500 per cent profit on the original outlay, had not the United States Government, being a little short of revenue at the time, promptly confiscated the lot of them because they were "on government ground" and sold them for its own profits!

After the first voyage the doctor had a profit of £5,000 as well as a little schooner bought for him in San Francisco. After the second voyage he had nothing.

But he began again, for all that. That was the spirit of these pioneers; they were always ready to begin again. And they very often had to.

One old whaling skipper, who in the course of his time had alternately been worth thousands and nothing several times, at the age of 80 found himself ruined again—tin mines, this last time. So he scraped together what he could and bought a fishing boat, though it is pretty cold and pretty hard fishing in Tasmanian waters through the long southern winter. Then he died, alone in the cockpit of his little craft, and was found there in his loneliness. There was nothing to eat in the boat, and from the look of the body it was some time since there had been.

Ships and men alike out of Hobart in the old whaling days possess now a fascinating interest. The ships have all gone, long since; here and there, old and pretty worn now, a man still remains. But their backs straighten and their eyes shine at mention of the old names: *Aladdin, Percy, Windward, Derwent Hunter, Flying Childers, Emily Downing, Marie Laurie, Runnymede, Waterwitch, Louisa, Zephyr, Grecian, Victoria, Pacific, Southern Cross, Litherland, Sussex, Cheviot, Maid of Erin, Highlander, Isabella, Julia, Lady Emma, Nautilus, Pryde, Asia, Fanny Nicholson, Othello, Planter, Offley, Velocity, Isle of France, Helen!* Names now—nothing but names, fast being forgotten; nothing of any remains but a figurehead, here and there, propped up in a garden, some bleached long-forgotten ribs upon a beach, and a logbook in a museum—few, too few of

these. For a long time a lovely old whaler's figurehead—
the full-length figure of a girl with a lovely face, hand outstretched, pointing ahead—stood incongruously above the
window of a second-hand furniture dealer's shop in Liverpool Street, Hobart. Passers-by walked beneath unnotic-
ing, but on rare and rarer occasions an old man straightened
up at the sight of that figurehead, and crossed to the Man
at the Wheel across the road for a better look.

But even that has gone now, and all that remains of the
Man at the Wheel is the name. All of its contemporaries
with the sea-flavored names from the high days of sail have
long since gone, and the clientele of the Man at the Wheel
to-day thinks that public house is named in honor of the
profession of bus driving.

The barque *Aladdin*, one of Seal's ships, was a very interesting old-timer to survive into this century. Charles
Seal was one of the greater of the whaling owners out of
Hobart—the Bayleys, the Crowthers, the Seals, the Saliers,
the McGregors, the McArthurs; all these are great names
in the story of the Hobart whalers—and his ships were always well-managed, well-manned, and generally well-filled
with oil. He had the English built ship *Pacific*, 347 tons,
the barques *Southern Cross*, 347 tons (Hobart built), *Aladdin*, 287 tons, *Litherland*, 305 tons, *Sussex*, 360 tons, and
Cheviot, 251 tons. The *Aladdin* had in her better days been
one of the wooden walls of Old England, being built at
Plymouth in 1825 as the *Mutine*, a brig then, though she
was made a barque later. Because of her name, she was for
many years thought to be the original French *La Mutine*,
cut out at Santa Cruz in one of Nelson's great engagements
at the close of the 18th century and later used to convey the
news of the victory of the Nile to England. So firm was
the conviction that the old *Aladdin* was *La Mutine* that on
the occasion of the centenary of the Battle of the Nile—on
August 1st, 1898—she was decorated with flags as she lay
in the Derwent; but she was a barque of 287 tons and *La*

Mutine was a "remarkably fine brig" of 349 tons. The *Aladdin*, too, was built of good old British oak, and carried the lion of England as her figurehead.

What exactly her career in the Queen's Navy consisted of it is now impossible to say, but at any rate after about 20 years of service she was sold for conversion into a whaler to Messrs. Bennett, whalers, of London. They called her *Aladdin* and sent her to the South Seas after sperms, and for them she was whaling in different parts of the world until brought to Hobart in 1846. At the time Charles Seal had recently lost the Hobart-built full-rigger *Marie Orr*, which was wrecked at Recherché Bay, and he sent Home one of his best captains to purchase a new vessel. So was the *Aladdin* bought, and set out for Hobart in 1846. She was 129 days on the passage out, whaling on the way, and Captain J. McArthur, who had his wife on board, took a sperm or two between the Cape and Tasmania.

From 1847 until the end of her days the *Aladdin* was owned in the port of Hobart. In 1860 Captain McArthur bought her outright for £500, which was pretty cheap although she was an old ship then. In 1867 she was recoppered, when she was found to be in excellent condition. A cannon ball, worn smooth by the rolling of the ship through the years, was found between her skins. On a whaling cruise off the coast of New Zealand, a child was born to Mrs. McArthur, who was to become, in after years, Captain Milford McArthur, Harbor-master of the port of Hobart and a wizard in the art of handling ships.

The *Aladdin* was actively engaged in whaling almost until the end of the 19th century. Then she saw service as a powder hulk, moored in the Derwent, for some time, but neglect caused her to leak badly and she was sold to be broken up. That was in 1902, 56 years after she had been brought to Tasmania and 77 years after she was launched. And she was still good then, had there been anything left for her to do.

Another old whaler with a rather interesting history was the barque *Emily Downing*. She had the distinction of being built by convict labor in the shipyards at Port Arthur in 1841. She was painstakingly built and solidly constructed, and so pleased was the Governor of Tasmania with her that he had her named after his wife. As the *Lady Franklin* she first took the water, for Sir John Franklin—distinguished Arctic explorer and no mean judge of ships—was then Governor of Tasmania; but Lady Franklin might have taken a fancy to the ship herself and had something to do with the naming. A strong character and a clever, forceful woman, she left a deeper mark upon the story of Tasmania than her husband; indeed, it was because of her energy and her efforts, very largely, that her husband was recalled to England.

The barque *Lady Franklin* was built for the transportation of stores and convicts from Hobart to Norfolk Island, in the Pacific, and in that pretty dreary "trade" she carried on monotonously enough until 1853. Then a shipload of convicts seized her. How exactly they managed that does not seem very clear at this late day, but it appears that a woman who was traveling as a passenger in the ship that voyage had a good deal to do with it. She plotted for the escape of one of the convicts and set out to hoodwink the guard and seduce the crew. She seems to have managed both quite well, for the vessel was seized without much trouble, and the master—a Captain William Willett—his officers, his guard, and all his crew, were clamped down into the ill-ventilated prisons in the hold while the convicts proceeded, in great joy, to drink up all the rum in the ship and generally to enjoy themselves. What became of the woman is not recorded, but in any case she was not one of the party flung into the prisons.

Then some of the convicts thought it would be wiser to abandon the *Lady Franklin*, rather than attempt to carry off a ship so well known as a convict transport. Others were for carrying on with their prize, now that they had won her, and making for some imaginary haven in the South Sea Islands where they could end their days in perfect peace, doing no work whatever. But the woman knew that such havens were imaginary and, even if they did exist, would play no part in the achievement of perfect peace to any one in that ship, so the *Lady Franklin* was abandoned.

It was flat calm then, and the barque's people were left foodless in the prisons it had been their duty to guard. The convicts, however, freed a small boy who had been the master's cabin boy and sent him to the main masthead, telling him to remain there until the boats were out of sight and then to come down, and if he could find the key, let the soldiers and the crew out of the prison. The boy went aloft as he was told, on pain of being shot if he didn't. Then the sails were systematically cut down, the braces and the halliards unrove and thrown overboard, the key laboriously hidden beneath the anchor cable, and the convicts cheerfully set off, taking all of the boats, and as much of the stores as they could with them. The boy came down as he was told and hours later found the key.

Weeks afterwards a battered and sorrowful *Lady Franklin* came sneaking up the Derwent with a pretty sorry story, a story that sent a good many of her erstwhile guard to face a court martial that treated them severely. The woman and some of the convicts got clear away, but others were recaptured on a Pacific island, and brought back for trial. The convict settlement at Norfolk Island—never anything in the nature of a desirable or pleasant haunt— suffered badly through the non-arrival of the *Lady Franklin*, and when at long last, recommissioned and newly manned, she put in an appearance, it was to find all hands, guard, convicts, and everybody, pretty near to starvation.

In 1855, the *Lady Franklin* was sold to a Mr. E. A. Downing, merchant, of Hobart, for £2,049. This included stores and sails and so on, worth a good many hundreds of pounds.

She was renamed *Emily Downing*, and put to whaling, remaining in that pursuit for at least another 30 years. She was owned by Mr. Alec McGregor and later by Mc-Gregor, Piesse & Co. for many years, and for them proved a very successful cachalot chaser. In 1885, when the value of sperm had dropped 50 per cent and more, and the sperms had become increasingly shy, she was sold for a coal hulk, still with her planks and frame as good as the day they were put in her, good for another century of service. Neglect finished her as the years passed by, and she was broken up.

What became of most of the old whalers nobody knows now, and probably no one ever will know. Some went missing, some were wrecked. Many passed into general trading, and so to coal hulks or the break-up yards. Sturdy little vessels all, magnificent sea boats, good carriers, good earners (if they got the chance), breeders of as fine a race of seamen as ever looked upon the Southern Cross, their work passed by and they departed. . . .

American whalers, too, were well known in old Hobart, and many a splendid old United States blubber-hunter was as well known in far Tasmania as in New Bedford and Old Salem. The port was always a great refitting base, and half a hundred whalers, upon a hundred occasions, put in to sell some hard-won oil, buy a bite to eat, and put to sea again and carry on. They were queerly named, these old New Bedford and Salem whalers—*Alexander Coffin, Rosalie, Young Eagle, Ansell Gipps, Lexington, London Packet, Awashonks;* there is the smell of the sea and the flavor of the salt in the nomenclature of these wanderers. These Americans often made cruises extending into three, four or five years, selling what they had won, now and again, and setting off once more to try their luck again.

It was a hard life, the old whaling, but at least it must have been a constant job. There were grand times too, when at last pay-off day came. The village constabulary retired, if they had not been sufficiently reënforced from the surrounding country, and left the whalers to it, and old Hobart with its Wapping, its saloons, its hostelries of ill repute, its dance-houses and its wandering, care-free whalers from the ends of the earth, was as colorful a spot as might be found anywhere south of the Line.

The old whaling died with the last cruise of the *Helen*, and then for 25 years and more no whaler came to the port of Hobart. In 1923, however, the once so great and prosperous whaling base entered into the industry once again, but this time in vastly different circumstances. In November, 1923, the Norwegian whaling floating factory, *Sir James Clark Ross*, a steamer of nearly 12,000 tons gross register, arrived in the Derwent from Sandefjord, Norway. She was bound on a whaling cruise to the Great Ice Barrier, in the Ross Sea, where explorers on their way to the South Pole had reported the great blue whales to be exceptionally thick; within a few days, five other vessels arrived. How different was this fleet from the ships of old! The *Sir James Clark Ross* had five whale chasers with her—little steamers, sharp lined and powerfully engined, of 100 tons or so, that sneaked upon the feeding whales, and fired great bomb-pointed harpoons into them that killed them inside seconds. Then they towed them to the factory ship that stripped their blubber off by machinery and boiled them down, ten and fifteen a day if she could get them.

The *Sir James Clark Ross* was commanded by Captain C. A. Larsen, veteran Norse iceman and whaler, but her first voyage to the Antarctic was not financially successful. She took some 17,000 barrels of oil despite the most appalling conditions, due to a heavy ice season and unavoidable (since no one had previous experience to serve as a guide) unsuitability of the gear. The following year she returned again, taking 40,000 barrels, and from then the Norwegian industry has thrived. Other great whaling ships, big enough to make even the *Sir James Clark Ross* look small in comparison, have come—huge tankers carrying 12,000 tons of coal to burn during the four months' icy cruise, as well as thousands of tons of oil for their oil-burning whalers. One of these ships has a slipway cut into her stern, up which she hauls the giant blue whales bodily on deck; another has a mouth cut into her bows, through which she chews up whales by the hundred. The *N. T. Nielsen-Alonso*, a Larvik whaler that was once the old Cardiff trader *Custodian*, and the *C. A. Larsen*, from Sandefjord, now carry on a yearly slaughter on a tremendous scale; the *Sir James Clark Ross*, and the *C. A. Larsen* with New Zealand as their base, and the *N. T. Nielsen-Alonso* from Hobart. Yearly their takes of whale oil grow and their profits must be tremendous. In 1926-27 the *Sir James Clark Ross* took 22,734 barrels from 250 whales, the *N. T. Neilsen-Alonso* 36,800 barrels of oil from 456 whales, and the *C. A. Larsen* 47,200 from over 600 whales. The following season— 1927-28—the *Sir James Clark Ross* took 45,000 barrels, the *N. T. Neilsen-Alonso* 57,000 barrels, and the *C. A. Larsen* 60,000 barrels, the three between them slaying something like 2,000 whales. Then in 1928-29 these figures even were eclipsed, and three huge whalers took between them 176,000 barrels of oil.

In three seasons these vessels have killed well over 5,000 whales for oil worth something like two and a half million pounds. The latest tidings are that four new great whalers are entering the field, but one might imagine that the whales would soon have had enough of it. . . .

"The only arrival from the whaling fleet has been the brig *Louisa*, Captain Thomas Davis, which came into port on the 6th inst. with only 15 tons of sperm oil, taken during an eleven months' cruise," reported the Hobart *Mercury* during February, 1872. "Captain Davis reported that during the last six months he had not seen any whales."

Captain Davis would stare in amazement at the figures quoted from these ships of later days and would find them impossible, almost, of belief. But perhaps he would not speak of the modern pursuit as whaling.

CHAPTER XIII

FROM CAPTAIN TREGURTHA'S LOG

AN interesting and enlightening picture of a cruise in
one of these old Hobart Town whalers is contained
in the log of Captain Edward Primrose Tregurtha,
who was master of the whaler *Caroline* for some time. Captain Tregurtha was one of the old band of real pioneers,
and his whole career makes the most fascinating reading.
Born near Land's End in 1803, the son of a naval lieutenant, at the age of nine he entered the King's Navy and
before he was 12 had taken part in several actions and gone
through adventures which would make the modern small boy
sit up and take notice, if he only saw them in the ubiquitous
movies.

At the age of 13 he was in charge of a ship. He was a
midshipman then when his ship took a small French brig
while on a passage from Madeira to the Channel, and young
Tregurtha was sent prize master in her with a crew of six
and a quartermaster, to take her into Cork. Later he left
the Navy, and while still in his early 'teens saw considerable
experience in merchantmen of various kinds, quickly rising
to be an officer in the East Indian and China trade. It was
while he was in this trade, at the age of 28, that the chance
came to command a Hobart Town whaler. Although he
had never been whaling previously, the life appealed to the
Cornishman's adventurous spirit and he seized the chance
gladly.

Captain Tregurtha remained a Tasmanian once he had
seen that lovely island, and long after he was finished with
the *Caroline*, sailed out of the port of Hobart with his own
and other ships. With the old brig *Henry* he played an

interesting part in the very early days of the state of Victoria; throughout his long life he appears to have had plenty of adventure, and when he sat down in his declining years to write up something of his "log"—for the log a sailor keeps for his ship is a prosaic and dull affair, in which one must dig deep to see adventure—he was not short of material. One uses here only that section dealing with the cruise of the *Caroline:* there are descriptions of whaling operations, of mates "whose sole aim seemed to be to make the fitting out of the ship as expensive as possible," of narrow escapes and boat voyages almost incredible, of colorful adventures and incidents each of which would be the romance of a life-time to-day.

On our voyage from Madras [writes Captain Tregurtha], a Captain Betts of the Engineers, lately in the Indian Service, had been a passenger. He had just returned from Van Diemen's Land and being an enterprising man had persuaded his brother-in-law and cousin, Alfred Betts, a rich Indigo Planter, to return with him to that Colony to establish a Whaling Firm and trade as merchants at Hobart Town. They had bought a barque named the *Caroline* (now on a voyage to China) but shortly expected at Calcutta. Having studied my character and ability on the passage he became convinced that I was a person well adapted for such an expedition, and he now came and explained the scheme and offered me the command with an eighth share in the vessel, to be on pay at once and commence preparations for the voyage.

This adventure just suited me, enterprising and bold, fearless and energetic, muscular and active. I immediately asked Captain Boyes to discharge me, and on the 25th January, 1831, I shook hands with my old Captain and shipmates and took a Palace in Calcutta, No. 43, Jackson Ghant Street. Here I kept my horse and gig and commenced a series of purchases for the intended voyage. I ordered whaleboats and employed a gang of tailors to make marryatts, signals and engagers, but time rolled on and the *Caroline* arrived. I had now my hands full. The ship had to be docked, new masted and sparr'd, and in fact new modelled, as she was in a most unseamanlike and unsatisfactory state. I placed her in Kid-

drapore dock and to be close in attendance myself, I lived at
the Bungalow with Mr. Kidd. It was here I had an attack
of rheumatism which nearly terminated fatally. Hurrying
my bearers through a storm of rain, I got home rather heated
and without a thought stepped into a marble bath in this
state. The sudden chill struck me like death. I hardly know
how I recovered but I did in a day or two. The rheumatism
remained for several years afterwards, but was finally cured
by hydriodate of potash. I soon got my vessel fitted, rigged
and ready.

On the 18th April we embarked 21 convicts of the most
desperate character for Sydney, with the intention of proceeding in tow of a steamer at daylight to be towed out to
sea. My crew consisted of a mixture of all nations, and all
trades, broken down gentlemen included; a Havildan Maig
and ten sepoys to keep guard over the prisoners, twenty-seven
Europeans of different nations, and eight boys as appren-
tices, natives of India, halfbreeds. I had been annoyed during the day three or four times by a Sheriff's officer taking
my 3rd and 4th Mates and Boatswain from the ship under
various pretences and at each visit he became more imper-
tinent, rude and insolent. The sun was now set when he again
returned half intoxicated and insisted on taking the Boatswain
on shore. I ordered him out of the ship adding, "There is
the Gangway." Not complying, I caught him by the collar
and seat of his breeches in my hand, but catching hold of the
manrope, he got in the boat unhurt. Pulling off a short distance he began a strain of abuse that sent my lady passengers
off the poop.

"Stop," I said, "you are not out of the reach of my dogwhip."

Having procured it, I called the dinghy whaler, and gave
chase. The Ghant was a long one, and before he could reach
his gig I had overtaken him. Turning suddenly round he
hit me on the nose, but catching him by the collar, we both
came to the ground. I rose, and holding him by the one hand,
I applied the whip to the naked part most dexterously until
he begged for mercy. The natives also interceded, saying,
"Hurt man, O Sahib." With a flourish of the dogwhip, I
soon cleared them off and released him, advising him to be
more civil and polite the next ship he visited. On getting
fairly into his buggy he shook his whip at me and roar'd out,

"You d—d rascal, I will have you in the choky to-morrow."
On which I made another spring at him, but lashing his horse
he drove off.   By this time Mr. A. Betts had brought a guard
of sepoys to my assistance, thinking I had been overpowered.
I got my passengers all on board with the luggage, amounting
to 43 souls.

After dark, the prisoners, 21 in number, came off.   These
convicts were of a most desperate character, chiefly murderers.   There was one in particular that I was cautioned
against, a Captain Wm. Humble, who had commanded a fine
country ship of 800 tons, but abandoned to profligate habits
had got transported for swindling.   He had publicly declared
that no bloody ship could convey him to Botany Bay.   I was
particularly guarded, being provided with a Havildan Maig
and 8 sepoys well armed as sentries, and Sergeant Major
Dobson to superintend them and serve out their victuals.   I
adopted the following plan with Humble: directly I left
Madras, I took him out of the prison forward, knocked off
his irons, and messed him in the half deck with the Boatswain
and carpenter.   During the day he worked with the carpenter,
at night he was forbidden to go on deck unless under the
charge of a sepoy.   I also cautioned him that from his un-
guarded threats to escape I had determined to shoot him
should any attempt be made on his part to agitate or effect
any rising of the prisoners.   The result was that he behaved
with great propriety all the voyage.

We had a scene notwithstanding, off Cape Leeuwin.   A
ruffian of herculean stature named Michael Duffy, an Irishman, was in the habit of committing great noises in the prison,
for which Mr. Dobson called him to account.   In doing so
he abused the Sergeant and threatened to throw him overboard.   I determined to punish him, and calling all hands aft,
I tied him up at the lee gangway, when after lecturing him
before all hands, I ordered the boatswain to commence flogging.   To my astonishment Mr. Alfred Betts drew his sword
and making a step forward requested the boatswain to desist
or he would run him through.

"Mr. Betts," I roared out, "put that sword in its sheath,
and you, Sir, walk on the poop or your life's not worth one
minutes's purchase."   (I was standing at the capstan with a
brace of loaded pistols in my hand.)

Captain Swanson close behind whisper'd, "Be steady, Tregurtha."

I answered that I was perfectly cool. "Boatswain," I said, "do your duty, and you, Sir, if you value your life," I said to Betts, "walk on the poop without delay."

Betts sheathed his sword and walk'd slowly up the poop ladder. I punished the prisoner with three dozen lashes, and heavily ironed him on his return to prison. Mr. A. Betts apologised afterwards for his interference, and this terminated a scene that but for prompt and energetic measures might have ended very differently.

We arrived at Madras on the 17th May, where we received our water and stock of fresh provisions. We were here joined by Capt. Swanson, Capt. and Mrs. Weston and family, Colonel Parker and 2 daughters, Dr. and Mrs. Kinny and Lieuts. Perrior and Onslow and a Mr. Grey for Launceston, V. D. Land, Mr. Steele, Mr. and Mrs. Flood, and in all 19 cabin passengers, 11 servants and 8 children besides Serg. Maj. Dobson, wife, and four children, and took our departure on the 27th for New S. Wales. The voyage was boisterous and tedious. On the 20th July having rounded Cape Leeuwin we encountered a heavy storm from the N.W. which carried away the Main Top Sl.yard, and I was obliged to round the ship to under a reef'd foresail. As the topsail was flying about none of the crew would go aloft to secure it. Taking a gasket round my neck I shinned aloft and stopt the yard arms together, enabling them to save the sail. It was the impulse of the moment. On entering the cabin for a glass of wine, "Oh, Captain," said a sensitive lady, "you *naughty* man, how could you dare to venture your life that way just now? If you had been flung overboard into the sea, what would have become of us?"

"Madame," said I, bowing, "I did not think of that, or I might not have ventured aloft."

We sighted Cape Otway on the 26th July and steer'd through Bass Straits. On the 28th while beating about off the Ninety Mile beach with light N.E. airs a passenger call'd me on deck to see what he termed a beautiful appearance of the sea. I instantly turned the hands out, furled the courses and commenced reefing the topsails. This remarkable appearance (which resembles the Bore in Calcutta) is caused by a sudden change of wind advancing against its receding opponent, and throwing the sea into the air in one crest of foam. Having placed the ship so as to receive the wind free, we were soon scudding before it for Sydney, at which port we safely arrived on the 31st July. I was what they call'd a new chum, and every person strove to dissuade me from whaling by marvellous tales exaggerated in the highest degree. I told them I made my mind up and no amount of alleged dangers of the sea would prevent me. I was ready and willing to encounter them.

One Sunday a party was made up of some young men to take one of my whaleboats and three men for the purpose of seeing the lighthouse on the Sth. Head. When on the point of starting, a Mr. Medly, who was passenger by the ship *Cairns* for Hobarton, asked me if I would drop him on board at Watson's Bay. As it lay in my way I acceded; however, when we got there it appeared that Captain Goodwin had proceeded to sea early that morning. The poor fellow was in an agony. His clothes were gone, he was left almost naked without money, and the situation he was going to would be fill'd by some other. He accompanied us to the Light House, and whilst on its summit, we discovered the ship with a very light air standing in shore. I proposed if he would procure two men from the Pilot, I would pull off and place him on board. Having got a full crew I started for the ship, having taken her bearings. We pulled about three hours ere we perceived her, and at sundown succeeded in placing him on board, to his infinite satisfaction. He gave the crew all the money he had, about £2 in silver. After allowing them time to refresh we started for the land, which was not visible. About 3 o'clock in the morning, I landed the Pilot's men and at the dawning was passing Pinchgut, when the one oar side stopped pulling for a minute. Being anxious to get ashore before daylight, I told the two oars to pull on or I would lay against them with the steer oar. In my anxiety to make a strong sweep, I missed the water and plunged overboard, a tremendous dive head first. I, however, turned and came up after the boat which I gradually reached and got in, the only casualty being the wetting of my watch.

At this time a great number of vessels were fitting out for whaling. In consequence all materials connected with it became extravagantly dear, and labour scarce. The time consumed in Sydney was dreadful. When the *Caroline* started for whaling on the 9th November, with 400 tons of oil butts, 2½ years' provisions, whaling gear, boats, etc., the outlay was estimated at £12,000. I had engaged an old whaling mate, whose sole aim appeared to me to make the vessel as expensive as he possibly could. Three months' residence in Sydney compelled to associate with the whalers in order to learn something of their craft did not improve my moral tendencies.

I, however, escaped much contamination by having charge of Mr. Betts' establishment during a visit he paid to Van Diemen's Land.

In November we set out and shaped a course for Howe's Island. My mate had assured me of some whaling treasures he knew of being buried there, which would only cost us the trouble of taking away. Our crew, full of hope, were very busy fitting their respective boats with all the requisite precautions for the quick and easiest method of killing the fish with safety, and securely stowing the different gear, oar mats, line, tubs, skeleton line, pins, whole pins for harpoons and lances, etc., etc., and finally the sharpening of the weapons. After being a week at sea, I was told we were ready for the encounter. On the 15th we sighted Howe's Island and at 10 A.M. lowered the two quarter boats, in which the mate and I proceeded for the shore. It took us, pulling and sailing, 7 hours to reach the beach, where on landing we shot a quantity of bronze-wing pigeons, which were so tame they would not go away until we had killed 60 or 70. Some persons had removed the gear we sought.

Whales now appeared and we started in pursuit. I was told that they were humpbacks and not desirable. It was near midnight ere we reached the ship, which had hove-to 4 leagues off the land. After remaining some days in sight of Howe's Island without success, we stretched away for the Three Kings at the N. point of New Zealand. There was still much to do on board a ship that had never been whaling before and a great deal of training and instruction to the crew, all new to the business. With the exception of about 20 all the rest had never seen a whale killed. We had the tryworks, coolers and tanks to fit, blubber room to prepare, cutting in gear, fluke ropes, etc., to prepare and overhaul; the cooper was busy fitting line tubs, breakers, boat kegs, etc., also small casks for stowage; the carpenter preparing drogues, whiffs;

the head men and boat-steerers, each painting and preparing their individual boats for the contest or chase. I had my work in preparing a code of signals for the boats, arranging the stowage and keeping the turbulent spirits in control.

On the 27th November made the Three Kings and standing close in sent two boats to fish and trade with the natives for potatoes and vegetables. The principal island only I found inhabited by portion of a tribe that had escaped being massacred by the natives of the Bay of Islands some years previous. They had climbed the summit of the Island, where a small portion of level ground provided them with the means of subsistence. I accompanied them to the settlement, consisting of about a dozen adults with their children. The approach was very difficult and easily defended by rolling fragments of rock down the precipice. I procured some baskets of potatoes in exchange for iron hoop, and some iron nails. The currents being irregular, I considered the ground rather dangerous so shaped my course toward the French rock and Macaulay's group.

On Decr. 4th, in Lat. 31° 42′ S. Long. 181° 24′ E. we sighted sperm whales and in the afternoon succeeded in killing a 60-barrel bull whale. I now commenced my duties, that of cutting off the fish's head. This is by no means an easy undertaking and the sinews resist the efforts to divide them by elastic opposition peculiarly fatiguing to the arms. Suspended on a stage over the ship's side in a canvas belt (similar to the position of heaving the lead) with a pole of from 14 to 16 feet long with a small steel spade at the extremity, keen as a razer, is hard work. This spade is from 5 to 7 inches wide. With this weapon you have to sever a bulk of from 8 to 10 feet diameter and about 20 in circumference, also to hit the joint of the vertebra so as to sever the head from the body. With the assistance of my 1st and 3rd mates we had got the blubber in and the case bailed out by noon.

Decr. 13th: sent two boats on shore at Macaulay's Island, where they shot five wild goats. I also landed on the Curtisses Rocks, where I found a boiling spring issuing through the sea. I obtained a quantity of sulphur from a lake on the Island, and severely burn't my feet by inadvertently getting over the tops of my boots in pursuit of some birds. On the 15th we had the fortune to kill another bull whale of 21 barrels. This day a remarkable incident occurred. I was work-

ing loose boat on the stricken whale, when turning on his
back he came at my boat with his jaws extended to bite
us in halves. It was only by fixing the spade in his neck
and backing astern rapidly that we avoided the monster's
jaws from champing the boat. Loss of blood soon caused
him to relinquish his efforts, which lasted 4 to 5 minutes.

We now continued to see whales daily, but they were so
wide awake and in so great a hurry we had no chance of
getting near them. On the 24th, being to windward of Sunday Island, which place my mate had described to me as desirable to wood and water at, as well as abounding in wild
hogs, I lowered two boats, and providing ourselves with fowl-
ing pieces and fishing gear, accompanied by the chief mate and
doctor, at 2 P.M. we pulled for the landing place which was
on the side opposite to where we started. Sunday (a lagoon
island) lying in latitude 29° 12′ S. and longitude 181° 47′ E.
is of about 16 or 18 miles in circumference, its greatest extent
being from east to west. On the E.N.E. side there lie 7 or 8
islands from a quarter to a mile and quarter off shore, with
various sunken rocks inside them, rendering the passage difficult in a boat. Off each of the heads (or extreme points) of
this island are shoals running ½ a mile off shore.

On the 24th December 1831, the island bearing W.N.W.,
I thought it a good opportunity of ascertaining the state of
the anchorage and conveniency of procuring water and firewood. I ran down the N. side and sent the other boat on
the S. side of the island. Neither of us could effect a safe
landing until we met on the W.N.W. side in a bay with a
dark, steep sandy beach. Having effected a landing without
seeing each other we were mutually surprised at meeting, the
boats being a mile apart or more. The evening proving tempestuous we agreed to remain on shore the night, the surf
being dangerous to launch through. We accordingly hauled
our boats well up on the beach and rigged a tent to pass the
night under the boats' sails.

Our men having caught some mutton birds we made a rousing fire, and those whose appetites were keen enough (and
not fastidious) partook, and then lay down to rest. At 11
it came on squally with very heavy rain so as to capsize our
tent and compel us to take shelter under the boat (which we
turned on her mouth). The rain beating in, I called the boat-
steerer and striking a light we turned our way towards the

cliff thinking to obtain shelter from the projecting rocks. This jungle proved too thick, so as to preclude the possibility of forming a passage. We got under the thickest foliage tree we could find and kindling a fire from the rotten wood about us, one attended the fire whilst the other lay down, alternately.

After enduring this for about 2 hours the rain ceased when we immediately facilitated our return to the boat, quite fatigued, and notwithstanding wet clothes slept soundly. At 5 A.M. seeing the dawning of day peeping under the boat, I roused out and finding the fire getting low ran along the beach (on which there was plenty of dry wood) and soon made a roaring fire. Removing the embers a short distance from where the old fire had been lighted, I rolled myself in the ashes and sand to warm my limbs which were stiff from being exposed and wet last night. 5.30 A.M. Come rouse out, my lads, don't you hear the pigs grunting? Let's get a roast one for breakfast, or it will be with Duke Humphries on a leg to nothing and no turnips. On rousing out the boat's crew and examining the guns found them wetted all over with salt water and rusty from the surf on landing. We, however, set to work, cleaned and loaded, then proceeded in different directions in search of something for breakfast.

On examining the bay it appear'd to be a pebbly beach of about 2 miles in length, utmost extent of depth between the heads ¾ of a mile. This is a reef of rocks nearly dry extending in a westerly direction from the S.E. Point. There is good anchorage in 4½ and 5 fathoms, sandy bottom ½ a mile from the shore but the roadstead is much exposed and landing is difficult. The sand runs in on a flat and meets the rising beach suddenly, which throws up a heavy breaking surf and renders it difficult to effect a landing.

After wandering through the valley two or three miles without even meeting a bird worth shooting, I sat myself on the bank of the lagoon, washed and refreshed myself and then proceeded to the boat. Here I met Mr. Kelly, my chief mate, who had as little success as myself. We mutually agreed as the most advisable plan to launch the boats and pull off the S.E. point of the island so as to get a fair view round, and discover whether the ship was in sight or driven off by the severity of the weather during the night. Shortly after Kelly had left, my boat-steerer came in having succeeded in killing a hog, so I came to the determination of roasting it before the start, and sent one of the boat's crew to inform the mate and invite him and his boat's crew to partake. This he declined but requested if there was any left to save it when we launched for their use.

At 10 A.M. I launched through the surf well. Joining the other boat we pulled out as agreed off the point, but not discovering the ship dropt our Kellicks and commenced fishing. In this we were successful, each boat had taken more than a dozen fine fish when the surgeon suddenly exclaimed "The Ship! The Ship! I see the Ship!

The Boat's crew, all rising at once overcome with joy nearly capsized the boat. Then weighing the kellick the mate directed his boat towards mine to communicate the tidings. It was now 1 o'clock P.M., blowing still very hard when Mr. Kelly's boat came near me for the purpose of asking my advice, but a sudden gust of wind taking his boat he proceeded off without any further instruction. I was much annoyed and considered it short of madness going off, the ship being scarcely perceptible (not larger to appearance than a seabird), but seeing that he was gone I did not consider it proper to allow him to proceed alone.

Weighing the kellick I started after him, and as soon as we were out of the influence of the puffs from the hills I dows'd the oars and set the lug sail, hoisted about three feet of the mast. Under this canvas she went like a little fairy and soon passed the other boat, whom I hailed by saying, "Where are you bound to? I am bound for Ushant!" just to keep up their spirits. We passed her very quick and shortly after I saw them make sail. At 3 I found the ship was going from us and that we were losing sight of the other boat. At 3.30. P.M. both the ship and the other boat were out of sight, with the wind and sea increasing and us twelve miles from the land and that right to windward.

I suddenly came to the resolution of pulling back to the island. I apprehended the ship might not tack, in which case we were lost totally.

You who have ever been placed in such a situation may fancy what I felt, but to those who have not, it is not in the power of language to describe the feeling of that moment. My orders were instantly obeyed, the sail taken in and each man stript with his oar on his hand. It was a desperate struggle between life and an inglorious death. Taking the

harpooner's oar I resolved to share and shew them I did not
shrink from the labours and perils they were encountering.

For the first hour, every 5 minutes a sea breaking would
overwhelm us and half fill the boat, knocking us off the thwarts.
But a strong weatherly tide assisted and found by the land
that we approached it. At 8 we had got within 5 miles of the
shore when the man at the stroke oar declared he could do
no more; he was so fatigued he could not lift his arm. I then
placed him at the steer oar and shortly after he recovered so
as to spell the rest at intervals.

At 11.30. we got close in shore but the wind had now increased to a gale, and it was in vain we strove to pull round
the point for the lagoon we had left in the morning. Fatigued
and thirsty we anchor'd close under the land awaiting the
dawn of day. It was at this time blowing a storm (the ship
had reduced to a close reef'd main topsail) and the squalls
that came over the hills were tremendous. Having allowed
the crew to lay down, as anxiety prevented me closing my
eyes, I had leisure to thank an Almighty Providence in preserving our lives so as to reach the land.

Our situation now was by no means an enviable one, six
men in an open boat with not a single article of food, water,
or covering, all wet to the skin, hungry, thirsty and fatigued,
so much as to lie in the bottom of the boat covered with water
to obtain rest. Several times during the night the squalls
were near capsizing the boat, she lay over so as to take in
water over the gunwhale before she had time to get head to
wind.

As soon as the first streaks of dawn appeared I roused the
crew to seek for fresh water. After weighing the kellick of
which we found the rope round several rocks, we pulled for
Lagoon Bay, but after struggling to get round the point upwards of an hour, we gave it up and bore away for the lee-
side of the island. (Just before we bore up three large sharks
rushed up alongside the boat and one of them seizing my oar
by the blade shook it voraciously; having disengaged it, I
struck him on the back. One of them got hold of the steer
oar but Brown striking him they disappeared.) We now
ran before the wind round on the S.E. side and having to pull
into the bay found ourselves so stiff and exhausted as to scarce
move the oars.

On arriving at the centre of the bay a shore appeared of

large round stones and the surf not very high I determined
to land and haul our boat up. This we providently effected
without injury, and having hauled the boat up in the wood,
all lay down to rest except myself, who instantly started in
search of fresh water. I so found, after a close search in
the hollow of some rocks and some old trunks of trees, two
or three gallons, so having quenched our thirst we lay down
to rest.

I believe we all slept soundly 5 or 6 hours as I did not
waken until near noon, it being after six at landing. Our
first consideration now was food, so kindling a fire we roasted
the fish from the preceding day and catching some sea bird,
called by the seamen "Mutton Birds," which we picked and
gutted and grilled on small spits of wood. After this repast
which although without bread or salt was not despised, I con-
sulted with the crew what was best to be done, and as they all
agreed that we could not expect the ship for three or four
days at least (if they had escaped the severity of the gale,
and perhaps as many months elapse before we should have
an opportunity of leaving the island) our place was to make
ourselves comfortable as possible, and make provision for
store in case of need.

I accordingly divided our numbers as follows, viz:—two
were to remain at the boat to cook out ferns (of which there
was a great abundance) and prepare a bed under the boat
(which we turned bottom up for that purpose); two were to
traverse the shore in an easterly direction in search of water;
and, in case of this party failing, I, taking a man with me,
struck up the mountain to cut cabbage tree as a vegetable and
to appease our thirst in case the latter party failed to procure
water.

Between 5 and 6 p.m. we had all returned. The water party
had only procured about 2 quarts of muddy sediment from the
hollows of trees. I found, however, plenty of cabbage palm
trees and the cook and his mate in cutting ferns had discovered
quantities of mutton birds on their nests, sitting so tame as
to permit of your removing the egg without quitting their
post, but unfortunately all the eggs proved addled, the birds
having sat some time. They secured a large quantity of birds.
(These birds when cleaned are larger than a pigeon and very
remarkably fat. After roasting their flesh was very good but
partook of rather a strong taste. I have no doubt if well

stuffed and seasoned they would be very nice, as there was nothing fishy in it.)

At 6 P.M. the wind had now shifted to the N.W. and blew a perfect hurricane. The sea presented one continued sheet of foam as far as the eye could reach. At the beach we landed at the sea rolled in mountains high. We all congratulated ourselves on our providential escape in landing, and each in secret while viewing the terrific scene before him murmured a prayer of thanksgiving to the Almighty disposer of events for having so miraculously preserved us from the fury of the elements. James Randal, an old seaman, turning round upon me made the subject of the following colloquy: "Tremendous sea, that, Sir. I'm afraid the old Boomer wuldn't ride it out to a raft in that. No. No! no chance. Must thank God we are here on mutton birds and cabbage. That's better than a salt water supper."

A quantity of palm leaves being placed upright against the open side of the boat, and secured with a door to go in, the inside was filled with ferns and leaves of trees which upon the whole was a good field bed. Before lying down a large heap of fire wood was collected so as to retain the fire during the night. Next day I roused them all up early to make provision for the day. The gale was now decreasing with misty showers of rain, but not sufficient to procure us fresh water. After breakfasting on mutton birds and cabbage tree, five of us set out for the purpose of crossing the island if possible (leaving one at home to cook) and endeavour to gain the lagoon for water, or perhaps procure a pig. After traversing up through the valley and ravine with difficulty through an opening formed by the descent of heavy rains (but nearly choked by the number of weeds and brushwood grown since) without being able to find about a pint of water in the rock, on a sudden a perpendicular rock of 70 or 80 feet presented itself with a front as smooth as a pebble. Looking round we perceived an area or space of 60 or 70 feet without bush or shrub. This was composed of small pebbles, gravel and sand, forming a large basin, apparently a reservoir for water, which overflows in heavy rains from the mountains, on the summit of which I am inclined to think there is a large lagoon, similar to the one in the N.W. Bay.

Our disappointment was very great but it added courage to our flagging strength, for I no sooner hinted that we might

get up on our right than three rose to assist me in the ascent.
I now commenced a climbing effort up the almost perpendicular mountain. I was on the point of achieving the summit at
the risk of my neck, when another obstruction offered itself of
perpendicular loose slate rock 12 or 14 feet high. My comrades who were following me at a little distance now gave up
all hopes of getting over, at my representing this fresh obsta-
ble, and it was in vain I sought among the rude and rugged
craigs for an opening to ascent. Spent with disappointment,
exertion, fatigue, and thirst, fainting, I looked round when a
large cabbage tree met my view about 100 yards below me. The
joyful intelligence was no sooner communicated than a few
seconds brought us together at its foot to enjoy so seasonable
a repast.

Refreshed by its copious juice, which flows in abundance,
and gratified with the view of numerous and diversified scenery,
I had an opportunity of surveying the prospect before me,
which although in a dejected state of mind from our late disappointment left an indelible impression on my memory. I
was seated in one of those numerous ridges which skirted the
valley on both sides of our ascent. Ridge and vale alternately
succeeded each other in wild and indescribable succession,
broken and irregular. The valley was filled with trees of
magnificent growth and foliage. On the ridges or cairns lay
scattered huge loose stones threatening to overwhelm the val-
leys beneath. Occasionally the cabbage palm shot forth with
its luxuriant leaves branching over the precipice like a thing
suspended in the air. The storm was now visibly abating, but
the distant sea appeared still dreadfully agitated and covered
with foam, while the wind swept by in hollow murmurs indi-
cating its falling power. On our right stood the huge pile of
perpendicular cliffs, over the summit of which myriads of sea
fowl were hovering and deafening the ear with their wild shrill
cries.

In vain our eyes were strained through the dusk with a wish-
ful hope of seeing the ship, scarcely daring to venture such
a delusive idea. We now cautiously descended and on reaching
the torrent bed, eagerly bent on our researches through its
several cavities in the expectation of finding water. Our
efforts were ineffectual, with the exception of a quart of dirty
sediment found in a hole. It was evident that vast quantities
of water had been there, but the heat and dryness of the

weather had absorbed it all. On our return we each caught about 20 mutton birds (a provision for next day) and after dining on our usual fare, felt too much fatigued for more researches that day. At night we procured a large supply of wood and setting on a good fire slept very comfortably under the boat (being more reconciled to our situation and recovered from the effects of the gale).

Tuesday the 28th; On awaking at daylight, I found the weather calm and clear, but the surf raged so violently on the shore as to preclude the possibility of embarking. Indeed it would be madness to risk our lives and frail boat through such a surf to gratify our thirst, however strongly it pleaded to be gratified. We knew that at Lagoon Bay there was plenty of water, but not any birds or cabbage palm. Here we had plenty of the latter but a very scant supply of the former. However, we could exist very well so long as the palm lasted. I therefore deemed it prudent to wait until the surf had moderated, rather than incur any risk of damaging our boat (the only chance of escape).

I now made a few arrangements, cleared an open road to the valley, opened a space for a hut, built a native oven, and laid a bench for a seat intending, should misfortune compel us to remain here, to commence fishing and dry them in the sun. I also had 30 or 40 mutton birds opened and split down the back in order to ascertain whether we could cure them before they took their departure seaward, which they do after the young are strong enough to undergo the fatigue of a long flight.

After breakfasting as usual, I sent three men to explore the eastern shore, and reserving one I took a westerly direction. Our intentions had two objects in view, viz., provisions and water, also should our unfortunate companions or ship be on the coast to ascertain in what direction. The day proved exceedingly sultry, and the exertion of scrambling over cliffs was almost overpowering under the influence of the sun in our dejected state. We, however, succeeded in reaching the S.W. point about noon. Clambering to the summit of the cliff, our sight was strained in vain to catch a distant glimpse of the ship. At times a sea bird turning on the wing caught our eye and again our eager researches combined swept the horizon.

My companion's name was Thos. Chance and after often

calling his attention to what I fancied was the ship in the following manner.

"Look at that, Chance! I think I see her, Chance!" and so forth.

I at length got angry at my own credulity and could not help exclaiming to myself. "Yes, it would be a chance! And it will be a chance if I ever see her again."

And yet at this time, at that very minute, the ship was not above twelve miles from us on the other side and hidden by the land.

After thus flattering and again repeatedly disappointing ourselves, thirst became very oppressive, and having heard bathing recommended, resolved to try its efficiency, and soon found its salutary effects. This was a speedy relief but its effects were merely temporary with us.

On our return to the boat the heat of the sun and the exertion made our tongues cleave to the roofs of our mouths, and we anxiously scrutinized every spot likely to afford even a drop of water. Once I thought I had found a prize, but after a copious draught discovered it was brackish, half salt and half fresh. It was also rather warm from the sun. The consequence was that a few minutes after I became dreadfully sick and cramped in the stomach. This disaster luckily soon passed off and at 3 P.M. I returned to our encampment. The other party had also returned quite dispirited, but they produced two quarts of muddy water which was very acceptable. They had seen nothing of the ship from the east point, but could not pass round for a precipice, so had turned their attention to procure cabbage palm of which they accumulated a large quantity, and informed me there were plenty in that direction, which was a pleasing intelligence. We all partook cheerfully of our usual repast, after which I called them together, and laid my plans of subsistence before them. This was cheerfully acceded to and we commenced gathering fuel and other articles as supplies and materials to commence building a house, provision, fuel, etc., for a winter stock.

While in the act of gathering wood from the beach, Thomas Chance began capering and dancing about like a madman, calling out "a boat! A boat" directing my sight towards the point we had been on in the morning.

I soon perceived a whale boat pulling and sailing round

towards us across the mouth of the bay we were in, and soon after another boat, and then a third.

It was now evident the ship was safe and seeking us, but the first word that escaped my lips and those of my companions was "We are preserved, but what is become of Mr. Kelly and his boat's crew?"

So completely overpowered were we that not one knew what he was doing, so unexpected and sudden was our delivery. Tears of joy and gratitude for our escape ran down our cheeks (the first appearance of anything of the kind). This was the first impulse, but it soon gave way to the most anxious solicitude for the safety and fate of our unfortunate companions.

Having recovered my composure and presence of mind, I requested that a large fire should be made at the edge of the beach to attract the observation of the boats, who had not yet perceived us. This was quickly effected. I then desired them to bring our bag of green ferns, place it on the fire and smother it so as to cause a huge column of smoke. This was no sooner done, than we had the satisfaction to perceive that the boats stopt, took down their sails and pull'd direct in for the spot where our fire was kindled. The surf was still most terrific, at times a perpendicular break of 8 or 10 feet which made us shudder at its consequence (more especially as a number of large sharks were visible through the transparent body of water) and prevented the approach of the boats so as scarcely to hold communication, but no language can express the joyous sensation I felt at beholding Mr. Kelly with his own boat and crew among the number who were seeking us.

CHAPTER XIV

FROM CAPTAIN TREGURTHA'S LOG (*Continued*)

THE particulars of Mr. Kelly's miraculous escape [Captain Tregurtha's log continues], I will relate in his own words: "At 2.30 when you passed me under sail, I immediately set my spritsail and finding I kept a better wind than you, took advantage in doing so. At 20 minutes past 3 I lost sight of your boat, and the ship getting very indistinct, I got very much alarmed for our safety. A little before 5 I perceived that the ship had tack'd and that she would weather the boat considerably. On this tack we took down our sail, and endeavoured to pull, but despair was painted in every countenance. We could scarcely keep the boat's head to the wind, so much had fear the effect of weakening us.

"We now endeavoured to hail her, making signals, and using most ridiculous gestures, like frantic men (in the midst of this tumult the sea was breaking over the boat so as to keep 2 men constantly bailing). A sudden commotion was seen aboard the ship, and in a few minutes they bore away and picked us up as soon as we got alongside. Lookouts were sent aloft to look for you and sail made in the hope of seeing or hearing something, and after cruising until 10 o'clock (when the storm was so severe) then we came to the conclusion you had foundered and hove the ship to under a treble reef'd main topsail. As soon as the gale abated we determined to search the island all round and in doing so have been amply rewarded for our labours, and thank the Almighty for His miraculous intervention in preserving us all so that not a hair of our heads has been injured. May I never forget Xmas day 1831."

Many plans were now suggested for our getting through the surf which I did not approve of, but being almost desperate from thirst and not fearing the consequences of losing the boat as before, I determined to hazard the launch. Having brought the boat to the beach, we put our stores and then set two men at their oars and peak'd three oars, the other 4 men launched the boat in the water as far as their knees and patiently awaited my signal for a start. After remaining in this situation about ten minutes, I waited for the last of three tremendous seas and as the third broke we made one simultaneous effort and just succeeded in clearing the beach before a successive wave broke which would have dashed us to atoms. The three boats anchor'd outside the surf watched our progress in breathless anxiety, and as the little barque skipt over the last breaker three cordial cheers revived our drooping spirits. The water keg and brandy bottle were instantly produced and a quart of weak mixture immediately administered.

This and a reasonable repast obtained from the boats quite refreshed us, and after a pull of 7 or 8 miles we reached the ship at 6.30 P.M. to the surprise of all hands who had entirely abandoned all idea of our safety.

Sunday Island was now most offensive after the drilling we had undergone; I therefore retraced my course to the Curtises and French Rock. On the 4th January we again lowered with success. I fastened first to a fish, which brought the whales to: the 3rd mate fastened, and then the 2nd mate, and the whales beginning to move in circles the other boats were afraid to fasten. The stricken fish after describing 4 or 5 circles with each other in which manœuvre we had very great difficulty to prevent our boats fouling, at a moment's notice the 2nd mate's fish and mine started off at a terrific speed. About 16 miles from the ship, my fish hove to and sounded; when down about 70 fms. the iron drew. The 2nd mate cut from his fish about 4 miles farther off. The 3rd mate killed his fish and towed it alongside.

On Sunday the 8th . . . at 2 P.M. saw the spout of a whale. In chasing came to the carcases of 2 dead fish slightly blown. On examination they proved to be the carcases of the whales wounded by us on the 4th, one fish having the irons on it with our ship's brand engraved. They lay about a quarter of a mile apart. We did not come near our indicator but proceeded to get the dead fish cut up. Hundreds of sharks and albatrosses disputed our claim. Of the latter we captured 30 or 40 for their feathers and killed a great number of sharks to the great annoyance of the carpenter, who had to sharpen each spade after killing or cutting a shark. The skin spoils the keen edge. These fish stowed down upwards of 6 tons of dark oil, worth £500.

On the 10th January we succeeded in killing another bull whale without accident. On the 20th being off Curtisses Island, I landed for the purpose of examination. I discovered the crater of a volcano still burning, a small lake of fresh water, also several boiling springs in full activity, in the vicinity of which I collected two buckets of sulphur. We also caught several fine fish. We continued cruising off these islands until the 25th January when I stretched to the southward for the coast of New Zealand. On the 3rd Feby., captured a sperm whale, and a sunfish. This latter I hoisted on board for close examination. This fish tried out 70 barrels.

On the 24th Feby., discovered a lad stowed away in the hold. The stowaway must have been there since the *Caroline* had left Sydney, about three and a half months previously. On cross examination he declared his name to be Joseph Harris, a prisoner of the Crown, assigned to a Mr. Robert Nichols of Goulbourne Street, Sydney. Having robbed his master of jewels, cash and notes to the amount of £100 and upwards, he had made away with all except a silver watch (which he put into my hands) and to escape punishment got secreted by some of the crew.

On the 25th, I was fortunate to secure a fish to-day after a chase of 7 hours. I sail'd on the fish to fasten, having distanced the other boats 3 miles, and before they could come near the shoal got restive and made off at full speed. The day's proceeding illustrates the beauty of perseverance in whale fishing. Had the boats kept anything near me we might have numbered 7 or 8 whales instead of one. Having fastened with the irons and rounded the shoal to, they came about my boat so very unpleasantly that I expected to be stove. A large cow whale was very solicitous to rub the irons out of the fish I was fastened to, that to get rid of her I imprudently threw my lance into her belly with all my strength. She only gave one shudder and turned on her side quite dead. It was this which caused the shoal to go off so rapidly and we also lost the dead cow, as my whale took off with the shoal and the boats were too distant to see her. I could not find her after I had killed my whale, it being late in the evening and I expect the carcase swam very low in the water.

We cruised from the French Rock to the East Cape of New Zealand and back to the Three Kings, from thence to Hokianga and back to French Rock. In the 3rd of March I bore

up the Bay of Islands to take in wood and water and refresh
the crew with fresh provisions. This at that time was a great
resort. Thirteen sail of whalers lay off Kororoideka Beach
and 4 at Trippona during our stay, which I made as brief as
possible. It was a beautiful afternoon when we approached
Torpena Point and as we closed with the land it fell calm, when
I ordered the five whale boats ahead to tow the ship as we
neared the anchorage of Kororoideka. Only one barque was
there. I ordered the lead to be kept going and to steer a close
berth for her. I hailed her.

"What ship? Where from and where bound? Capt's
name?" . . . Answer: "*Caroline*, from whaling bound to Hobarton, Smith. What ship is that?"

"*Caroline*, from whaling to Hobarton. Tregurtha."

"Not Tregurtha that was at Rangoon?"

"The same."

"I will come on board."

It turned out that our respective ships, the *Sulumany* and
Hashing, had been lashed alongside each other 3 months at
Rangoon . . . when we were chief matės and close friends, and
we now met as masters commanding two vessels belonging to
the same port, on the same pursuit and of the same name,
without either having the slightest idea of it.

Our meeting so opportunely enabled us to act together in
dealing with the natives, who were inclined to be very capricious, refusing permission to wood and water unless most
extravagantly paid in powder and blankets. A couple of old
tower muskets quieted their scruples. The women on the contrary were too familiar. Upwards of seventy swam off and
located themselves on board with the officers and crew, which
obliged me to turn some of them out. Their demands on the
bread cask becoming a nuisance to supply and a heavy drain
on our sea stock, I ordered the steward to put all hands on an
allowance of biscuit and casked all the loose bread so that it
could not be procured without my knowledge.

In about 5 weeks we completed our stock of wood, water,
and provisions, taking an ample supply of pigs, poultry and
vegetables, especially potatoes and pumpkins. These we got
in exchange for powder, tobacco, and slops. I also got a
young lad named Tommy, about 17, native of the Bay of
Islands.

On April 18th we took our departure for the Curtiss Rocks

again, but met no success during a month's cruise. We now
steered to the northward for Tougataboo and the Fiji Isles.
Here the currents were very rapid but we saw no whales. In
the latter end of May I sighted the Island of Rotumah.
Canoes coming off, I hove to for the purpose of trading with
the natives. In a canoe I observed a white man whom I invited to come on board. I found him to be Mr. Platt, late
master and owner of a schooner called the *Brisk* which he lost
at the entrance inside the reef at Wallisses Island. He related
to me a barbarous account of the massacre of the crew of the
barque *Oldham* there. He said he lost his vessel trying to get
in by not being able to back off the rocks, and the *Oldham*
would be worth getting as there was 60 tons of oil in her.

I agreed to take the master and the mate of the *Brisk* with
me and proceed direct to recapture the vessel. Having traded
a day with the natives for cocoanuts, bananas, fowls, etc., I
bore up for Wallis Island. We now prepared ourselves for a
conflict with the natives, firearms furnished up, and two brass
swivels foxed in the sterns of the spare whaleboats. The whaling gear was also subsidiary as lances. The wind being light
it was five days ere we sighted the land. I had arranged to
stand off and on until daylight when a sail appeared bearing
down upon us which proved to be the *Lebra*, sloop of war, that
had arrived two days previously. They had made an attempt
to pass through the reef, but were carried out again by the
tide, but the previous day had sent two armed boats' crews on
board the *Oldham*. They found the vessel about 5 miles inside
the reef moored off the native town, completely stripped to her
lower masts and cargo. A rupture ensued with the natives,
and from what I could learn several had been severely wounded
if not since dead. It was arranged that I should go in with the
Lebra on the following day, the 23rd of May.

As the evening came on we perceived that the natives had
set fire to the vessel, which burnt with great fierceness. It soon
became apparent that the fire had reached the oil from occasional outbursts of the flames during the night. On the following day we effected a passage in by taking advantage of
the flood tide. The *Lebra* and *Caroline* attained an anchorage
about 3½ miles inside the reef, but still full 2 miles from the
wreck, which was still burning afloat. Carpenters under an
armed force were sent to scuttle the vessel which was accom-

plished in about 3 fms. water. Some portion of the oil was eventually recovered.

We now endeavoured to effect amicable intercourse with the native chiefs. A boy of the *Oldham*, about 14 years of age, had been rescued by one of the females, being the only survivor from the miserable crew whose atrocious conduct to the native females on board had caused their murder. This boy after a day or two was brought on board the *Lebra* by the head chiefs, and an amicable meeting was arranged to chew the betel and drink cave to our renewed friendship. The following day about a dozen officers with 30 or 40 men armed repaired to the village where we were regaled with a mess stewed before us by four virgins, one of which was as beautiful a creature as I ever saw. Cook gives a full description of this ceremony at the Friendly Isles. Their huts were erected with great ingenuity and taste. The greater part of them were built from the masts of the *Oldham*, constructed in the following manner:—a pole of 20 feet high stood in the centre forming a circle of from 20 to 80 feet according to the size; other poles were driven about 8 feet from the ground, and distant from them other poles of 6 feet about 6 feet apart. The whole was covered in with beautiful mats and curtains of mats placed all round. These were drawn up at pleasure for air and light. In the centre a square was formed covered over with boards which constituted the private store, having access by a ladder. I was anxious to peep into these repositories to see their contents, but the natives were averse. I however got a peep at one, where I perceived harpoons and lances, canvas, biscuit and several other ship's stores. This was the secret of their refusal.

I now moved my vessel nearer the entrance for the purpose of getting to sea, but was foiled in my first attempt, as the flood tide setting in before I had cleared the strait, I had to throw all aback and drop out of the channel. About the 10th of June I succeeded in getting away, having secured a supply of cocoanuts from the grove on the reef. We now shaped our course for the Kings Mills group.

On the 3rd day we sighted an island not laid down in the charts. It was uninhabited. I accordingly lowered the boats and heaving the ship close to under its lee, proceeded on shore. We had no difficulty in approaching and as the bushes were covered with sea birds I fired several shots, before I was aware that the birds were unacquainted with man, and would allow us to approach quite near and handle them on the perch. This Island was about ten miles in circumference, extremely low, with only a few bushes and intersected by shallow lagoons, in which abounded reef sharks of from 4 to 6 feet long. In traversing through the water about knee deep these sharks rushed through your legs and leaped around you so as to cause considerable alarm. We shot several, but this did not prevent them constantly attacking. The reef shark of the South Seas is a distinct species of shark. From what I have seen they do not exceed 8 feet in length. Their fins and one end of the tail are tipped with black, while the body is of nearly a fawn colour. This renders them nearly invisible although lying in two feet water while they remain quiet, and the velocity of their motion when in pursuit can scarcely be followed by the eye. They were in the midst of us, through our legs and off like a burd flying.

Towards evening when we returned to the beach I found the tide receded so as to leave the reef dry ½ a mile or more, and we had no alternative but to pass the night or run a great risk of staving the boat. In the morning I found thousands of boatswain birds on their nests and contented myself by taking scarlet red feathers from their tails as they sat. A species of small rat was also very numerous, which were very busy on the reefs picking up what they could find. It was near the following day ere we got away as the tides rose and fell only once in the 24 hours. I observed the wreck of a large canoe but no mark of the island having ever been inhabited. The sea slug (Beche-du-Mer) and clams were abundant on the reefs and I procured some good specimens of coral. Sharks we could have killed in any quantity. They even ran ashore in pursuit of us, yet not one person was bitten by them although several were cut by their fins, and tail. It would answer taking possession of this place as a depot for shark fins and Beche-du-mer.

We now pursued our course for the Kings Mills group, the first of which we reached by the 20th of June. Here I adopted the following plan. Finding a strong current to the N.E. at sundown, I hauled close on the wind and worked to windward all night with a good look out to leeward. On the 22nd while working under the lee of an island almost level with the sea but some 20 miles in length, several canoes came off bringing women who were anxious to come on board. Their primitive costumes made me curious for a closer interview. It consisted of wet seaweed tied round the loins, the leaf hanging down to the knees. This forms nature's figleaf. The men wore a small band.

I continued off and on until the next day, when I understood some mother of pearl and turtleshell would come off to trade with. They only brought a very small quantity and in the afternoon several robberies were committed. One was the tin filler for the compasses, in endeavouring to regain possession of which one of the unfortunate natives was shot.

The following morning I was wakened about 3 A.M. by the copper grinding over the coral reef. By instantaneous exertion in wearing ship and crowding a press of canvas I carried the ship over it without injury. On the Line we fell in with a whale or two but these shoal whales were not like our Southern fish, 8 or 10 barrels of oil a fish being all they would yield, unless you got hold of an old bull. While fishing on the Line is a different employment to the Southern fishing. Here exposure to the sun and rain are very injurious. The water in general is so smooth and quiet that instead of a spout, black skin is reported, which is the whale or a pod of whales basking in the sun. In this case, the boats are lowered very quietly and with great caution. The oars are placed a-peak, and each man uses a paddle bought or bartered from the natives for the purpose of paddling near the fish ere the iron is thrown. The oars are seized for the purpose of retreat. In this manner when one fish is fastened to, if cows they will remain until you secure several, but if bulls they are off instanter.

In July we proceeded to Pleasant Island, which well deserves this name. The natives came off freely, bringing cocoanuts and a kind of herring which they grow in ponds for the purpose of trade. They told me that they got the spawn off the reefs and threw it into sundry salt water ponds in the interior where the young fish came forth, when they fed them with chewed cocoanut until fit to sell. When full grown they were larger than a herring. I purchased several hundreds from them, had them opened and salted and dried and kept them on board nearly a year It was here we observed a shoal of small fish attached to the ship which never left her. In a calm they swam alongside and darted at any object that came near. I rigged a pinhook and succeeded in catching 4 or 5 very much resembling a shad. Two or three having dropt off the hook they bit no more. I now made a net on a bucket hoop, and slinging a grating over the stern by the assistance of a spade pole, we caught as many as we required at any time the ship was moving 4 or 5 knots as they then hovered near the rudder. This continued 3 or 4 months until they grew 8 inches long, and 3 were enough for a meal, when they suddenly disappeared.

We obtained several whales about this island but one old bull gave us a drubbing. We had to cut from him with the loss of 4 lines, irons and several stopwaters after being fast 8 hours without being able to use a lance, five boats down, three loose. He dodged us so effectually we could not get near to him. I had an adventure here with the *Toward Castle*, Capt. Bren. We had lowered after whales and Bren was fast. I pulled up and fastened to a loose fish close by. Bren accused me of fastening to his fish. Angry words passed when suddenly his whale darted ahead and across mine causing his boat to pass nearly athwart ours. We each killed our fish.

The latter end of July I steered to look out for Shank's Island, stated as "doubtful" in the charts. I could not discover it although reported several times from the crow's nest. Returning back to Pleasant Island in September we departed for Melanthe and that group, with the intention of passing to the northward if the search was successful. We here met with several vessels cruising whose success was on a par with our own. They were all from Sydney, the *Proteus*, *Lynx*, *Lyndsays*, *Wolf*, *Lady Blackwood* and several others.

One day I had fastened to a young bull whale which sounded and whilst we were anxiously looking out for him, I felt the boat lifted out of the water. He had got us on his back with the hump nearly through our garboard streak. On finding the weight he gradually sank again and rose about 50 yards from the boat. Although we closed the aperture with shirts, our boat filled rapidly. No other boat being near us, and the whale taking off, for our own safety I very reluctantly cut him adrift. With 4 baling and two pulling we reached the ship at sunset. This was off *Guadalcanar*. I saw the rocks under our bottom several times while cruising here. The water is extremely clear. I also landed on the island in these Straits. The appearance of the natives is very much against them. Their canoes were some of them of great size, carrying from 60 to 70 men. On the prow they have some carved figure standing from 15 to 20 feet from the water. They were constructed from the trunk of one large tree, hollowed out. At the sides a plank was laid on its edge and sewn with fibres of bark very securely, the whole pitched over with a resinous gum. These large canoes very seldom leaked; at least I never saw any baling. They were propelled by paddles on each side, two natives at each end steering. They did not require to turn, but would go either end first if required. A platform was usually raised at one end for the Chief. I never allowed them to come alongside, but ordered them astern, yet they had little to trade except tortoise-shell and cocoanuts.

On Christmas Day we were 4 sail in company, and I invited the Captains to spend the day. There was a fine fresh breeze, and in the morning a pod of whales hove in sight. They were very wild. I could not get near them, but as they bore to leeward I determined to sail one down. I set my sail and had stood up to fasten when the whale fluked and we lost him. In the afternoon we all met. The other Captains who had witnessed my morning's trick, wished me joy of my lucky escape, if I had fastened they said I must have been stove. We dined and were smoking our pipes very quietly, when crack went a pistol in my cabin with the following exclamation, "Missed him! No, winged him, by G—d!"

We rushed in expecting to see a corpse. There was Capt. N—d on his back on my bed, bursting his sides with laughing. A cockroach had been crawling on the beam, and he had taken one of my pistols and fired it. The ball flattened and fell on his breast.

That evening each master shaped his own course, and we parted. We cruised through the group with very little success, and passing down by the Solomons Archipelago on the east side, I cruised off New Ireland about a fortnight. We lowered several times after whales but were unsuccessful.

One day when our boats were near the shore we observed the natives pursuing a man, who threw himself into the sea, and although hotly pressed succeeded in swimming to our boats, which took him on board. His story ran that he and another seaman had been left behind by the vessel they belonged to about 5 weeks previous, that the natives had murdered his comrade, and seeing our boats he had made a desperate effort to escape. His name was Black, a natural son born in the West Indies of Dr. Black of Edinburgh. He became very useful on board as a fancy carver. A few days afterwards I took two boats into St. Mary's Bay to trade with the natives. I took good grapnels which we threw out 100 fms. from the shore to haul the boats into deep water should the natives prove treacherous.

It was well we did so, as they would have murdered us all. On our approaching the shore, the natives came down in numbers. We had the boats near each other and two men on the line, one with a musket and two pushing the boat in. They were all in a state of nudity. Some brought fowls, some cocoanuts, and others tropical fruit and vegetables. We had commenced to barter, when a gang of naked women came to the beach and by lascivious actions invited us on shore. The chief mate called to me that he did not like their actions and be on my guard. I accordingly got the tomahawk. Suddenly a yell was made and 8 or 10 men tried to haul the boats on shore. Seeing their plan, I ordered the men to swing their oars round. At the same time I rushed forward, tapping the hands of all those who had hold of the boat, and the others hauling on the rope. To their great chagrin we slid from their clutches. Stones began to fly and I could see the bows coming down. We pulled off rapidly but not before a discharge of arrows was sent after us. They did not strike any person. There were about 200 natives assembled, and they evidently contemplated our capture. We did not fire at them, but had any person been injured, I should have astonished them with our 12 muskets laden with swanshot.

Cruising off Cape St. Mary one afternoon we sighted a sail standing towards us. As we approached each other we discovered each vessel had a different wind. We passed, hailed, and exchanged news. In a minute we exchanged winds, and sailed from each other. This was a phenomena I had never before witnessed; neither have I since.

In the middle of June I stood for Gowna Harbour to wood and water. This I found by far the most commodious place for the purpose I have ever seen. We found the *Lady Blackwood* moored. I ran my ship in and let go my anchor in 6 fms., then ran a warp on shore and moored to the Trees, my stern being in 3 fms. completely landlocked. Natives were very scarce and I did not encourage them. A mountain stream ran down about two hundred yards distant. Wood we could cut ad libitum. I took the boat well armed to a river about 24 miles distant. There is good anchorage inside the island and 4 fms. water at the entrance. I pulled about a mile up, but was cautious of the natives. The Trees were magnificent. I never had seen such splendid straight sticks for masts, and the water perfectly clear and transparent.

Having completed our refreshments, I again bent my voyage by Guadalcanar, Bougainville's Group, Gorgia, and Malanthe; thence to Mallicole and Santa Cruz. When near the volcano I obtained three whales. I cruised round this island whose natives vied with each other in friendly trading with us, although hostile to each other on shore. It was amusing as the ship approached a projecting point to see the 40 or 50 canoes who were trading push off, the warrior standing in the centre with his bow ready. Scarcely are they half a mile distant ere you perceive a similar fleet issuing from beyond the point prepared to fight or fly, making for the vessel to barter their goods. They brought off nuts from Volcano Island, yams, cocoanuts, shells and all description of war implements. These they exchanged for iron hoop, gimlets, nails, mirrors, and various coloured beads and nicknacks. There was an eruption of the volcano one evening which covered our decks some inches deep in ashes. The lava ran down a fiery stream, illuminating the heavens bright enough to read. It only continued the one night.

On getting near Mallicole, I felt very anxious as the charts were imperfect and the currents rapid. One afternoon when 7 or 8 leagues from the land, I was surprised to see two small canoes making for us. On approaching the ship, they held up a fiery oakum wig and effigy of a man and shouted "Peter, Peter." I exchanged for these articles and sent them away contented but it was some days before I acquired a clue to their what appeared to me strange conduct. I had a work of Dillon's voyage in search of La Perouse, and this was the island where the unfortunate navigator was shipwrecked and for which discovery he became Sir Peter Dillon. The natives of Mallicola had dubbed him Peter and cherished his memory by ochr'd beard and wig.

I now made the attempt to pass through Banks Islands and get to the northward of New Caledonia, but I found these islands so very little known and imperfectly described that I was glad to avail myself of a fair wind and run to the southward. I passed twice between two of these islands keeping the lead going and obtaining ground occasionally at 20 fms. I observed a remarkable fall of water on the southern island, and one evening when about 4 miles from the shore, the sailors were dancing to the fiddle, a naked savage popped his head out of the forechains. I had him brought aft and treated kindly. We hoisted in his catemarian and gave him a blanket to lie down. After sauntering about for an hour he suddenly jumped overboard and struck out for the shore.

The weather remained fine. About 3 in the morning we observed several fires lighted on the shore, which we expected was a signal from our late visitor. On the following day it came to blow dead on the shore. Standing to the southward late in the evening, land was reported extending far on the weather bow. This was unknown land to me. The island was not more than six miles under our lee, and a very stormy night. I crowded a press of sail and wore ship at midnight. As the dawn broke and the sky cleared we were near enough to see the surf breaking. This determined me to get to the southward. To the great joy of all hands the order was given to bear up and run through to the Hebrides. Passing Aurora Island on the starboard hand and having sighted the Isle of Pines off New Caledonia, I steered for Norfolk Island, in the neighbourhood of which I got a large whale.

I cruised off and on the island three weeks, sighting it occasionally, and then bore up for the Bay of Islands where we arrived in March 1833. I found upwards of 20 sail of whalers in port refitting and recruiting the health of their crews. This occasioned much desertion among the unfortunate and discontented, which was encouraged by a native Chief called Bumurray, or Beaumurrey, who had a Pa or fort up the river strongly situated at the junction of two branches and commanded by a Dutchman named Johnson. A meeting of masters was called on board my ship to consider what steps we should take in this matter. A complaint was put in by the master of the Achilles barque, lying at Tippoonah, that 6 men had taken a whaleboat to Beaumurray's Pa where he kept the men and boat and refused to give up either one or the other. It was agreed and after dinner all the masters would proceed to the Pa and remonstrate with Beaumurray, but I could only persuade two to accompany me. I took two boats fully-manned and proceeded to the Pa. The Chief was absent with all his warriors on a marauding excursion, leaving the Pa and fort to a chief named Mayflower and the Dutchman called Johnson. We walked round the place and were leisurely re-

turning to the boats when Mr. Waddell, a young Irish gentleman who belonged to my crew and accompanied me said
"There is Mayflower; you and I can make a prisoner of him
and carry him on board as a hostage."

We accordingly walked up to him, and planting ourselves
on either side we partly by persuasion and partly by force
conducted him to the boats, but here not a fellow would leave
the boat to assist us in securing him. Whilst we were struggling another New Zealander came running with a long club
at which Waddell pulled out a pistol with a spring bayonet,
but in doing so he loosened his hold of Mayflower, who making
a spring left the waistband of his trousers in my hand and
started off for the fort. I instantly shoved off and pulled
away, but the alarm was given and ere we had made 100
yards they began to pepper us with ball. I pick'd up my
double barrell'd gun but merely as a threat, we having been
the aggressors. The balls passed through the boat between
my legs, but not an individual was injured.

Having got beyond the musquet range, we lay on our oars
a minute or two, when bang came a 3 pounder from the Dutchman, which fell outside the boats about 50 yards. Laying
out at the oars ere he could reload we were beyond range of
the fort. My crew were highly indignant and wished me to
carry the vessel abreast the fort and demolish it. I took my
revenge in a different manner. Beaumurray prided himself
on having a very fast whale boat, so I challenged to pull two
of my whale boats against her for a wager. This was accepted. The boats pulled and we beat him hollow by about
half a mile in a race of 4 miles. We became fast friends.

Having recruited the health of the crew and laid down a
sea stock of potatoes and other vegetables, with a plentiful
supply of firewood and water, I turned our ship's head in a
new direction. On the 12th of April I left the Bay of Islands
and directed our course towards the coast of Australia near
Moreton Bay. We remained cruising between Cato's Reef
and Mount Warning from May to the beginning of July, when
the weather became tempestuous and I moved towards Howe's
Island. We had very good success from Cat's Reef towards
Sandy Cape and had my crew exerted themselves we ought
to have secured 200 tons of sperm oil, but the spirit of in-
subordination had got hold of my chief officer, he having become jealous of my acting on my own judgment in securing

the whales and pursuing them. He had given himself up to drink and I had to reprove him more than once. The consequence was that he managed to lose his lines and harpoons and we the whales.

I had a most singular adventure here on the 26th May. We had killed two large lone or single male fish on the 25th and on the morning of the 26th, whilst employed cutting these in, several spouts were seen by the lookout. I ordered the chief mate and 5th boat to lower and go in pursuit. About 9 o'clock A.M. they were observed to fasten and were soon lost sight of from the masthead, which had taken their bearings. At 1 P.M. having taken one fish in and cut off the other, I lowered my boat and proceeded in the direction of their boat. I left orders that as soon as they had rolled the body in, the 3rd mate's boat was to follow us. We pulled about 9 miles from the ship and lay on our oars for a look round, when we perceived a large whale spouting about a mile from us. I determined on attacking him, and on his next rising we fastened at about his 4th spouting. He did not sink for more than a minute and I was dancing with rage thinking my boat steerer had darted a flat iron. I had thrown the turns off the loggerheads when the line began to run out having taken a turn round my leg and was dragging me forward very rapidly. My crew seized the line and holding it fast a few seconds, enabled me to disengage myself and get my turns on again, when the whale sounded rapidly and took out 180 fms. ere I could bring him up. I, however, succeeded in planting two or three deep lance wounds which enabled us to get the line in, and I killed him in less than an hour. The 3rd mate's boat came to assist me, followed by the 2nd, but going on the fish to windward he fluked and cut her nearly in two, which employed the other boat to pick them up and take them to the ship ere he could return to me, by which time I was towing my dead whale. At 4 P.M. the other two boats came to our assistance having lost their lines and harpoons, and a very large whale into the bargain.

From this date our voyage ceased, for although we saw plenty of whales they killed no more and I was determined not to go in a boat again to risk my life for the benefit of such ungrateful rascals. Cruising gradually to the southward we saw a great many large lone whales, but there was always an excuse and having about 140 tons on board I con-

TASMANIAN CAPE HORN TRADER, *HELEN*, IN HARD WEATHER

THE LAST OF THE HOBART WHALERS BEING TOWED TO SEA, *CIRCA* 1899

sidered I had better take care of that on the ship as there was a headsman shipped to head my boat whenever I thought proper to send him. We cruised about from Latitude 23 degrees S. to 25 degrees 30′ S., sometimes in sight of Mount Warning, at other times 200 miles from the land, but whales became scarce, and the weather unsettled. Towards the latter end of June I edged to the southward for Howe's Island. While cruising here a large whale baffled all our attempts to fasten to him. I hoisted my boats up and pursued him with the ship before the wind. Having passed him I dropt the boat at equal distances for his next rising. He rose in the middle of them and they did not succeed in fastening. This decided me to close the voyage.

Two days after we experienced a very gale from the S.E. with which I steered for Tasmania, but on the 3rd day it slopped round suddenly from N.W. and blew a hurricane. I had now to heave the ship to, and for safety of position with her head to the N.E. I could not shew a sail to it, but lay to with a bolt of No. 1 canvass secured in the mizzen rigging wrapped round by lines, for about 12 hours. The wind then moderated and I steered for Flinders Island, Bass Straits. On making land, the weather appeared very cold after our sojourn in the torrid zone. On the following day spouts were seen and lowering the boats the Chief and 3rd mates fastened to and killed a very large bull right whale, but it being a dry skin he sank so fast that both the boats were compelled to cut their lines to prevent being pulled under. Thus I lost my fish and four harpoons, which induced me to make as straight a course for Hobarton as weather and winds permitted.

At this period the only guide to the entrance of the River Derwent was a feeble lanthorn on the Iron Pot, but it being a very fine day after rounding Cape Pillar I pushed on towards Bruni Island as the light variable winds permitted. After dark several fires sprang up in different places, which on nearing the land I could plainly see were whaling parties trying out their fish. The wind changing from the westward I was standing on the port tack going about 4 knots when we discovered a light ahead. It was presently extinguished and a voice hailed "Ship ahoy, are you agoing to run your boom into our Iron Pot?"

We however luffed and weathered the danger, the said voice

proceeding from a man on a ladder who was endeavouring to trim the lanthorn. Although we were entire strangers and had a signal flying no pilot came near until the ship had passed Sandy Point. I was only too glad to give him charge after a good scold for his tardiness, as I was ready to drop from fatigue, having been on my legs 36 hours.

On arrival I found the principal owners had failed, which would eventually close my agreement in the whaling business. I accordingly arranged to load and command the ship to London. I directly commenced discharging the cargo for the purpose of examining and coopering the oil for the voyage and overhauling the ship. The cargo being discharged on the new wharf turned out 133 tons of sperm oil.

CHAPTER XV

THE ADVENTURE OF THE "ESSEX"

IN the very early days of Hobart, and indeed during most of that period in which the far southern city was dependent upon the ships of sails for its communications, ships came into the port now and again with wonderful stories of the sea and extraordinary adventures to relate. But generally the newspapers of the day were too interested in quarreling with each other and whatever government there might happen to be to trouble much about things that really were interesting, and to discover details of the most extraordinary incidents now is difficult indeed.   Fortunately, however, a full account is preserved of one of the most extraordinary of them—so unusual a yarn that it is almost beyond belief.   But it is true enough.

Some time in 1821 the ship *Surry*, Captain Raine, arrived at the port of Hobart on the termination of a voyage from Valparaiso, and reported having relieved three castaways from the American whaling ship *Essex* whose story was an extraordinary one.   The *Essex* was a ship which really did meet Moby Dick, and Moby Dick—or Moby Dick's counterpart in real life—attacked her and sank her, thousands of miles from the nearest land.   Her crew had to take to the boats, in one of which the survivors were sixty days at sea before they were saved, and in the other they were *ninety* days!   The horrors of their sufferings are almost indescribable; in one boat they fell to eating each other, and when at last the boat was found only the captain of the *Essex* and a boy survived.   The other came upon a barren island where, despite its barrenness, three of the survivors preferred to remain rather than to go on in the boat,

and it was these three the *Surry* found.   One's particulars
are from an article on the subject written by J. E. Calder,
in the Hobart *Mercury* of June 7th, 1873.

The *Surry*, he writes, lay at Valparaiso in March, 1821,
when there came into port an American whale ship having on
board two persons whom they had rescued from an open boat
in which they had been at sea, in the most shocking state of
suffering, for the long period of sixty days, before they were
picked up.   These two unfortunate persons were George Pollard, master of the ship *Essex*, and a boy of the crew of the
vessel, that had been wrecked through an accident so extraordinary that belief would be refused to the story they told had
it not been confirmed exactly by the narrative of three others
of the sufferers of this most marvellous wreck, whom the
humane Captain Raine afterwards released from a desert rock
in the Pacific and carried on with him in the *Surry*.   Some
of the *Essex* men, who belonged to the same boat from which
these three had landed, were also rescued after being *ninety*
days at sea, and told the selfsame tale of distress as the rest.

The ship *Essex* sailed from the island of Nantucket, Mass-
achusetts, on August 19th, 1819.   She was registered two
hundred and sixty tons, the master being George Pollard.
She was a whaling ship, bound for the fishing grounds of the
South Seas.   She was provisioned for a long cruise, as usual
in American ships bound for the fisheries.   At fifteen months
out she had taken between seven and eight hundred barrels
of oil, and at the time of the accident that destroyed her was
in 47 degrees of south latitude and 118 degrees east of Green-
wich, in other words, about 1,150 miles to the west (but a
little to the southward) of Tasmania.

The morning of November 13th, 1820, was one of promise
and pleasurable excitement to all on board, for the ship was
then sailing amidst a vast school of whales that were spouting
all round her.   All her boats were lowered and in chase, and
all were fastened before noon, and everything at this moment
seemed hopeful of success.   About noon, however, an accident
happened to one of the boats, the chief mate's, which was
struck by the whale he was fast to and so badly stove that
he was forced to cut and pull back to the *Essex*, the fish escaping, of course.   The accident being seen by the men of the
ship, who were all anxiously watching the chase, she bore

down to her relief and boat and crew were all got safely,
though none too soundly, aboard. The boats of the captain
and second officer were still fast, and had well near killed,
when they saw, almost simultaneously, the ship herself heel
over and fall on her beam ends.

They could scarcely believe what they actually saw and
doubted for some moments the evidence of their senses; for
what was there that would make the ship behave so? They
knew that she could not have struck, for the sea was there
blue and near bottomless; they knew that the cargo could
not have shifted, for it was well stowed and lashed down. And
then there was no wind to make the vessel roll and shift it,
even if that had been possible. But there their ship lay, a
helpless wreck before them, without visible cause.

The day was fine, the wind steady, and the water as still
and unbroken as it ever is upon a good day at sea. With no
thought of the real cause of so strange a calamity, they cut
at once from the fish they were fast to and pulled rapidly
alongside, both to see what was the matter and to give assistance to the overturned ship. To their intense amazement
they found that she had already filled; she had not gone over
on her beam ends, but she had been stove and was sinking!
What could have caused so inexplicable an occurrence? What
could possibly have happened? They did not know. They
saw that the ship was low and heavy in the water and were
amazed that she had not already sunk; probably the force
of the airtight empty casks piled in her hold was keeping
her up.

Pollard was on her deck in a moment and, without stopping
to enquire into the cause of the accident, gave orders to cut
away all the masts immediately and, axe in hand, cut through
the standing rigging himself to clear the wreckage from the
deck. As soon as this was done the vessel slowly righted again,
but her hull was found to be as hopelessly damaged as if she
had received a broadside from a line-of-battle ship. When
he had time for inquiry, Captain Pollard found that it was
caused by an accident without precedent in the annals of
whale fishery, and of which, as far as is known, there has been
no subsequent example.

A little after the damaged boat of the chief officer was
taken aboard, a sperm whale that is described as of very
unusual size, rose near to the ship, and from some inexplicable

impulse of the moment, attacked the vessel itself, and dashing savagely at her with extraordinary force, dealt her such a blow as knocked away a portion of her false keel just abreast of the main channels. The ship fairly reeled under the shock, but was not fatally damaged by it. The fish then lay along-side for some minutes, probably stunned herself after the vio-lent force of the impact. After a while, however—so it is reported in all the accounts I copy from—she renewed the attack, trying to bite through the planking of the ship's bows as fish of this species have so often smashed up the boats of our own port. But as nothing came of this style of assault she renewed the onslaught in the manner in which she had begun it. She now dived under the vessel, but this time missed her mark and came up again on the other side. Swimming under the stern she turned and went ahead of the ship about a quarter of a mile, the seamen now trusting that they had seen the last of her. But this hope was of momentary dura-tion only, for the strange occurrences of this eventful day were not yet half over.

The vessel was at this time under easy speed, about five knots, when the furious monster turned upon her, as if deter-mined to finish her before leaving her. On she came again, straight at the *Essex's* bows, more madly than at first; she struck the ship under the catshead with such violence that the men on board, who were anxiously watching her, fell every one of them just as if they had been shot through, or as if the ship had been knocked from under them, as indeed she was.

The crash was tremendous, the bow planking giving way to the blow like matchwood, and such was the force of the contact that it was solemnly declared by all on board that for a moment or so "the vessel had sternway at the rate of three or four knots," while the ship's bows were momentarily so lifted up out of the water that the sea rushed in at the cabin ports, which were open.

The collision was probably as fatal to the fish as it was to the ship, for she was seen no more afterwards. But her work was finished, and the ill-starred *Essex* done for as com-pletely as if she had been flung headlong on a rock. She filled, of course, and then fell over.

It would be useless to attempt to describe the feelings of the crew that ensued on so terrible a calamity, but that the change of sensation from hopefulness to bitter despair was

terrible beyond expression will readily be understood. But it
has been truly remarked by one of the greatest writers of
modern times that men of the profession of these hardy fellows
bear up under calamity with greater equanimity than others
do, and that under no ordinary accumulation of misfortune
are they as hopelessly prostrated as we are. And thus it was
with the crew of the *Essex*.

With not the slightest chance of saving the water-logged
vessel, and with almost as little of saving themselves, they
stuck by her for three whole days, not in a state of despond-
ing inactivity, but in preparing for a dreary boat voyage
across the illimitable ocean, and in securing such provisions
as they could to support it. From the accident that had
happened to the chief officer's boat just before the fatal assault on the ship, only two others were serviceable for sea,
and in the natural confusion that followed such an unheard-
of attack, all the boat sails seemed to have been lost, so that
they were unprepared at the moment for a long ocean voyage.
But the weather continuing pretty moderate, they employed
themselves variously about the derelict ship, some in making
new boat sails, others in getting together what they could to
support life at sea, and one or two always on the lookout
from dawn to day-close for a passing sail, if Fortune directed
one hitherward, but the Fates ordered it otherwise and no
relief came to them.

The food supply of the boat's crews was scant enough at
best, for in the condition of the ship then very little could
be got at, and nothing like enough to keep life from going
out altogether, if the voyage proved a protracted one as
seemed very likely. In those days the southern seas were
little frequented by ships and the nearest land of relief was
Tasmania. From this they were separated by an expanse of
water of nearly 400 leagues and they had no chance of reaching it despite the fact that the permanent winds of those latitudes were westerly. It was summer in the high south then,
and the winds were easterly. Their only hope of salvation
lay in sailing for higher latitudes in which they knew the
whale ships of their countrymen were at work. To this course
they all agreed, and at the beginning of the fourth day after
the accident they quitted the still floating wreck, and stood
away to the south with the wind a little before the beam. To
this circumstance, as well as being among ocean currents un-

favourable to their course, it must have been due that they
made more lee than headway and thus missed the ground where
they had hoped to meet with some ship of the American whaling fleet. After this misadventure, I presume they headed the
boats for the South American coasts though this is not stated,
at least in direct terms, in any of the published accounts of
this voyage of disaster.

The little stock of provisions they had managed to obtain
from the derelict before they left her were obtained with great
difficulty by scuttling the deck just over the provision room,
and through this breach a small quantity of damaged supplies
were fished up. It was hardly enough to support the crews
for a week, much less for the sixty or ninety days the boats were
at sea before they were picked up.

Of the proceeding of the boat that was the longest at sea
not much has been published, at least in English or Colonial
works; and only after a dreary voyage of two months, or
something very like it, she reached the dreary islet from which
the excellent Captain Raine rescued the three poor sufferers
whom he brought on with him in the *Surry*. But as it does
not appear that her crew hungered quite in the same degree
as Pollard's people did, it must be believed that after separating from their companions they were fortunate enough to
take either birds or fish on their passage, that enabled them
to support existence—a very wretched one—without having
recourse to the dreadful expedients that the other crew were
compelled to resort to, that some of them at least might be
saved from death by starvation. After resting for a week
upon this miserable rock that produced almost nothing to
sustain existence, the bulk of her never despairing crew pursued their cheerless voyage, leaving the three whom Raine
afterwards released from their Promethean captivity, who had
preferred to perish ashore rather than take another chance
for life in the chief officer's boat. The boat was eventually
picked up by a passing whaler, *ninety* days after the *Essex*
had been abandoned.

From the day on which the boat voyage commenced, the
people of both crews were put on short allowance, two or
three ounces of damaged bread and a mere driblet of water
being the scale at which the daily ration to each person was
fixed. But even at this reduced rate of supply they could
not hope to hold out long, as the entire stock of provisions

aboard the two boats was not sufficient to serve them for more than a very few days, or a fortnight at most, at the end of which time all their provisions were exhausted. The two boats kept together for some space but eventually parted, though in what circumstances I cannot say as the cause has not transpired. But it most probably occurred in the dark.

The effects of hunger and protracted exposure were soon visible enough in the looks of the men who were along with Pollard, producing a ghastly sharpness of feature and general attenuation such as we see in the disease called Atrophy, or *wasting away* of the body, which contrasted painfully with their healthy vitality of a few weeks before. This debility, acting sympathetically on their minds—especially of the weakest—induced a sensation of despondence that was almost as distressing as starvation itself. Their anxiety to be released from this state of endurance was so intense as even to prevent them getting anything like sufficient rest, if indeed this were possible in a boat in high southern latitudes; and weakened as they were from cold and fasting, few of them sought repose during the long hours of daylight (for the days were long down there) so long as they lasted, but sat up watching the dreary expanse of the horizon in the faint hope of discovering a sail. But day after day passed, and none was seen. . . . Their sufferings from hunger grew keener and more intolerable every hour until they could be endured no longer, and the conviction gained ground that something must be done to prevent the skeleton crew from perishing one and all from starvation.

And so the horrible proposal was at length made and assented to, that some one of them should die to support the lives of the rest. This dreadful expedient was at last put into action, and as usual in such cases the selection was made by the drawing of lots. The name of the victim has not been recorded, nor the manner in which they dispatched him. Nor is it necessary to prolong the account of his death which in their unfortunate circumstances may have been preferable to a continuance of life, for the mind may be reduced by extreme bodily suffering to such a state of apathy and prostration as to cease to value existence. Of this the early annals of this very Tasmania of ours have furnished manifold examples.

It would be a revolting task to describe the sickening details that followed their first sacrifice, and none too pleasant

a one to describe the natural processes by which men who
are neither naturally depraved or cruel may, under protracted
and hopelessly endless suffering, become as remorseless as wild
beasts, and in whom every sentiment unconnected with self-
preservation is temporarily extinguished.   Thus it was with
these unhappy men.   Their natural sympathies were dead or
dormant and if they looked upon each other at all through
these ghastly days it was only when contemplating another
sacrifice. . . . The fearful process of lot-drawing was soon
repeated, and so frequently afterwards by the crew that they
became, at length, cruel and callous from habit.   In this manner, and from being so long at sea, four-fifths of their number
were destroyed.

At the morning of the 60th day of their boat voyage none
remained alive but Captain Pollard and a boy.   On that morning lots were again prepared and drawn, the fatal one falling
to the boy, but for this once no execution was necessary, for
relief came.   The sacrifice was stayed by the appearance of
a sail above an horizon that had not shown one for two months,
and the survivors managing to attract her attention, they
were rescued.   The ship (the name is not preserved) was an
American whaler bound to Valparaiso, and it was from the
captain of this vessel, as well as from Pollard himself, that
Raine received particulars of the loss of the *Essex* which he
afterwards made public.

Valparaiso was then a place of resort for American whalers,
and it so chanced that the ship which had picked up the other
boat of the *Essex* had also put into that port a little before,
bringing the intelligence that three of that vessel were—if
still living—on one of the Pacific Islands.   On March 10th
Captain Raine took the *Surry* to sea from Valparaiso, bound
across the Pacific, and on April 5th he came up with the
island.   There he found the three in a fearful state of emaciation—"little better than skeletons in trousers"—and was able,
despite a heavy surf and other difficulties, to take them aboard
the *Surry*.   They were in the last stage of emaciation that
precedes death by starvation, and so enfeebled that they could
scarcely speak.   Yet they felt some elation at the suddenness
of their relief and, says Raine, directly they found themselves
in the boat "each devoutly expressed his gratitude to that
Benign Being who had so providentially preserved them from
sharing in the destruction to which their unhappy shipmates

had fallen victims." They were ultimately restored to health, and their names were Thames Chappell, William Wright, and Seth Weeks.

It is all indeed a remarkable story, and maybe the boat voyage is even more remarkable than the sinking of the *Essex* by the whale.

BOOK IV

CLIPPERS, AND LATER DAYS

CHAPTER XVI

THE HOBART CLIPPER SHIPS

BECAUSE of the difficulty of obtaining shipping, and the high freights charged when ships were obtainable, quite early the colonists of Tasmania decided that if they were to prosper they would have to build ships for themselves. Having made the decision they proceeded to put it into effect, and before long they built ships so well that practically the whole of the regular Hobart-London trade—considerable in those days—was carried on in Hobart-built and Hobart-owned square-riggers.

The banks of the Derwent were ideal for shipbuilding; excellent timber abounded both for ribs and for planking, and skilled labor was readily available. In the very early days design does not appear to have mattered much, and if most of these old ships wandered along at an average speed of about three or four knots that was all that was required of them. They were deep, bluff-bowed, and homely. They carried small sail plans and big crews. Their masters were in the habit of putting into port—any port—upon the slightest pretext, and nobody seems to have objected to the practice. Every ship had some passenger accommodation, of a kind, and there was always use for it. They sometimes carried their own cow on deck, and always had pigs, sheep and fowls. They were high in the sides, buoyant, dry, and ugly. They sailed long voyages and took a long time; nobody ever looked for quick passages. They never lost anything over the side and were rarely dismasted. And they generally managed to earn good enough profits for their owners, and the increasing prosperity of

Tasmanian trade—the whale oil export, the wool, the wheat, and later, minerals—gave a soundness and steadiness to the colonial shipbuilding industry which no one imagined could be taken away from it.

So the years passed, with a steady improvement in design; whalers were built of the same old homely pattern, but the regular traders had now to be fast. Shipowners brought old clippers to the port, and those who stuck to the local product demanded more and greater speed. It was always given them; in the early 70's splendid, beautiful little barques first felt the kiss of blue water upon the Derwent's broad deep, lovely little vessels that caused highly appreciative comment in a London which had previously held only contempt for these "axman's jobs." Indeed, for many years the British shipowners and shipbuilders never lost a chance of belittling and harming, if they could, the colonial shipbuilders. Their ships were referred to always contemptuously as "colonial barques" or "colonial ships," as if the "colonial" were part of the rig. They were not barques or full-rigged ships, or brigs or schooners; they were colonial barques, and as such held to be vastly inferior to the true English product.

Harassing restrictions and provoking discriminations were made against them; on her first arrival in London after a fast passage from Hobart, the "colonial barque," *Harriet McGregor*, was forced to strip all her first-class copper and to use, instead, a very inferior metal which soon hung from her bottom in strips, though even that could not take her sprightliness and grace from her. She was classed for five years less than she would have been had she been built half as soundly in an English port, and the compulsory stripping of her copper was not the only vexing move that was made against her. And yet in the end her excellence prevailed, and her grace of line shone through all the scowls of the shipbuilders upon her, until the tiny "bluegum battler" came to be affectionately

A 1926 NORWEGIAN WHALING EXPEDITION ALONGSIDE IN
HOBART, BOUND FOR ANTARCTICA

THE NORWEGIAN *N. T. NIELSEN-ALONSO* SETS OUT FROM
HOBART FOR THE ROSS SEA ON THE SAME EXPEDITION

THE GHOST OF A VANISHED PAST, PHOTOGRAPHED AT KING ISLAND, TASMANIA: THERE WERE MANY SUCH WRECKS

known as the yacht of the India Docks. Her goings and comings were so regular, her lines were so taking to the sailor's eye and her rigging so uniformly well cared for, and she was always so neat and trim, that it was not to be wondered at that even in the world's greatest port she came to be looked upon as a little yacht rather than as a humdrum regular Cape Horn trader.

Tasmania is, of course, an island. As such it had a need of ships, and it bred sailors. It had to build ships; it bred the sailors naturally. Its first-born were born into the sea air—not a cold and clammy sea air, but fresh and healthy. Settlement was around the coastline first, naturally, and the early inhabitants looked upon ships and shipping as one of the most important factors in their lives. The very first convicts were first turned to shipbuilding, at Macquarie Harbour, and made a good job of it—here in this wilderness upon the west coast of Tasmania many a deepwater man and coastal trader was launched, during the few years the place was used as a convict settlement. Here the barque *William the Fourth* (later a well-known Hobart whaler) was constructed from Huon pine and bluegum; the brigs *Derwent, Tamar, Isabella, Adelaide* and *Frederick* (of pirate repute) ; the schooners *Penelope, Shannon, Badger, Kangaroo, Industry, Sorell* and *Despatch;* the sloop *Opossum;* the cutters *Charlotte, Clyde* and *Shamrock*—all these arose from the curses of tired convicts, the excellence of Tasmanian timbers, and the skill of man. Most were for government use, of course, and at least began their careers under the banner of officialdom. Later the shipyards at Port Arthur also turned out fine vessels—the barque *Lady Franklin,* the *Pilot, Lady Denison, Ellen, Elizabeth, Wallaby* and *Victoria,* among others, sloops, cutters, and schooners for the most.

Early Governors and legislative bodies did what they could to encourage the shipbuilding industry; the *Maria Orr,* which was the first full-rigged ship built at Hobart, was given a complete suit of sails by the government in 1838. She went whaling later and was lost in the 40's in Recherché Bay, Southern Tasmania. The growth and prosperity of whaling out of Hobart was naturally a great incentive to the shipping industry, and for about half a century Hobart turned out its wooden walls as regularly and as well as some of the greatest centers of the United Kingdom. Hundreds of men were employed regularly in the shipbuilding industry, and when a patent slip to take vessels up to a thousand tons was imported and set up in 1854 the proprietor made a fortune out of it. At the time it was the only slip of its size in all Australia and New Zealand, and ships came from far and wide to be overhauled on it. The slip was owned by one John Ross and remained in active use in Hobart, though several times changing hands and once changing its site, until 1911 when it was dismantled and shipped away to Devonport, on the northwest coast of Tasmania. There it still stands, and still finds work to do; but when it left Hobart its work there was gone.

Here many a lovely vessel was molded, and from this old patent slipway many a graceful barque and towering full-rigger first took the water. The slip stood on an ideal spot at Battery Point, in one of the oldest quarters of the old seaport town, and through the gates that led to it night and morning a steady stream of shipwrights, carpenters, and sailmakers passed. Now the site is grassgrown and the slipway weedy, and through what once were the dockyard gates now only come an old man and his dog. Of the slipway nothing but the scar remains; of the clipper ships that were built there, nothing. . . . *Isabella Brown, Lady Emma, Nautilus, Acacia, Runnymede, Flying Squirrel, Flying Fish, Flying Fox, Freetrader, Southern Cross, Middleton, Star of Tasmania, Grace Darling, Waratah, Oceania, Harriet Nathan, Silvenus, Esperanza, Margaret*

Brock, Tasman, Thomas Brown—barques and ships, all these, where have they gone?

But they played their part and played it well; it is to be regretted only that the splendid race of colonial sailors they bred passed with them, and now there may be bred no more. What ships remain out of the port of Hobart— and these are few—are steamers or auxiliary-engined, and the natural bent of the Tasmanians for the sea must now find its chief outlet in yachts. . . .

And what a fuss was made of a ship-launching in those days! The figurehead and catheads were festooned with flowers, and bunting hung from all the masts and yards in the port; thousands came to wish Godspeed to the new vessel, and a day of it was made indeed. Nothing but the best of wines would do to smash against the prow as the vessel slipped down the greased ways to the sea, and generally the woman from whom she had taken her name was there to perform the ceremony. Many of these old sailers were named after women; nearly all carried fair maidens as their figureheads—maidens with outstretched arms, and sweet gentle faces that looked benignly down upon the sea, with an amiability and loveliness in their eyes that could still even the wrath of the waves, or at least quieten them that the brave ship to which the carved maiden was guard might ride the more gently on.

A good many of these old figureheads were carved in the anteroom of an undertaker's shop, with shelves full of waxen and horrible wreaths about them and a coffin or two waiting ominously by, and now and then a corpse. Some were brought from Scotland and from England, but the most were carved where the ships were made; no one dreamed of sending a ship down the slipways without her figurehead. They would as soon give her a straight prow.

It was steam, of course, that in the end sent the Tasmanian clippers from the sea. When the great English companies took to steam, and put on services to the colonies that grew in regularity, speed, and importance as the speed and the size of the steamers they used grew, there was little chance for the tiny 300-ton barques and 400-ton full-rigged ships. They could be Home in ninety days, or with luck in eighty-five or less; but the steamers could be Home in forty-two. The outward freight gradually moved more and more to steam in the London trade, and, perhaps a little more stubbornly but none the less surely, the Home-ward trade had to follow in its trail. The wool had to go in steam, or it would miss the sales; there was no more whale oil to send, and no more wheat from a Tasmania that no longer grew enough for itself. The intercolonial trade with Australia and New Zealand passed rapidly to steam and the sailer began to be derided; "old windjammers," they were called, and their people were looked upon con-temptuously by the deckhands washing paint in the steam-ers. No one dreamed, as a very few years passed by, of booking a passage in London in a sailing ship. Quickly, once steam had become established and Suez shortened the Australian route by weeks, the sailing ship passed from the stocks and no more were built; as the old ones were lost or sold no new ones were bought to take their places, and the fleet dwindled gradually at first, and then rapidly, until not one remained.

It is a good many years now since a sailing ship bigger than a three-masted schooner has been built at any Derwent shipyard, and the port of Hobart owns no more square-rigged ships at all. The iron barque *James Craig* was the last—a lovely little barque that had once been the Glasgow full-rigger *Clan McLeod*, sweet-lined, economical, and fast —but she was rigged down for a coal hulk some years ago. Outside a few old hands who still look with scorn upon steamships and regard motor ships as no ships at all, it is doubtful if there is any one left in Hobart now who could prepare the sail plan of a barque, or send up a topsail yard. But who wants to send up a topsail yard these days? And what *is* a topsail yard, anyway?

Of all the Hobart clippers, the little barque *Harriet Mc-Gregor* must be the most interesting. She was no high-sided, bluff-bowed, homely wagon; she was a stately clipper ship, tall and fleet, for all her tiny 331 tons; and the wonderful consistency of her record shows that in her lines she must have caught something of the marvelous secret of the albatross which sails on majestically which way it will in all winds, and in all calms. The *Harriet McGregor* certainly was a remarkable little vessel. Built by Mr. John McGregor for the firm of Alec and John McGregor, at the Domain slipyards, in Hobart, in 1871, she went straight into the London trade and remained in it while she was under the Tasmanian flag, regularly making a round voyage to London and another to Mauritius every year. There were famous clippers, of course, which could show passages 20 days and more better than she could, but there must be few vessels which have a more consistent record. She was small for the Cape Horn trade, too; it is difficult to understand, indeed, how she managed to survive so long and to do so well.

Cape Horn has always been the sailing ship's most bitter enemy, and in the heyday of sail it counted its victims by the dozen year by year. Ice took some, and these were not again heard of; many were wrecked on the unlit coasts down there; many more were dismasted, or suffered so great weather damage that they could do nothing but limp sadly away for some port—Port Stanley, in the Falkland Islands; Montevideo, Cape Town—and perhaps never go to sea again. The list of sailing ships that Cape Horn has claimed or driven from the seas would be a great one: here is a small list from one month in the declining years of sail:

August 5.—American ship *Shenandoah*, Baltimore to San Francisco, put into Melbourne in distress, leaking (damaged off Cape Horn). British ship *Glencairn*, Rochester, England, for Seattle, wrecked at Cape San Paulo (near Cape Horn), about August 9. British ship *Indore*, from Hamburg to San Francisco, wrecked about August 10 on Staten Island. American barque *Prussia*, from Norfolk, Va., for Bremerton, wrecked on Staten Island about August 10. British ship *Loudon Hill*, from Liverpool for Vancouver, arrived at Cape Town August 17, damaged by storms off Cape Horn, with 13 in. water in hold, pumps broken, and deck badly damaged. On August 21 the Italian ship *Elisa*, after being buffeted off the Horn, had put in there with binnacle and compass carried away, steering gear damaged, and loss of sails. American ship *Tillie E. Starbuck*, from New York for Honolulu, abandoned at sea; heavy weather nearing Cape Horn.

And yet for nearly 30 years the tiny *Harriet McGregor* regularly rounded Cape Horn in her Hobart-London run, and always had good passages. She encountered her share of terrible weather, but she always survived. Surely no vessel sailing regularly in the Australian trade made more regular voyages than she did, and no barque had a better record under the one commander. From February, 1871, to November, 1889, she was commanded by Captain A. S. Leslie; his private log for the period from 1871 to November, 1885, gives the following as the *Harriet McGregor's* record:

	Miles
From Hobart to London and back to Hobart, 15 voyages; average passage out and home, 88 days.	431,639
From Hobart to Adelaide and Mauritius, back to Hobart, one voyage.........................	10,083
From Hobart to Adelaide, back to Hobart, five voyages	9,800
From Hobart to Mauritius, back to Hobart, eight voyages; average passage, 29 days............	86,007
Total distance sailed	537,529

The *Harriet McGregor* had then sailed half a million miles and more and had never had an accident; her average speed during the whole of the time had been over 1,000 miles a week. That is the better when one learns that she was not considered a very fast ship, as far as occasional bursts of speed are concerned. She was no 18-knotter, and no one who had been in her fo'c'sle ever told yarns about "touching 20" afterwards. She was just a lovely little model that did her best in strong winds and never lost steerage way in a calm; the flap of her sails gave her breath enough to steer, and in the great winds she would reel off her twelve and fourteen knots. But she was nowhere with the great steel clippers with their steel yards and their great spreads of canvas; she set no skysails and carried no kites, and she had no enormous crew. She was just an ordinary little barque, built of good Tasmanian wood—bluegum and pine—and her sail plan was the usual one of double tops'ls, single t'gall'nts, and royals. She rarely lost a sail and was a very dry ship, although she was well loaded always and carried all the cargo that could be stowed into her. Her beauty was in her lines and the symmetry of her rigging, and throughout her long career she was kept on deck like a yacht.

The *Harriet McGregor* left Hobart on Christmas morning for London for a good number of years arriving there usually about the second or third week in March. Her smartest passage to London up to the time of Captain Leslie's retirement was seventy-nine days. She used to leave London again with general cargo about the end of April, and if she did not put in an appearance in the Derwent within ninety days Alec McGregor—so 'tis said—wanted frequently to know "what the devil the *Harriet's* Old Man had done with her this blessed voyage." If she wasn't in in less than one hundred days, he began to fear she was lost. Her best passage outwards was seventy-eight days, and her fastest day's run was 287 miles.

That does not sound so very much in comparison with the runs of over 300 and sometimes over 400 miles of the lauded clippers, but the very fact that her best day should be so comparatively poor and yet her voyages so consistent and fast is the best proof there could be of the little blue-gum lady's handsome qualities. So far as that goes, maybe it is not the ships that have been most written about that have greatest claim to fame; the records of the voyages of the big iron and steel wool clippers during the years the *Harriet McGregor* was at sea make interesting reading. For instance, in the year 1881, when she was eighty-two days from Hobart to London, here is a list of the better known ships' voyages from the better known ports for comparison:

MELBOURNE TO LONDON

Leander	119 days
Dara	118 "
Rolf	118 "
Ladoga	117 "
Theophane	115 "
George Thompson	112 "
Winefred	121 "
Asterope	121 "
Shannon	113 "
Thessalus	105 "
Loch Sloy	103 "
Bothwell Castle	104 "
Avenger	98 "
Cardigan Castle	91 "
Drumlanrig	91 "
Parthenope	88 "

SYDNEY TO LONDON

Darling Downs	131 days
La Hogue	121 "
Mitredale	132 "
Soukar	137 "
Sophocles	126 "
William Duthie	120 "
Carnatic	110 "
Candida	98 "
Jason	117 "
Loch Etive	103 "

Ramsay	120	days
Ben Nevis	110	"
Greta	105	"
Parramatta	96	"
Brilliant	86	"

NEW ZEALAND TO LONDON

Wave Queen	125	days
Waikato	127	"
Lutterworth	121	"
Wairoa	107	"
Dunedin	98	"
Ned White	110	"
Rangitiki	98	"
J. W. Parker	102	"
Alexa	107	"
Wanganui	106	"
Taranaki	83	"
City of Tanjore	105	"
Glenlora	103	"
Jessie Readman	95	"
Ardentinny	90	"
City of Lahore	89	"
Nelson	87	"
Hermione	104	"

ADELAIDE TO LONDON

Barossa	120	days
Hesperus	109	"
Argus	108	"
John Rennie	128	"
Alice Platt	119	"
Richard Parsons	104	"
Monaltrie	107	"
Glen Osmond	127	"

TASMANIA TO LONDON

Wagoola	100	days
Ethel	108	"
Westbury	114	"
Lanoma	89	"
Lufra	87	"

The *Harriet McGregor* beat them all.

Of course 1881 was a bad season in the North Atlantic for the wool clippers, and years could be easily selected, one has no doubts, which would make the *Harriet McGregor* look very small in comparison with the bigger and better known ships. But at least this table shows that at times the lauded clippers were no better than their box-like sisters of later days—*Hougomont*, *Grace Harwar*, *Olivebank*, *Woodburn*, *Lawhill*, *Juteopolis*, *Monkbarns*, and all the rest of them, which though never built for speed would write "bad" against a passage of over 120 days from Australia. The curious point about the *Harriet McGregor* was that she *never had* one of these bad passages.

In 1885, for the first 35 days after leaving Hobart, she averaged 211 miles a day which put her well on the other side of Cape Horn. On the 64th day out that voyage she was within six days' ordinary sail of London, being beyond the Azores, but from then on she had no chance to make anything like a passage.

On that occasion there were 32 big sailing ships in company with her, including such well-known clippers as the *Aristomeme*, *Aristides*, *Patriarch*, *Orontes*, *Serapis*, *Samuell Plimsoll*, *Collingwood*, *Avenger*, *Ben Cruachan*, *Loch Katrine*, and others, all signaling to each other at 8 o'clock in the morning and at noon all hove-to in a heavy northeast gale. Out of that company of clippers the *Harriet McGregor* arrived second in London, being beaten only by the *MacDuff* of Banff. The *MacDuff* being the bigger ship got a tug first, but both vessels docked on the same tide.

Sailors who were in the *Harriet McGregor* for years said that she was rarely passed by any ship, especially in light winds; in five years once she was passed only by the *Ben Voirich* and the *MacDuff* of Banff, both of which could have stowed her in their main holds. Her passages to Mauritius were just as good; going from Hobart to Mauritius she had to weather Cape Leeuwin, the extreme south-west corner of Australia, first, and then stand up into the Indian Ocean for the tail of the south-east trades; coming back she would make, of course, down for the west winds and let them blow her to Hobart.   Her best passage from the wharf at Port Louis to Hobart Wharf was 21 days 8 hours; this was beaten only by the brig *Jumna* with an extraordinary passage of four hours less, but the *Jumna* was lost with all hands upon leaving Hobart on her next voyage.   The *Harriet McGregor's* succession of masters included Captain Richard Copping, Alex. Leslie (who had been chief mate in her), C. Knight (who had been chief in the *Lufra,* another McGregor clipper), Brown (he was chief when Captain Knight died on his first voyage as master, and had her for three years after that), and Captain Boon, who took her Home to London in 1896 when she was sold to the Danes.   On her first voyage after changing flags she was burnt in Rio de Janeiro harbor.

Captain Leslie was accompanied by his wife in the *Harriet McGregor* for upwards of 15 years, from 1874 to 1889. Four of her six children were born aboard the clipper: Harriet McGregor Leslie was born in the London docks, Alex. McGregor Leslie in the Derwent, Agnes Mary Leslie within sight of the Scilly Isles, from which she took her name (the islands were St. Agnes' and St. Mary's) and Robert William Leslie was born in the north-east trades. Mrs. Leslie was as well known as the barque she sailed in, and the little wooden sailer was known as an ideal ship both before and abaft the mast during the whole of the 15 years she sailed there.   In all that time the average of the *Harriet McGregor* for the round voyage between Hobart and London, cargoes both ways, was seven and a half months.

Each one of the *Harriet McGregor's* voyages would make grand reading now, and a detailed history of her career— if one could be obtained—would be well worth while.   But there are few records of her voyages in existence. In 1929 Mrs. Leslie lived, in a hale old age, near London; here and there a shipmaster may be found who served his time in the little barque, and round the sea-salt flavored streets of Hobart's waterfront there are still old-timers who felt the kick of her wheel and laid into her rigging in the shriek of the down-south gale. From one such I had the story of one voyage, at any rate—from an old salt named Garde, ashore these many years now but still with grand memories of his years in sail. He made a voyage as A.B. and carpenter—a responsible job in those days, with plenty to do and no small skill required in the doing of it—1894, and he still remembers it as if it were last year.

He joined the barque on January 2, 1894, and her crew for the voyage was 14 hands all told—none too many, one is inclined to think, though small vessels like that must have been very handy and much easier to maneuver than the modern sailing ship with her huge 3,000-ton bulk, her great steel yards, and her sails of thousands of square feet of canvas. She was loading wool and whale oil at the Hobart Wharf, and four days after he shipped she went out into the stream. There she lay, in the time-honored manner of sailing ships, until January 11, in company with the well known old barque *Ethel*, and early on that morning the two of them hove anchor together and stood down the Derwent out to sea, making a beautiful sight in the early morning with their white sails spread to catch the breeze. Outside the *Lufra* was passed, and the two London-bound barques ran into a nice nine-knot breeze that soon saw the old *Ethel* hull down astern of the speedier *Harriet McGregor*. The course was set E. by S. for the Horn, and the long stormy run across the worst seas in the world began. And it was stormy! Not long after setting out some of the livestock that had been taken on board at Hobart—the list included Tasmanian bears, parrots, and opossums—died owing to the severity of the weather.

By January 20—nine days out—the little barque was off the south of New Zealand, which was not so bad considering that good sailing breezes had not been plentiful. Usually she was that far in four days. On January 22 the Antipodes were passed, and next day the 180th meridian was crossed. That was January 23, and in accordance with sea usage the ship had two January the twenty-thirds, much to the disgust of the crew who had not only to work an eight-day week but had to put up with two days of salt tack and hard biscuits. Somehow shipmasters seem to have an uncanny ability in avoiding crossing the meridian on a Sunday, for that would give the crew two days of rest and that would never do. Later strong winds and gales; these were only to be expected down there and the crew put up with them.

For three days she was hove-to under reefed storm stays'ls, while the only progress she made was to drift slowly before the hurricane which shrieked through her rigging and swept the huge seas down upon her, and right over her at times. With lifelines rigged round the decks the crew had difficulty in getting about; the galley fire was out and things were pretty miserable in general. There was the smell of ice in the air, too, and a sharp look-out had to be kept. Ice was always the greatest danger on the Cape Horn road; gales, hurricanes, mountainous seas, treacherous calms—a sailing ship might go through these and stand a chance, but the cruel ice looming suddenly ahead gave her no chance. Many a ship has sailed that stormy road and never reached a port because of the ice that has come between her cutwater and the sea.

Perhaps an entry from Mr. Garde's own journal, written when his ship was actually in the passage of those dangerous seas, will best serve to illustrate the life.

"Sunday, Feb. 11," one reads: "A very bad sunrise; our watch—six hands all told—had to shorten her down to lower tops'ls. We have to reef the tops'ls before we set them fast, and we have reefed them about 15 times up to now. It is a tough job, they being new sails and always wet down here and as stiff as iron; a hail squall or a good shower of Cape Horn rain does not make them any the easier to handle or us any the more inclined to handle them. It would be a lot better to be home in bed rather than upon a tops'l yard here this Sunday morning. . . . Last week we had a baked fowl for tea, one that had died from cramps. Three have died now with the cold and we look forward to more. On Sunday the crew have to prepare the vegetables to make the seapie. On week nights we make for ourselves dry-hash, etc. The cook has very little to do and we have very little to eat." That cryptic sentence brings home a lot! And it meant a lot, too, to the fourteen hands all told; it was not to be wondered at that they surveyed the prospects of the approaching deaths of further fowls with neither outward nor inward manifestation of sorrow. Baked fowl is good down round Cape Horn, whether the fowl died of cramps or not.

On that Sunday the hard work of the early morning watch and the trimming of the vegetables for the seapie did not by any means end the day's work, and when Mr. Garde's watch came on deck for the afternoon they found the wind back to gale strength and getting worse. There was nothing else for it then than to get her down to storm stays'ls and heave to, though on this occasion the gale was not long abating sufficiently to square away again on course. The sea was very big, with something like a mile from crest to crest; the great Cape Horn sea is an awe-inspiring sight at any time and must have been grand viewed from the decks of a tiny 300-ton barque, running under shortened canvas for her life. On the following day the ship had again to heave-to because of the elements, and from then on her run to Cape Horn was a succession of gales and heavy, heart-breaking work aloft and below. On February 15 the little ship came round the dreaded cape—35

days out: she usually came to the Horn in less than 30—
and bore away for the milder latitudes of the Atlantic. On
February 18 the Falklands were passed, and after that the
weather quickly improved.   On the 24th a Norwegian
barque was sighted, 44 days out on a voyage from New
Zealand to Falmouth for orders; shortly after that a British
full-rigger was sighted and passed, and within the next two
days two more big square-riggers were seen.

The trades were good; the flying fish came and some
flew on board and into the cook's pots; it was pleasant to
sleep on deck at night and the sailor's lot was a vastly different one from Cape Horn. The coming of the tropics
did not mean an end of danger, however, and on February
28 the old barque was caught in a pampero that made
things look very nasty for a while and all but dismasted
her. Then came the doldrums, to the vast annoyance of
the fourteen hands, but at last the north-east trades came
fresh and strong, and the good ship sailed on for the Channel. The north-east trades had a little too much northing
in them for a start and drove the ship to the westward,
much to the skipper's displeasure, and woe betide the helmsman who did not keep the weather clews of the royals well
shaking! So came March 23 and Good Friday, with no
work and hot cross buns for breakfast.

"It surprised every one to have a holiday," the log recalls; evidently the master of the old *Harriet McGregor*
that voyage was no believer in easy times for the crew. On
Sunday, April 8, the Azores were passed, with the balminess of the tropics gone again and a return to something
approaching the conditions of the run to the Horn.   A
northwest gale came along and the ship sailed through "a
lot of wreckage and timber"; after that she got in the
steamers' tracks and asked one of them where she was.
She was near to her landfall then, and the captain wanted
to be sure of his instruments. It is no fun fooling round

the Channel mouth in a fog with half a gale of wind aloft
and an uncertain chronometer below.

There was more bad weather in the Bay, but on April 16
the ship was off Falmouth, 95 days out from Hobart, and
three days later she was in London docks. Next day the
crew paid off at the Weld Street home, and remained ashore
until it was time for the barque to go to sea once more.
An incident worthy of recording happened when the vessel
was in the dock mouth waiting for the dock to open. There
was, of course, the usual considerable crowd of bystanders
watching the square-rigger just in from the sea; "they were
all so honest," the log recalls, "that they would not take
away anything they could not carry." Dinner came with
the ship still hung up, but the officers did not like to allow
the crew to go to dinner and leave the decks while the
collection of very honest persons on the dockside came on
board and helped themselves to everything they could lift.
It looked as if poor Jack was to have no dinner, but one
of the crew had a brainwave and let all the Tasmanian bears
free to wander around. The sight of these weird, and perfectly tame, beasts had the desired effect, and all hands
went to dinner and the loafers remained mere spectators
of the proceedings.

The *Ethel*, by the way, did not arrive that voyage until
11 days after the *Harriet McGregor* had docked.

The McGregor vessels were particularly smart. Besides
the *Harriet McGregor*, they had the ship *Lufra* in the regular London trade. She was built as a China tea clipper
by Hall, of Aberdeen, in 1870, and was magnificently lined.
A beautiful full-rigged ship of 672 tons, she was very popular amongst passengers. Steam and Suez drove her out
of the China trade, along with many another splendid vessel,
and she was fortunate to be bought into a trade in which
she would retain something of her glory.

Other square-riggers that were regularly on the London
berth in Hobart during the latter part of the last century

included the *Wagoola* (550 tons), *Windward* (620 tons), and the two *Ethels*, the first a barque and the second a 556-ton ship. The populace took a fierce pride and a great interest in the doings of these ships, and the hoisting of signal flags at the old Battery Point station that one of them was in the river was the immediate motive for a general downing of tools and discarding of aprons and office stools while the populace hastened to the New Wharf to await the arrival. As she drew in intelligent comment would greet her appearance: "The old *Harriet's* given the *Ethel* and the *Lufra* what-oh this passage, Harry," it would be; or "She's lookin' a bit strained on it: must 'a' got it bad round the Cape. Per'aps he's been drivin' her a bit hard; they say old Mac went mad last time when he was 100 days."

Everybody knew the old ships, and everybody followed them. They were greeted, upon each arrival, as old friends come in from the sea yet once again to renew acquaintanceships; there wasn't a boy within ten miles of the Hobart waterfront who hadn't sampled the *Lufra's* biscuits, or climbed (when the mate wasn't looking!) to the *Ethel's* royal yards. The grandest ambition of half the small boys in the port was to be bound 'prentice in one of these sweet deepwatermen, and a good many of them began their sea careers in the Hobart barques.

During the whole long year round, there would be square-riggers tied in tiers to the quays round the waterfront and more swinging to their anchors out in the stream, during the heyday of sail—whalers and bluff-bowed merchantmen, tall clippers and lovely little intercolonial and China barques; and the waterfront on Sundays was the promenade of the town. Here there was nothing of the squalor that surrounds the great docks of the world; no ugly walls or high guarded fences screened the clippers from view, nor did they lie with their yardarms braced incongruously to avoid warehouse windows and their figureheads looking

out gloomily over a stagnant pond. The freedom of the
sea outside still followed them to the Hobart wharves, and
the bright sunshine was reflected in their polished brass.
The old time sailors took a grand pride in their ships and
always kept them at the very acme of efficiency. One recalls
a trim little clipper barque named *Mary Blair*—she was
only 322 tons—that carried a beautiful girl figurehead
with outstretched arms, and every Sunday morning in port
a posy of fresh flowers was placed in her extended hand.
The outstretched arm was rigged down at sea, and taken
inboard and stowed away that it should not be lost; the
name "*Mary Blair*" in letters of gold paint on highly polished teak was taken, too, from the counter and the bows,
and underneath the name in white paint had to do for the
sea.   This same *Mary Blair*, by the way, was another of
the old China clippers; she was a Duthie Aberdeen built
barque of 141 feet in length and 27 feet beam, with a hold
14 feet 6 inches deep. She sailed out of Hobart many
years, to China, Mauritius, New Zealand, and the Cape,
and always was kept most beautifully.

Another beautiful little vessel owned and sailed out of
Hobart was the ship *Heather Bell*. She was built by Duthie
in Aberdeen to the order of Brown & Co., merchants, of
Hobart, and for many years was a regular trader between
Australia and England. In 1856 the *Heather Bell* made
a passage of 64 days from Melbourne to London. Captain
W. H. T. Brown, one of the old Hobart master mariners,
who died in Tasmania as recently as 1927, was in her that
voyage, although not then as master.

"We took our departure from Port Phillip Heads," he
said, years afterwards, "on October 15th, 1856, with a
strong easterly wind that made us pass down the west coast
of Tasmania instead of making straight out through Bass
Strait on our way to the south of New Zealand and Cape
Horn. We made the Horn in 26 days despite the bad beginning, and despite also five days of easterly winds which

harassed us later on.   From Cape Horn to the Line we were
18 days, and from the Line to Start Point 20 days.   That
by the way, was the longest run from the Line to Start
Point that I ever knew the *Heather Bell* to make.   It was
nothing for her to cover that distance in 16, 17, or 18 days.

"From Melbourne Heads to Start Point we were 64
days, which was not beaten even by the *Cutty Sark*.   Our
longest day's work was 330 knots, being an average of 13¾
knots an hour.   The longest week's work was 1,855 knots,
265 knots per day, or an average of 11 knots an hour for
the seven consecutive days.   The whole distance from Port
Phillip Heads to the Line, a little over 10,000 miles, we
covered in 44 days; that is 227 knots a day or 9½ knots
an hour.   It is very doubtful if such a rate of speed was
ever maintained so long by any other sailing ship that ever
floated.   The steamer *Royal Charter*, 2,000 tons, carrying
the Royal Mail, left Melbourne the same day as the *Heather
Bell* and was reported in London the day after her."

Besides these London traders there was a host of smaller
vessels which traded between Hobart and Mauritius, or to
the Cape of Good Hope, China, New Zealand, the South Sea
Islands, and the mainland of Australia.   Wherever they
went the little Hobart-built barques made a good name for
themselves because of their sturdiness and fine lines.   The
Loongana—another McGregor barque—was one of the
best of them.   Of 260 tons, she was two years on the stocks;
she was built by John McGregor to the order of his brother
Alec.   Her keel, kelson, stern, sternpost, and main clamps
were all of one length of timber, while her framework, bottom planking, and inside planking were of the best seasoned
Tasmanian bluegum, some of the planks being 120 feet long.
There was not a bolt in her.

"She has an eliptic stern which has a remarkably neat
appearance," states an old account, "appropriately orna-
mented with carved work.   Her figurehead represents a
young and handsome female of modern fashion."   Years

later the "handsome female of modern fashion" followed the
little *Loongana* when she was sold to Oh Ching, of Sydney,
for the Pacific Islands trade, and afterwards she was burnt
somewhere round the Gilbert Islands, I believe. The fate
of almost all these ships seems shrouded in impenetrable
obscurity; no one appears to have taken much notice of
them when information was on hand, and now it has gone.

The barque *Thomas Brown* was another smart vessel.
She was mostly in the Mauritius trade, bringing sugar to
Tasmania to be used in the making of Tasmanian jam.
The ship *Isabella Brown* was another fine oldtimer; both of
these were single topsails ships. *Italy, Kassa, Wild Wave,
Acacia* (later lost with all hands), *Harrowby, Wellington,
Tasman, Bella Vista, Bella Mary, Glencoe, Helen, Irazu,
India, Southern Cross, St. Brycedale, Victoria*—all these
were square-riggers out of the port when Hobart was the
fourth port in Australia. That was in its declining years,
when the whaling had largely gone; earlier it was for years
second to Sydney alone.

The *Wild Wave* was the last of these barques in commission, at least in Australian waters. Cut down aloft and
about as sound below—so sailors said—as a crayfish pot,
for years and years she continued to wander monotonously
backwards and forwards in the timber trade between Hobart
and Port Adelaide. Many a time I have seen her in both
ports, descended upon sad times, with her crew, for the most
part, adjourned indefinitely to neighboring hostelries, and
a weary boy pumping up the clear sea water from her hold.
She never had been a beautiful ship, even in her best days:
it is told of her that when her owner first saw the barque
he sent his best captain home to buy, he took one sad look
and turned on his heel and strode away. Nor did he ever
speak to that captain again. . . . It was said of the old
Wild Wave, too, that she had wandered for so long between
Hobart and Port Adelaide that she knew the way instinc-

tively and brought herself into port, which from the look of her now and again, she might have done.

Then in the end she was sold for a hulk in Melbourne, in 1925, but upon this last voyage she refused to sail and piled herself up upon the shore on the north-west coast of Tasmania. And there she remains.

Some of the very small vessels—schooners, cutters, and the like—built in Hobart are well worthy of mention. There was the little schooner *Kingston*, of 38 tons, built by John Lucas at Battery Point, that went pearling from Hobart to the Timor Sea about 50 years ago and had all her crew murdered. That was a queer business that has never been satisfactorily explained. She was doing well enough in the pearling with 40 wild Malays doing the diving; then one night she was lying quietly at anchor and was spoken by a fishing boat, anchored close by. In the morning there was nothing of the *Kingston*, or of anybody who had been in her, to be seen; nor has anything ever been seen, heard, or learnt of them or their schooner since. The fishing boat's people heard nothing at all. The *Kingston* just vanished into thin air.

No one else went pearling from Hobart after that.

For many years the Royal Mails between Hobart and New Zealand were carried in a tiny 16-ton cutter called *Royal William*, that two farmers had built on the banks of the Derwent in 1833. She was a queer little snub-nosed square-sterned vessel, that looked to the inexperienced eye as if she would not be the best of craft even in the sheltered waters of the Derwent; yet she took the mails for years, when New Zealand was in the days of its infancy—there was not so much mail to take—and it is said of her now that she lived through many a Tasman Sea gale better than ships a hundred times her size. She was deep and sharp bottomed, and had a big sail plan for her size; she was so soundly constructed that she sailed for over three quarters of a century —not carrying the New Zealand mails all that time, of course—until she was broken up at Hobart about twenty years ago. She wandered as far afield as King George's Sound, West Australia, and Sydney, and for some time ran more or less regularly between Melbourne and Hokitika. As larger and better vessels came she ceased to carry passengers, and was eventually reduced to carrying firewood for Hobart housewives.

But she was a staunch old sea warrior to the end.

CHAPTER XVII

TREASURE TROVE!

THERE are many stories, mostly along the conventional lines, of buried treasure still waiting to be found along various parts of the coasts of Tasmania and its adjacent islands. Perhaps some of them are true and perhaps they are not; at any rate it is certain that, if any of it exists, none of the treasure has yet been found.

There is the *Britomart*, for instance, which has already been mentioned. As the different banks were established in Tasmania, it was necessary to ship bullion to them; and various persons who had nothing to do with the legitimate receipt of that bullion were frequently aware of its coming. These were the ships, naturally, which special effort would be made to entice upon some lonely island in Bass Strait, if there were any means of doing so. According to some stories, the *Britomart* had a considerable treasure of this kind aboard, and, though she was lured to her doom, the treasure was not secured and it has never since been found. She was lured on to a reef in the blackness of a stormy night and all her people murdered, but she slipped back off the reef again before the treasure could be secured. It was in a heavy iron safe, which the pirates could neither open nor move, and it was while they were endeavoring to move this from the hold that a storm came and took their prize from them. It slipped into deep water where they could do nothing, and there it remains.

According to this story, the *Britomart* had £150,000 in that safe, and if any one can find the wreck the safe should still be there. Various attempts have been made to locate it, but all have failed. In quite recent years costly and am-

bitious endeavors have been made by persons who claimed
to possess priceless information; one of these was a descendant of the sealers of the islands and information as to the
position of the wreck had, he said, been handed down to him.
But the difficulties of salvage proved too great, although
while there are persons who believe that the treasure is there
there will, of course, also be adventurers to go and look for
it. The whole circumstances of the loss of the *Britomart*
are so surrounded with mystery that it is difficult to say
what real expectation there might be of discovering £150,-
000 in her sunken hull to-day, but in any case there is no
record of such a huge sum being shipped to any bank in
Tasmania about that time. Still, if a bank were importing
such an amount, it would probably be very quiet about it—
and quieter still when it was lost.

Then there is the *Hope*, a quaint old ship that would be
worth a story even if it had not also been mixed up in a
treasure episode—a much more probable one, by the way,
than that of the *Britomart*. The old *Hope*, an ancient bar-
rel-bowed, tubby old drifter, was well enough known in
Hobart in the earlier years of the Tasmanian capital's history. She was chartered by Peter de Graves, who later
spent some years in the debtors' prison in Hobart and had
to be ejected before he would go, to bring out a party of
Wesleyan migrants from London. The Wesleyans went
aboard and began their journey right enough, but head
winds in the Channel and generally miserable weather kept
the *Hope* at anchor off the Downs so long that the migrants
had to eat all their provisions for the voyage.

They had many complaints about the ship, too; she
leaked; she wouldn't sail; she was poorly rigged; she was
incompetently manned, inefficiently officered, insufficiently
stored. She would never, they said, reach Tasmania; they
doubted, after she had been at anchor a month, whether
there was any intention that she should try. The motion
of the ship at anchor was a sickening one, and the migrants

put in a wholly unenjoyable time of it. The ship became such a hell of discontent, abuse, and misery, that in the end the Wesleyans, with a strong deputation to the authorities ashore, had little difficulty in getting themselves and all their belongings transferred back to the shore. Later some of them came out in another vessel, but others had such a sickener of it that they never came on at all.

Peter de Graves, however, was not to be put off by long delays at anchor or by the abuse of impatient Wesleyans; the *Hope*, as far as seaworthiness was concerned, was no worse than a great many other ships and better than some, and if he could not bring out the Wesleyans then he brought out a brewery instead. With *that* he did not fail.

After she came out to the Colonies, the *Hope* remained trading between Hobart and Sydney for a while, and while in this trade she was lost. On a voyage from Sydney to Hobart with general cargo and some passengers in 1827, she was thrown ashore not far from the mouth of Derwent River, on a night when Storm Bay, into which the Derwent flows, was doing a valiant best to act up to its name. The *Hope* was always a lubberly wagon, and under short canvas she would do nothing except drift sideways like a floating cask. She drifted sideways on to the beach between Betsy Island and South Arm, coming to rest on a sandy shore that is still called Hope Beach. The weather was very bad and seas broke right over her as she lay stranded, and she was in such a serious state that the master, crew, and passengers hurriedly abandoned her, thanking Providence that they were able to do so without the loss of their lives.

The *Hope*, according to the stories now told, had a considerable quantity of bullion aboard—which is likely enough —and two soldiers had been sent with the ship to guard this. When the order came to abandon ship, the bullion was forgotten by crew and passengers alike, all of whom were too concerned with the safety of their own lives to worry about money. But the two soldiers were in a different

position. During the voyage down they often discussed the
treasure they were guarding and each expressed the hope
that they might be able to lay hands on a share of it, return
to England, and live more or less happily ever after. There
was little enough hope of getting any of the money, however, had not the vessel been driven ashore.

That gave the guards their chance, and when everybody
else was abandoning the ship they were concerned with the
treasure. In the general confusion, the blackness of the
night, the roar of the wind, the thrashing of the blown-out
sails, the terrifying crashing of the splintered masts, they
were neither missed nor thought of; it was every man for
himself without thought of others. The soldiers had decided beforehand that, if a chance came to get the bullion
they would take it. Here was their chance. They were not
so much concerned about their lives, without the money; at
least, they had brooded so long over it—they had little else
to do—that possession of the money, or at any rate the
endeavor to possess it, had become of more importance to
them than their dull, uneventful lives.

So throughout the whole of the night, while the *Hope*—
strong, well-timbered old wagon, despite the wailings of the
Wesleyans—still held together on the beach, the soldiers
worked furiously shifting the heavy sacks of sovereigns out
of the strong room and over the side on to the sand. They
had to wait until the other people abandoned the ship before
they could begin, and it was a desperate business; at any
time she might have broken up, or been drawn back into the
sea. But oblivious of everything but their purpose, the two
kept on; at dawn they had the whole of the bullion safely
ashore and hidden, temporarily, behind some tufts of grass
growing on a sandbank just above the beach. Then they
made their way, unnoticed, to the proximity of the main
party, and threw themselves down on the beach with a weari-
ness that was very real, and a disinterestedness that was not.
Nobody had the slightest idea that they had not abandoned

the vessel at the first crash; until hours afterwards nobody thought of the money.

The soldiers now hoped, of course, that the *Hope* would break up or be swept out to sea; saying that they would look along the beach to see if there was anything to eat washed ashore, they set off like good fellows and securely hid their treasure; they found some firewood and returned. The *Hope*, however, did not break up or drift away off the beach, and when the salvors came later to collect the treasure they were amazed to find that there was none there. But there was no suspicion against the soldiers.

The discovery that the treasure had gone, however, made complications for them. They planned to return to the beach as soon as possible and recover the buried bullion, but when such a hue and cry was raised about its loss it would obviously have been a false step to do that. Then they would not be able to get away from the colony with so vast a sum of money, when inquisitive officials were looking for it; all their plans had been for a clean getaway without any knowledge even that the treasure had gone. In the end, the two were sent, with their regiment, to India, not so very long after the *Hope* went ashore, and much against their grain they had to go away and leave the bullion still buried in its hiding place.

Then followed years in India, still with the secret shared strictly between them and mentioned to no one else. In India one of the soldiers died; after years the other returned to his native Ireland, and at last set about getting back to Tasmania and recovering the treasure. But he had no money then, and could not get a passage to Tasmania. He took a countryman into his confidence—it was the only thing he could do—planning that the two of them should voyage out to Hobart, wander aimlessly down to Hope Beach, secure the treasure, and at least remain sober long enough afterwards to get clear of the country.

But the confidence was misplaced; instead of helping the

ex-soldier, the Irish farmer to whom he entrusted the secret
set off alone, leaving his confrere to do what he liked. Since
he did not care to share the secret with any further double-
dealers, that was not much.

In the course of time the Irishman reached Tasmania,
bought an outfit—ostensibly for mining—in Hobart, and
set off for Hope Beach. But he had been so excited when
he bought that outfit that the curiosity of the inhabitants
was aroused. They had no faintest idea of the Irishman's
real aim, of course, but they followed him, when at length
he set out, in the hope of coming across the rich strike of
gold that he must have found to be so excited. So when he
came to Hope Beach the Irishman found his efforts watched
by a curious gallery, the interest of which was insatiable.
For a while he humbugged around pretending to look for
gold—uncoined gold—hoping that his unwelcome visitors
would go. Some of them did, but not before they noted his
repeated references to a mysterious chart. Then, digging
furiously in the dead of night at the place marked by a
cross on the chart, the Irishman discovered that the further
he dug the more evil was the smell of the sand. He made
no further discoveries.

Then he returned to Ireland.

Here he came, chagrined but putting a bold face on it—
at first he denied that he had been to Tasmania at all—to
the soldier, and the soldier laughed at him.

"The cross was in the wrong place!" he said. "I did that
to double-cross whoever might be fool enough to try to
double-cross me!"

He explained, then, that the real position of the treasure
was a little way from the cross, from which bearings had to
be taken which he did not confide. It was then arranged
that the two of them should journey again to Tasmania and
at last secure the treasure, the soldier concluding that one
who had tried to fool and had been fooled himself would be
less likely to try any tricks again than any new confidant,

and the farmer raising the necessary funds for the voyage.

Then the soldier died, without having disclosed the nature of the bearings to be taken from the cross on the chart to discover the treasure. He died suddenly, in Liverpool, on the eve of setting out. He was a fairly old man then.

Whether the Irishman found, in his friend's papers, the bearings that he so much desired is not known; at any rate he came on to Tasmania alone, bought another outfit in Hobart with his last pence, hurriedly (but quietly this time) decamped to Hope Beach, dug for three days, and then contracted pneumonia and died. He *did not* find the treasure. Neither has anybody else since, although many have looked.

To-day fond parents encourage the sand-digging efforts of their offspring along this fair Tasmanian beach, and staid and plump city fathers may be seen steadfastly assisting energetic small boys in the romantic task of turning over tons of sand in the hope of suddenly discovering the treasure from the *Hope.* It would be a curious thing, if, some day, somebody did.

Most of the stories of piracy and treasure center around Bass Strait, and here indeed there is ample background in fact. When the first of the convicts came to Hobart, with Bowen when he founded the capital of Tasmania in 1803, one of the first events recorded is the seizing of a boat and the decamping of a desperate party. With this boat they made up to Bass Strait and led a wild life there; it is certain that whatever attempts at piracy they could safely make they would be pretty sure to embark upon. They became probably, the first of the wreckers; Bass Strait was always a bad place for the old sailing ships to navigate, with its rocks, its hosts of islands, its currents, and its strong winds. When the menace of piracy was added it was much better, if one were bound to Sydney, to go round the South of Tasmania and give it the go-by altogether. Indeed, upon the rare occasions when great sailing ships still set out for the New South Wales capital from European ports—now and again there is an odd cargo of rock salt to be picked up in Liverpool for delivery in Sydney and Newcastle—they prefer to go round the south of Tasmania rather than through the strait, though the islands are lit now and the wreckers have long gone.

In the earlier years of last century life was primitive on the Bass Strait islands, and rough characters were to be found there—runaway convicts from Tasman's Peninsula who had managed to secure a haven there, deserters from Botany Bay, die-hards, adventurers, desperadoes. Ostensibly they made a living by hunting the game that was to be found in abundance on most of the islands; really they lived in any manner that best suited them. One of these men, one David Howie, is popularly supposed to have been in possession of the secrets of several treasure hoards in the Bass Strait islands, and it is quite likely that he was. He lived on King Island, for the most part—one of the most notorious coffin grounds for ships in the world—and knew what was to be known of the wrecks there.

In those days it was the custom for ships to carry much more ready money than they do now. They had to. I happen to be writing this in the fo'c'sle of a full-rigged ship—one of the last in the world—making up through the South Atlantic for the south-east trades, somewhere about the latitude of Buenos Aires. Here in these seas pirates once had a great hunting ground for the treasure ships from Peru, but if any pirate happened to come across this ship now I suppose that in ready money he would find about £5 among the lot of us aboard. There would be no need to carry money, even if we had it. But it was different in the old days when the Bass Strait pirates were in the business.

Then it was customary for captains to buy their cargoes wherever they went, and for that they had to carry their own money; in the course of a long and profitable voyage they might accumulate a goodly sum in the strong room aft. It was a pretty sure thing that if one were fortunate enough to discover an abandoned wreck—or if one enticed the ship ashore and murdered the crew—one would also find at least some treasure. Howie, at any rate, seems to have found some. There are various stories about him, all more or less improbable. There is, however, a reliable record that he had a curious habit of visiting, whenever he was short of money (which was pretty frequently) Three Hummock Island, in the strait, and there, penniless and alone, he always pulled himself ashore in an old dinghy. He never allowed any one to come with him, or permitted any to watch where he went. And when he came back, it was always with plenty of money, in heavy minted gold.

Howie is also supposed to have known of the hiding places of different hoards on King Island. In his time he discovered many rich and varied cargoes in different wrecks—he said they were wrecks—and in the course of his lonely wanderings round the strait in a little eight-ton cutter he might have found anything. No one else ever shared any of his secrets and his treasure hoards have never been found. Howie and his cutter disappeared on one of these cruises; he set out from Stanley, in the north-west of Tasmania, and never returned.

There have, of course, been many attempts to unearth the treasure hoards of the strait islands, but if any has succeeded the discoverers have been silent about their luck. From time to time persons have come forward with charts and so on, claiming to have a knowledge of the whereabouts of some treasure, and costly expeditions have been fitted out to search for it. But the most interesting thing that has happened was that once, not many years ago, two fiercely antagonistic parties, both of whom had set out with much shouting and great noise on a treasure hunt in the islands, happened to have as their objective the same cave, and when they met in it there was a pitched battle from which they emerged treasureless, breathless, and bruised of coun-

tenance. On another occasion somebody heard that treasure
was buried in a lagoon. The lagoon was drained, but not
even an old stove that a resident had thrown in there as
some encouragement to the seekers was discovered.

Somewhere in these islands, however, it is quite likely that
a very great treasure is hidden—such a treasure that would
make "Treasure Island" seem dull discourse. In the quite
early days of Australia, an old sea buccaneer wandered
across to the West Coast of South America and pillaged
several of the wealthier towns. If there had been a war on
at the time everything would have been in order, of course,
and he could have brought his treasure to port—vast sums
of gold and silver, ingots, valuable treasures stolen from
churches—but there was no war and he had no excuse for
his wanton piracy. He therefore sailed across to Australia
and hid the treasure upon an island in Bass Strait—all this
is dull fact, recorded in his trial, although it may read
rather along the conventional lines of such stories—intending to come back and get it as soon as war broke out again.
(He rightly guessed that he wouldn't have to wait very
long.) Then he put into Sydney where some of his crew,
in a drunken spree, talked too much and the whole secret
was out. The sea rover was arrested and imprisoned, and
died there; the government insisted "that the exact location
of the treasure should be disclosed to us" and was sent upon
a wild goose chase; and as far as is known that treasure
still remains buried in its Bass Strait hiding place.

Then there is the *Catherine Shearer*. She was a small
barque lost in D'Entrecasteaux Channel on the last night
of her voyage to Hobart in 1855. She took fire and had
to be hastily abandoned because of the large quantity of
explosives aboard, and she blew up and sank in deep water.
In 1928 the wreck was located by a diver from Hobart, and
all those persons who had stoutly maintained for years that
there was a vast treasure aboard were on the tiptoe of excitement. The *Catherine Shearer* was supposed to have a

large amount of money on board, variously stated as anything from £3,000 in pennies to £250,000 in gold. Great
preparations for an exhaustive survey of the wreck were
made, and a large party went down with the diver to wait
for good weather. Then the great day arrived and the
diver went down again. After a long search, he discovered
several jars of pickles which were still intact and a very
large, heavy jar which when brought to the surface and the
barnacles scraped off, was found to be labeled "Captain's
Rum." But of treasure there was not a moldy penny.

No; no matter how much of buried treasure there may be
scattered around the Bass Strait islands and the coast of
Tasmania, the best way to secure coin of the realm in that
dominion is exactly the means which work best in every
other land there ever was. That is to earn some.

CHAPTER XVIII

"GRAVEYARD ISLAND"

IN the days of sail many a handsome clipper, lumbersome whaler, and unseaworthy convict transport piled up on the coast of Tasmania, which was peculiarly well situated for the wrecking of vessels. The west coast, ill-lit and ceaselessly stormy, was particularly bad; here the odd exploring and prospecting parties that came now and then were never surprised to discover, half buried in the sand on some beach, the rusty and battered hull of some old sailing ship that had been driven there in the storm. Survivors were not often found; there were several cases where the identity of ships so discovered never was established. When they were found there was nothing left to know them by: battered masses of twisted and shapeless wreckage, boatless, with neither spars nor sails and no papers of any kind in a cabin which perhaps for years had been at the mercy of the constant rain-sodden gales down there, with not even a skeleton of a man in sight—what might there be to know them by? A number carved upon a hatch, maybe, but the hatch was gone; a name carved upon a counter perhaps, but the counter was gone too, with all else that a man might recognize.

But bad as the west coast of Tasmania undoubtedly was, its record is not the worst. It could be avoided; there was not much excuse, when its danger was known, for being stranded there. There was no port to make, except Macquarie Harbour, and few ships went there. There was not further need to sail round Tasmania in ships bound for Sydney, once Bass Strait was known; the nearer and the better way for bold sea captains was to run through the strait and save 500 miles. But that was just the danger. The strait, ill-lit and worse charted, subject to suddenly changing winds and varying currents, crowded with precipitous and often scarcely perceptible rocks, soon became known to mariners as one of the worst places in the world. But that was not before many a fine ship had gone to her doom there; so many were lost upon one island alone—King Island—that it was known to sailors by the expressive but horrible name of "Graveyard Island"—a name it had well earned.

To-day the very bays and headlands of this fair island, almost all of them, carry the names of the ships they wrecked—Admiral Beach, Waterwitch Point, Netherby House, Harbinger Reef and so on. Five ships have gone to pieces on the one patch of rocks. Now and again, even now, a strong wind exposes some skeletons on a beach, forgotten victims of some long-lost ship. The number of persons whom the sea has taken is to be reckoned in tens of hundreds, and the ships by the score. Most of the ships were wrecked when on the eve of their arrival, and destruction wrought upon their human freights when at last, after often a long and trying voyage—all very well in the retrospect, but not very enjoyable to go through—they were looking forward to coming to the land again with all that it meant.

It would be impossible to compile a full list of the ships that have been lost on King Island; some have been forgotten and some were never recognized.

One of the earliest, and perhaps the first, of many wrecks occurred almost at the beginning of last century. Captain Campbell, of the *Hetherington*, and his men discovered on the island on March 18th, 1802, a quantity of planking from some ill-fated vessel. Captain Campbell sent a man to walk round the island in the hope that some trace of survivors, or, at least, some clew to the identity of the ship might be found. Kangaroos, porcupines, badgers, and emus were seen, as well as black swan, teal, and ducks, and sea elephants, which afterwards provided the *Hetherington* with a cargo of blubber and seal-skins. The searchers came upon a quantity of staves, a small Quaker gun, and water butts, leading them to assume that the vessel had come from Britain or the United States. There was one survivor of the disaster.

"We did our utmost to discover whether any of the people had escaped from the wreck," reported Captain Campbell, "but perceived only one English cat."

Subsequent research failed to reveal the name of the vessel, much less how the cat came to be so strangely among the native fauna. Captain Campbell does not tell what became of the cat—whether the seamen took it with them for a charm, or whether, startled in its solitude, it dashed back into the bush there to attain the total independence which all cats are assumed to seek.

"We regret to report that on the 28th ultimo the barque *Rebecca*, Captain McTaggart, from Batavia, bound to this port, was wrecked on King Island," reported the *Port Phillip Patriot*, on October 23rd, 1843. From Batavia to the Straits the *Rebecca* had an adventurous voyage, buffeted by gales, and it was no doubt with a feeling of some relief that the northern part of King Island was at last sighted. The wind was blowing hard from the north-west, however, and the captain found himself surrounded by reefs and obliged to anchor, as darkness was approaching. In the morning the only way out of the maze appeared to be the channel by which the vessel had entered. The captain waited until the following day, when a violent south-west wind sprang up, and steered to clear the Harbinger reef.

The barque was soon in danger, driving towards the reef, and as there was every indication of a tempestuous night with no chance of saving life by getting out the boat, at 7 o'clock in the evening—the barque being then a quarter of a mile from the breakers, and the wind blowing hard from the north-west—the captain ordered the sick and a woman passenger into the longboat, and pushed off with 12 hands, to make room for the quarter boat to lower. The night was very dark, and the longboat was pulled to windward to wait for the quarter boat. Getting into this boat, the men swamped it, and several were drowned. The mate, finding himself without a boat, and the barque close to the breakers, drove her on to the beach. The longboat and its passengers reached the shore safely. It suffered some damage, but when this was repaired the survivors, with the exception of one man who was left in charge of the stranded *Rebecca*, set out on a hazardous voyage to Victoria. On October 21st, they arrived in Hobson's Bay.

Two years later an appalling disaster occurred in comparison with which the wreck of the *Rebecca* was trivial. The immigrant ship *Cataraqui* in command of Captain Charles Finley, from Liverpool, broke up on a reef on the west coast of the island, and more than 400 persons, many of them women and children, were drowned. A gale was blowing and a course had been set for Cape Otway, when suddenly, at four o'clock in the morning of August 4th, the vessel struck a rock. Frightful confusion occurred. Seas were pouring over the vessel, and above the tumult planks and timbers could be heard crashing and breaking. Water poured in from below and rushed down from above, drowning the unfortunate persons between decks. The attempts of many to reach the deck at once blocked the hatchways, and few who escaped drowning below were not injured in the crush. Huge seas broke over the deck, sweeping the people overboard. More than 400 had set out from Liverpool, and when day broke only about 200 remained. All those who could not be got up from below were drowned, owing to the list of the ship. About 4 o'clock the captain, the boatswain, four seamen, and the doctor launched the quarter boat, but it capsized immediately. Worse was to come, however, for with a crash the *Cataraqui* parted amidships, and half the vessel slid into the sea, carrying with it 70 to 100 persons.

Lines were stretched along the deck and the survivors lashed to them, but many dropped off the wreck during the night.

At dawn on August 5th only about 30 remained alive. Mr. Guthrie, the first mate, clutching a spar, plunged into the sea and was carried over the reef to the shore. There he found a passenger who had escaped during the night and one of the crew who had got ashore in the morning. Six other seamen swam, or, with pieces of planking, floated ashore. Soon afterwards, the remains of the *Cataraqui* disappeared beneath the sea. These nine men were all who survived; only one migrant reached Australian shores.

The newspapers of the day were conservative. News of wrecks was printed in the shipping column under a small heading "Wreck," or in the form of a letter to the editor. The *Port Phillip Gazette*, although appreciating the horror of the *Cataraqui* catastrophe, seemed to be particularly concerned in its material aspect. "Inasmuch as the district was starving for labour and we find this supply of healthy immigrants snatched from us when almost within our grasp," it says, "could anything be more tantalising to the country?"

So the *Cataraqui* joined the *Neva*, the *Isabella*, the *City of Edinburgh*, the *Harbinger*, and the *Rebecca* and the unknown vessel in which the English cat was a passenger. The sole surviving immigrant of the *Cataraqui*, it is said, was afterwards found dead in a bush creek with only two feet of water in it—a strange fate for one who had come unscathed through such perils. The first mate, Mr. Guthrie, later returned to Australia as Captain of the *Tigress*. The vessel was wrecked on the South Australian coast, and he was drowned.

Another account states that the master of the *Cataraqui*, fearing that he was in proximity to land, hove to about midnight but at 4 A.M. he changed his mind, and gave orders for the ship to be put under way again. It was blowing hard from the west, and when the vessel struck there was no hope for her passengers and crew. In addition to her ordinary cargo, according to this version, she carried a treasure of gold, and Davy Howie was busy in an attempt to obtain this by means of his black divers when a storm came up and drove the remains of the wreck off the ledge into deeper water. In later years a Victorian resident who had diving experience contemplated fitting out an expedition to try to find the wreck, but the depth of the water and the unsheltered position forced him to abandon this project.

Then there was the female convict ship *Neva*, Captain Peck, which left Cork on January 8th, 1835, bound to Sydney, with 240 persons on board. Of these 150 were female convicts, with 33 of their children; nine were free women, with 22 of their children, and 26 were crew. The voyage passed without incident until May 13th, when the *Neva* was 125 days out, bowling along for the entrance of Bass Strait with all sail set to a favoring wind. The weather was good and conditions were ideal, and all on board were looking forward to a speedy end of the voyage. The course, according to the ship's navigators, was set to clear King Island by 90 miles. At two o'clock in the morning the lookout reported land, but the ship stood on; about four a reef of rocks appeared suddenly right ahead. Instantly—it was at the changing of the watches and all hands were on deck— the helm was jammed hard down and the ship brought into the wind to go about.

She never accomplished the maneuver, for while in stays she struck and the rudder was torn off. Then the helpless ship was at the mercy of the sea; she was altogether unmanageable and was driven hard up on the rocks. She swung round and heeled heavily over, while the seas which had seemed so gentle while she ran before them, swept over her and broke all round. The masts began to go, and it was evident that the ship would go to pieces quickly. The boats were lowered, but each of them in turn capsized, and every one in them was speedily drowned. In a few moments more the ship broke into four pieces—an indication of her sea-worthiness; or lack of it—and, with the exception of twenty-two people who clung to fragments of wreckage, every one on board was drowned. The women had been asleep in their prison in the hold when the ship struck, and so little time passed between the striking and her falling to pieces that they were still barricaded behind their bars when they went to their doom.

The few who survived the tragedy said that they could never forget the horror of those moments, the terrible screams of the helpless women mingled with the crash and grind of broken timbers, and pervading all, the appalling roar of the thundering breakers. Of the twenty-two who reached the shore, two went mad with sheer horror of the calamity and wandering into the bush, died there. Five others died from exposure, leaving only fifteen survivors from the whole 240. Of these six were prisoners and nine were crew; no child lived. The prisoners who survived came out of their prison when the ship fell in pieces and floated ashore on hatches, broken beams and the like.

"What can be the reason of these shipwrecks?" asked the newspapers of the day. "The investigation that took place into the circumstances attending the loss of the *George III* shewed that that ship was almost too old and frail to have been chartered for so long a voyage with so many souls on board, and if the enquiry which we learn the Government is now instituting into the circumstances of the present dis-tressing wreck should come to a similar conclusion, which, from the so abruptly falling to pieces of the vessel, we almost anticipate, it will appear that some more care in these points is necessary at headquarters than appears to have been used. Neither can we shut our eyes to the fact of the recent ar-rangements adopted almost single-eyed with a view to econ-omy and saving, by which vessels of inferior size and quality have been engaged for this important duty."

The Blackball liner *Netherby*, wrecked at King Island in

1866, was more fortunate. She had over 500 persons on board, and all were saved. A baby was born after she struck, and that baby was still hale and hearty in Melbourne in 1929. But the *Netherby* was fortunate in striking good weather, and her principal trouble was in the commissariat department.

The *Netherby* was a Blackball liner, and they were not proverbial for providing too much or too dainty fare for their patrons. She was, besides, 120 days out, so things were only middling in the stewards' department, the allowance to each person being one pannikin of flour and one packet of cocoa per day. And this was from the cargo. By the time the shipwrecked 500 were rescued and brought to Melbourne they were practically starving.

In 1871 the ship *Loch Leven,* bound for England with a cargo of wool, tallow, hides and preserved meats from Geelong, ran on to the island near the lighthouse. She had been seen about 15 miles off the land on the previous evening, but in the night the weather became thick and foggy. At daylight next morning she was seen ashore with all sail set, and made a beautiful picture. The crew got ashore safely but, as the captain wished to procure his papers, an attempt was made to board the vessel in the lighthouse boat. After launching the boat an attempt was made to reach the vessel, but a heavy sea broke into her and completely filled and capsized her. Three men clung to the boat, and four swam ashore, but Captain Branscombe, of the *Lock Leven,* was drowned.

In 1874, the ship *British Admiral* was wrecked, with the loss of 79 lives.

On the night on which the *British Admiral* was wrecked, the wind and sea were terrific. The vessel struck at 2:30 in the morning on a reef about two miles south of Currie Harbor. She remained on the reef for a short time, and then slid off into deep water. One boat got away, carrying ten persons, but near the mouth of Currie Harbor the boat capsized and four were drowned, including the chief officer, whose body was recovered. The six who escaped were cared for by the hunters, and later three more survivors arrived. They had clung to a spar and been washed ashore in Fitzmaurice Bay. The beach was strewn with the bodies of men and women, and the hunters had the task of burying them. The cargo salvaged was very valuable, and for more than a year salvage work was carried on at the wreck by means of lighters, which were towed out from Currie Harbor when the weather was favorable.

While operations to recover the cargo from the *British Admiral* were going on, another fine ship, the *Blencathra*, on her maiden voyage, ran ashore at Currie Harbor. The crew and officers were taken off and next day the diving gang set to work to dismantle the ship and to send sails and valuables ashore, and for this they received salvage. The captain and crew of the *Blencathra* were taken to Melbourne by one of the vessels which was running the salvaged cargo from the *British Admiral*.

The wreck was bought by L. Stevenson and Sons, and they proceeded to salvage her. Among cargo salved were about 800 cases of whisky, which were placed on the rocks, and a watchman, with firearms, set over them. Notwithstanding this watch, about 75 cases "evaporated" in the night. The vessel lasted for many months, and hopes were expressed that she might be floated. This was attempted, use being made of clay and green hides placed over the holes, but in the end she had to be abandoned.*

And so one might go on almost indefinitely recounting the details of these wrecks of King Island—the *City of Melbourne* in 1853, the schooners *Bruthen* and *Maypole*, the ship *Brahmin* and the barque *Waterwitch* in 1854; the ship *Whistler* and the schooner *Elizabeth* in 1855; the schooners

---

* I am indebted to the writings on King Island history by George R. Leggatt, B.A., in the "Australasian" for the particulars of the *Netherby*, *British Admiral, Lock Leven* and *Blencathra* wrecks.

Favourite and *Kathleen* in 1864; the schooner *Arrow* and
the cutter *Dart* in 1865; the ship *Netherby* in 1866, and
the ship *Lindisfarne* in 1867; the barques *Flying Arrow*
and *Omagh*, the brig *Europa*, and the schooner *Helen Ann*,
in 1868; the ship *Lock Leven*, the brig *Ocean Pride*, and the
schooner *Martha Lairina* in 1871; the barque *Anna* in 1873;
the ship *British Admiral* and the cutter *Cape Pigeon* in
1874; the barque *Blencathra* and the schooner *Flying
Squirrel* in 1875; the ketch *Dart* in 1876; the barquentine
Ablona and the schooner *Garfield* in 1877; the barque *Kala-
home* and the schooner *Mary Ann* in 1878—and so on.
. . . One hopes that at last the list is ended.

Other Tasmanian islands in Bass Strait have taken their
toll of wrecks, especially of the latter day steel and sailing
ships—*Farsund, Songvaar, Speke* (giant full-rigger), *Falls
of Hallidale*, and the like—but none approaches the grim
record of King Island.

Tragedy has overtaken many a ship bound for Tasmania
too, and some that have been bound Home; they had all a
stormy road to sail, and it would have been miraculous if
it had not claimed a few. In the "good old days" ships were
wont to go to sea much less fitted for the contest with the
storms of the ocean than they are now, and even now great
steamers, to the consternation and alarm of the maritime
world, are not infrequently lost. Between 1793 and 1829—
36 years—the average number of British ships wrecked an-
nually is given as 557. In 1829 over 800 were wrecked;
more than 2,000 British sailors were drowned in each of
those years, nor did the figures decline at all rapidly for
some time. There was no Plimsoll line then, nor was there
a strict classification and supervision of vessels before they
were allowed to cater for the carriage of goods and passengers at sea. Charts, too, for the most part were pretty poor
things; coasts were badly lit or not lit at all; navigation was
far from the exact science it has become to-day, and masters
were sometimes drunken.

Of a good many of the ships that set out from England for Tasmania and did not arrive, there is now no trace at all. They just set out, and were swallowed up. Now and again a story of shipwreck and privation survives; such a one is the tale of the loss of the *Lady Munro*, which was lost on the rocks of New Amsterdam Island, in the Roaring Forties, in October, 1833, while bound to Hobart Town with passengers and cargo. On October 11, 1833, the *Lady Munro*, according to the account of an Indian army officer who survived, was within about one hundred miles of the islands of New Amsterdam and St. Paul's which are more or less commonly sighted by sailing ships running their easting down to Australia. There were many children in the ship, and nightfall found them looking forward to awakening on the morrow to see the sights of New Amsterdam well astern. A good many of them, however, never wakened on the morrow.

It was a cold, dark, foggy night (states the officer's account), with drizzling rain and a stiff sea breeze, and the ship was dashing along 9 knots an hour, with all sail set, and the wind on the quarter. I went below and turned into my cot, thankful that I could make myself so easy and comfortable while so many poor fellows on deck, unused to such a cold temperature, were shivering with cold, drenched with rain, and thinly and poorly clothed against such inclement weather. I had not fallen asleep, indeed, I had not turned in a quarter of an hour, when I heard a sudden alarming voice from the forecastle. It was instantly answered from the poop, a confused sound hurried along the deck; all the watch seemed in motion, and immediately afterwards the ship struck with such violence as almost to pitch me out of my cot. An awful pause ensued, as if the ship were stunned with the concussion and incapable of motion; a few seconds after she struck a second time with increased violence, till every plank in her frame trembled and every bolt rang aloud. I heard the sea roaring and gurgling around my port, and dashing over the deck, I rushed up the companion ladder with nothing on but my shirt and trousers. The water was rushing down it in cascades. The serang was rushing about calling "Captain sahib! Captain sahib! Jahaz lagga, kya kurenga! Hum kya kurenga!!!" and crying like a child.

The ship staggered about from rock to rock, groaning and labouring and writhing from side to side like a dying thing in its last agony. The sails and rigging were torn to tatters: the masts and yards went crashing overboard piecemeal one after another, and fell seaward. Wild shrieks of despair were now heard in the cuddy. "Save my children, Oh, save my children!" pierced me to the very soul. The united roar of the surf, the wind and the crash of falling masts and spars soon drowned every human cry; and the hull at one time heaved high into the air, at another dashed with destructive force against the rocks, gave one last lurch and went all to ten thousand shivers. I was torn from my hold on the poop without knowing how, and amongst the dreadful breakers before I was aware of it; and swam strongly for the shore amidst floating wreck and groups of drowning men.

I felt the fatal grasp of desperate hands pass two or three times round my thighs, and once or twice felt my foot strike against some one struggling beneath me. Sometimes I got entangled among pieces of sails and rigging but less dreaded their folds and coils, and frequently was struck by planks and spars, and floating boxes. The first wave hurled me along in its crest with the velocity of a whirlwind, and I thought I should never again ascend to the surface; the second followed with equal impetuosity and hurled me upon the rocks. I grasped a pointed rock with both hands, until this sea receded, and after a moment of distressing anxiety lest a third should overtake me and sweep me away, I was high and dry and my danger was over.

By this time all the cries of the drowning had ceased, and nothing was heard but the rending of the wreck and the thunder of the devouring element.

But the loss of the emigrant ship *Northfleet*, with over 300 lives, is by far the most terrible thing in the annals of Tasmanian maritime history. The *Northfleet*, which was taking out navvies for the construction of the Tasmanian main line railway from Hobart to Launceston, was run down by a steamer while anchored in the Channel, a few miles from Dover, on the night of January 22nd, 1873. The steamer did not stop but, having administered her death blows to the helpless sailing ship, backed out of her splintered sides and sneaked hurriedly off on her voyage.

The *Northfleet* was surrounded by other vessels, but none of these noticed her plight, and though she sent up distress signals and burnt flares these were mistaken for requests for a pilot, and the emigrant ship went down at her anchor unassisted and unwatched by the vessels all round her. In the meantime, the steamer which had caused the tragedy made good its escape. It was a clear night, with some stars visible, and the *Northfleet* was burning anchor lights and had set an anchor watch. There was no excuse for the collision, and no reason.

There was ample sea room for the steamer, which had no need to lay a course anywhere near the *Northfleet*.

The *Northfleet* was a fine old vessel of some 900 tons, built in the fifties by Pitcher at the Kentish river-side village from which she took her name, and for a while she was run by Duncan Dunbar. At the time of the disastrous voyage she had about 450 tons of railway iron in the hold, while the whole of the 'tween decks were taken up with the passengers, many of whom had their wives and children with them. She had got as far as Dungeness where head winds forced her to anchor in the midst of a fleet of other sailing vessels similarly delayed. There was no cause to apprehend the slightest danger and the passengers were making everything ready for the long voyage; most of them were asleep when, about half past 10, there suddenly rang out the startling cry of the officer of the watch: "A steamer is right into us!"

Before any one could reach the deck the collision had occurred, and the sailer reeled in her death agonies inside two minutes. The force of the collision was so great that everybody who was standing was knocked down; the steamer rebounded and came a second time in collision with the

Northfleet. Water began to pour in, and in a very short time the passengers' quarters were swamped.

The women were slower to rush on deck than the men, and many were not in a condition to go till the water rose threateningly round them. When the first of the passengers came up the steamer was so near that it would have been possible for them to jump on board it. She was described as a two-funneled schooner-rigged steamer. No one on board her was heard to speak, though loud and eager shouts from the *Northfleet* must have made her aware of the danger that existed. She backed for two or three minutes, and then, steaming rapidly away, was soon out of sight.

The scene on the *Northfleet's* deck was of a most appalling character. The women shrieked, the men cursed and swore and fought their way towards the boats, while the captain and the first mate roared commands to the men to keep back and allow the women to get to the sides of the vessel. During all this time rockets were fired and blue lights burned. The signals of distress were seen by several vessels anchored round, but they appear to have been regarded as signals for a pilot, so that no notice was taken of them by surrounding ships and steamers and the *Northfleet* was left to sink. This she rapidly did, and in a few moments dived to the bottom, head first, with awful suddenness, and with 327 souls on board. At the moment the first boat that left was about 100 yards away, and the second not twenty. The ship lurched suddenly and seemed to take convulsions, and went spinning under the gray Channel surface as if she had dived. . . . Only three women were saved.

A survivor who rushed on deck the moment the shock of the collision was felt said that he saw a lot of the colliding steamer's crew rushing along their decks with a piece of tarpaulin which they threw over the figurehead, so as to hide her name. With that she backed water and got clear. The mate was shouting at them all this time, and when he saw this he cried out, "Oh! my God! Stop and save us, for we have 400 emigrants on board."

But it was not a bit of use, for she backed water and shot ahead across the *Northfleet's* bow, and was away with her black smoke driving in the doomed emigrants' faces before they could do anything. No one saw her name.

The steamer, however, was identified. A few days after the night of the collision, the Spanish steamer *Murillo*, a two-funneled schooner-rigged vessel, came quietly into the Tagus with new paint on her bows and a slight indentation by her starboard anchor davit. The news of the *Northfleet* disaster had been spread abroad and consuls and port officials were on the lookout for the steamer that sneaked away from the ghastly catastrophe she caused; the sharp eyes of the British consul at Lisbon noticed the condition of the *Murillo* and investigations followed. The engineers on board were British and there was an English passenger. They all said that she had come into collision with a large sailing ship on the night the *Northfleet* went down, and they were amazed to see the vessel proceed on her way without the slightest endeavor to render any assistance. They had, they said, protested to the master and his officers, who said that they did not think the ship was damaged much. *Their* ship wasn't.

"I rushed on deck," said the engineer of the *Murillo* in his statement to the Consul, referring to the night of the collision, "and saw that we had come into collision with a large ship at anchor. I had felt the shock below. I saw distinctly that the ship had a very brilliant light burning at the head of the foremast, and she appeared to be riding at anchor. Instantly returning as was my duty, to the engine room, I received orders to put on easy speed, and we continued at that pace all night." The passenger was more explicit in his details, and distinctly said that he heard the cries of the *Northfleet's* people not to leave them. He was horrified to see the Spanish ship back out and go off,

but the officers and the crew took no notice of his entreaties
to stand by. He spoke no Spanish and they did not understand English.

The *Murillo's* master and the watch of the night of the
disaster were arrested, and such was the public outcry
against them that they had to be protected from the fury
of the mobs which gathered at the enquiries.

One of the most striking things about this whole terrible
story is the fact that at the time of the collision there were
200 craft of different kinds anchored within a three-mile
radius of the *Northfleet*, yet not one heeded her signals of
distress and not one aided her. The simple explanation was
so extraordinary that, if it had been written about in a book
instead of having happened, nobody would have believed
that such a tragedy could possibly have occurred. A
steamer under full control collide with an anchored sailing
ship, displaying brilliant lights in the midst of a fleet of
anchored sailing ships, upon a clear night, when all the sea
was open to her! It seems impossible, even now.

But it happened.

A story of a different kind comes from the Hobart
barquentine *Guiding Star*, a small three-masted vessel of
some 300 tons or so. The *Guiding Star* was on a voyage
in ballast from a port in the Dutch East Indies to Hobart,
sometime in the latter part of last century, when without
warning, a virulent fever suddenly struck down practically
the whole of her crew. Until the fever came the weather had
been fine, and it was not until the available crew consisted
of the cook and a small boy that the trial of almost unendur-
ably bad weather was added to the list of tragedies under
which the small vessel labored. One by one the crew died,
and their bodies were thrown overboard. Quickly no one
who was not fever-ridden remained; still they had to work
on, trying to keep the barquentine above the surface, and
to shape some sort of a course towards West Australia.
The ballast was volcanic mud, and with the constant work-

ing of the vessel in the heavy sea this turned to a sloppy mixture little better than water. The little *Guiding Star*, bad enough before, now became a floating hell indeed. With her ballast shifting with every roll, all the sails long since blown away because the dying sailors could not handle them, death stalking through the forecastle and the cabin day by day and always claiming victims, it was not to be wondered at that one sailor who was not yet quite dead with fever went mad at the prospect of his fate, and jumped overboard.

Still the remnant stuck to the ship, since there was nothing else to do; they actually tried to sew a new sail or two, and to bend one of them that they finished. They managed it, and it fell calm. Then came storm again, with the crew reduced to a mere fraction of its proper strength. . . . Three were alive, when at last a Dutch steamer came upon the scene, and picked them up. These were so far gone that they did not know they were rescued. One went mad and another died. The *Guiding Star*, according to the story of the rescuing steamer, was abandoned in a hopeless condition.

Years afterwards, an old Hobart mariner who had once been master of the *Guiding Star* happened to be in Batavia. There he saw a little wooden three-masted barquentine, lying at anchor, and there was something about her that looked strangely familiar. He looked at her more closely, and went aboard. She carried a Javanese crew and was painted black; there were some houses on deck that were not as old as the ship. She was built of Tasmanian timber, and despite the changes wrought by the years and other changes made by human hands, that master mariner still could recognize the *Guiding Star*.

APPENDICES

The following is a copy of a typical female migration advertisement appearing in a London newspaper in the thirties:

FEMALE EMIGRATION TO AUSTRALIA

Committee.

Edward Forster, Esq., Chairman	Capel Cure, Esq.
Samuel Hoare, Esq.	William Crawford, Esq.
John Taylor, Esq.	Charles Lushington, Esq.
Thomas Lewin, Esq.	George Long, Esq.
C. Holt Bracebridge, Esq.	Colonel Phipps, Esq.
John S. Reynolds, Esq.	Nadir Bazter, Esq.
John Pirie, Esq.	S. H. Sherry, Esq.

THE COMMITTEE for promoting the EMIGRATION OF SINGLE WOMEN to AUSTRALIA, under whose management the Ships *Bussorah Merchant* and *Layton* were last year despatched with Female Emigrants, acting under the sanction of His Majesty's Secretary of State for the Colonies, hereby give Notice, that a fine Ship of about 500 tons burden, carrying an experienced surgeon, and a respectable person as superintendent to secure the comfort and protection of the Emigrants during the voyage, will sail from GRAVESEND, on Thursday, 1st of May next (beyond which day she will on no account be detained) direct for HOBART TOWN, VAN DIEMEN'S LAND. Single Women and Widows of good character, from 15 to 30 years of age, desirous of bettering their condition by emigrating to that healthy and highly prosperous Colony, where the number of Females compared with the entire population is greatly deficient, and where consequently from the great demand for servants, and other female employments, the wages are comparatively high, may obtain a passage on payment of Five Pounds only.

Those who are unable to raise that sum here will be allowed to give notes of hand payable in the Colony within a reasonable time after their arrival, when they have acquired the means to do so, as they will have the advantage of the Government grant in aid of their passage.

The Females who proceed by this conveyance will be taken care of on their first landing at Hobart Town; they will find there a list of the various situations to be obtained, and of the wages offered, and will be perfectly free to make their own selection; they will not be bound to any person, or subjected to any restraint, but will be, to all intents and purposes, perfectly free to act and decide for themselves.

Females in the country who may desire to avail themselves of the important advantages thus offered them, should apply by letter to "The Emigration Committee, London," under cover addressed to "The Under Secretary of State, Colonial Department, London." It will be necessary that the application be accompanied by a certificate of character from the Resident Minister of the parish, or from some other respectable persons to whom the applicant may be known; but the certificate of the Resident Minister is in all cases most desirable. Such females as may find it expedient may when approved by the Committee as fit persons to go by this conveyance be boarded temporarily in London, prior to embarkation, on payment of 7s per week.

All applications made under cover in the foregoing manner, or personally, will receive early answers, and all necessary information, by applying to

JOHN MARSHALL, Agents to the Committee,
26, Birchin-Lane, Cornhill,
EDWARD FORSTER, Chairman.

NOTE.—The Committee have the satisfaction to state that of 217 females who went out by the *Bussorah Merchant* 180 obtained good situations within three days of their landing, and the remainder were all well placed within a few days, under the advice of a Ladies' Committee formed in the Colony expressly to aid the females on their arrival.

ARTICLES OF AGREEMENT made at Hobart Town in Van Diemen's BETWEEN George Chase of the first part and the several seamen whose names are hereto subscribed of the second part WHEREAS the several seamen have respectively agreed to engage in the Whale Fishery in the service of the said George Chase for the consideration hereinafter mentioned NOW THESE PRESENTS WITNESS that each of them the several seamen for himself agrees with the said George Chase that in consideration of the Lay or Share hereinafter mentioned and hereunder written opposite to his name he will at such time during the now approaching whaling voyage or voyages as he shall be required proceed in such vessel or boat as the said George Chase may direct to any River Creek or place on or near the Coast of this Island New Holland New South Wales New Zealand or elsewhere on the High seas as the said George Chase or his agents may require for the purpose of killing and taking whales and trying down the same and obtaining and preserving the oil and whalebone thereof and that he will continue in the employment of the said George Chase during the whole of the whaling voyage or voyages (or from the first day of September one thousand eight hundred and fifty-five and up to and until the thirty-first day of August one thousand eight hundred and fifty-six if so required) and each of the several seamen hereby promises that he will diligently and faithfully do his duty by day and by night during the continuance of his term of service under this agreement and obey the lawful commands of the said George Chase or of the officer or officers from time to time appointed over him and that he will take care of all matters and things from time to time committed to his charge and assist in carrying them out as he may be required AND it is distinctly agreed that in case any such seaman shall on any pretence unlawfully desert from the service of the said George Chase before the term of service hereby agreed for shall be fully ended he shall forfeit the whole of the said Lay or Share or proportion of Oil and Whale bone and all right to remuneration of any kind under this agreement or otherwise AND it is agreed that absence from the vessel or boats to which any such seaman shall for the time be attached for more than twelve hours without lawful excuse shall be deemed a total desertion and shall render the person so absent liable to such forfeiture AND it is agreed that at the close of the said term of service and as soon as the quantity of Oil and whale bone procured by the said George Chase's whaling vessel to which such seamen shall belong shall have been ascertained and shall be ready for exportation (whether landed at its final port of exportation or not) the said George Chase shall pay to the said seaman for the said Lays or Shares of and in such oil and whale bone at the rate of Fourteen Pounds for every marketable ton of black oil Forty Pounds for every ton of sperm oil and Forty Pounds for every ton of clean and marketable whale bone and the said seamen agree to accept the same in payment of such Lays or Shares and in lieu of all wages or other compensations IT BEING UNDERSTOOD NEVERTHELESS that out of such Lays or Shares the said George Chase may deduct all advances previously made to the parties in money clothing slops or tobacco PROVIDED that in every case the seaman shall be bound (if required so to do) to assist in the actual shipment of all such Oil and Whale bone or in conveying the same to Hobart Town or Launceston (as the case may be) for such shipment and the service under this agreement shall not be deemed completed until such shipment or conveyance (if so required) shall have been effected LASTLY the said George Chase agrees to provide for and supply to each seaman weekly during the said term of service the following provisions and other necessaries of good quality viz twelve pounds of beef or mutton or ten pounds of pork twelve pounds of bread or flour one and a half pounds of sugar and a quarter of a pound of tea all extras to be chargeable against the said seamen as in the case of clothes or money any wilful or negligent destruction or loss of any of the owner's property or other misconduct on the part of any seaman to the owner's damage may be set off against the Lay or Share or other claim for wages under this agreement IT IS AGREED that the said George Chase's whaling vessel shall man two Boats

DATED IN Hobart Town this first day of September, 1855.

(Signed) GEORGE CHASE.

Name	Capacity	Lay or Share on Sperm	Lay or Share on Black Oil and whale bone
John M. Luke	Ship Keeper	30th	20th
George Tilley	Boat steerer and carpenter	25th	20th
Robert Jeffrey	Boat steerer	30th	20th
Henry Madge	Seaman	50th	40th
George Cafley	Seaman	50th	40th
Thomas Storey	Seaman	55th	40th
John Duncan	Seaman	55th	40th
Sydney W. Ellery	Seaman	55th	40th
George Gillham	Seaman	55th	40th
Samuel Miles	Cook and Seaman	50th	40th
William Gubby	Seaman	55th	40th
John Scutchings	Seaman	80th	70th
Laurence Millar	Seaman	55th	40th
Alex Donaldson	Boat steerer	30th	—

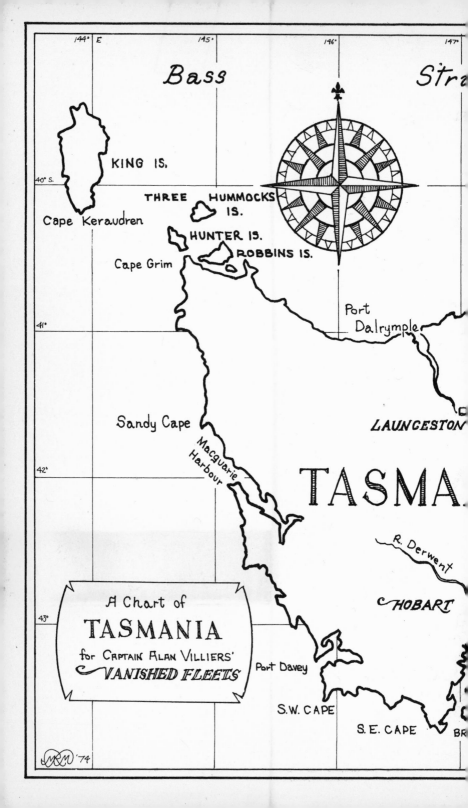